The Politics of Prayer
in
Early Modern Britain

The Politics of Prayer
in
Early Modern Britain

Church and State in
Seventeenth-century England

RICHARD J GINN

Tauris Academic Studies

LONDON · NEW YORK

Published in 2007 by Tauris Academic Studies, an imprint of I.B.Tauris & Co Ltd
6 Salem Road, London W2 4BU
175 Fifth Avenue, New York NY 10010
www.ibtauris.com

In the United States of America and Canada distributed by
Palgrave Macmillan a division of St. Martin's Press
175 Fifth Avenue, New York NY 10010

International Library of Historical Studies 48

ISBN: 978 1 84511 412 1

A full CIP record for this book is available from the British Library
A full CIP record for this book is available from the Library of Congress

Library of Congress catalog card: available

Printed and bound by Thomson Press India Limited
camera-ready copy edited and supplied by the author

CONTENTS

ACKNOWLEDGEMENTS

I am glad to acknowledge my many debts to those who have furthered this work: to my beloved and patient family - my wife, Linda, and our children, Sarah, David and Andrew; to the parishes of Darsham, Dunwich, Middleton, Peasenhall, Sibton, Theberton, Westleton and Yoxford; to the congregations of their churches and chapels; to my colleagues Ann Bayman, Andrew Campbell, Elizabeth Cole, Barbara Michie, Elizabeth Morris, Olive Reeve, Roger Smith, Frances Trower, and Susan Warne; and to David Hubbard, who so often sheltered me under his roof in London, as well as giving me his generous support. Somehow Professor Alan Ford did not give up on my remarkably protracted labours. His sensitive probing of my research and his robust criticism of my writing helped to shape the resulting work in all sorts of ways. The University of Durham was graciously flexible in accommodating the successive and severe personal problems that delayed the writing and completion of the thesis from which this work is formed, and for which a degree of Master of Letters was conferred. I am pleased to record the support and encouragement that I received from my late mother, Dorothy, whose gentle words often sustained my commitment to these studies.

My research has used principally the collections at the Bodleian Library, the British Library, Cambridge University Library, Canterbury Cathedral Library, Dr Williams's Library, Lambeth Palace Library, and York Minster Library. The patience and helpfulness of their staffs have been enormously appreciated. Living and working about one hundred miles from the nearest national libraries at London or Cambridge has entailed frequent recourse to local library facilities. Acknowledgement must therefore be made to the staff at Saxmundham Public Library who excelled in their cheerful willingness to deal with my enquiries and requests for Inter-Library Loans.

Appropriate thanks must also be rendered to Dr Lester Crook, who surprised me with the assurance that this work could be published, and to his colleagues at IB Tauris. I would also express thanks to Sarah Ginn for her detailed scrutiny of the text. No doubt shortcomings will be found in this book, but I hope that any defects only reflect upon the author and not upon the subject matter of an era that continues to fascinate and from which we can learn about the handling of issues of central regulation, local variety and the way that ultimate truth can be a rallying point that contributes meaning to human association.

INTRODUCTION

This study derives from a survey of printed literature containing evidence of the Anglican perspectives of prayer in the period 1641-1700. The themes, concerns and leading ideas of this large deposit of material have been given a structure and related to features of the life of the parochial system of England. This study includes the voices of centralised authority within dioceses and nation, as well as many witnesses to life at parish level. Accordingly there emerges an interesting interpenetration of official requirement and voluntary sincerity. Prayer operated in many ways and differentiated many aspects of society, as well as offering an overall pattern of integration.

Some Preparatory Perspectives

Within the period 1641-1700, the Church of England was faced with rapidly changing circumstances which compelled exploration of its own identity and which required the explanation of Anglican practice. A recent study has affirmed that there was a definite shift in the presentation of material after 1660. Religious teaching was simplified to aid popular communication.[1]

In the years 1641-1700, Anglican practice was successively proscribed, then established as a monopoly and was plunged finally into a legitimated Protestant pluralism. Within such a sequence of rapid change, it is possible to examine Anglican understanding from many different perspectives. To draw close to the concerns of the day it is necessary to explore how the vocations of the church, the clergy and the laity were articulated and nurtured. One significant aspect of the self-understanding of the Church of England was the matter of prayer. As this study reveals, the Church of England did not acquiesce passively in the sequence of abolition, re-establishment and dilution. The Church responded by enthusing about its devotional programme.

Inevitably, the sources reflect the opinions of the writers and can sometimes provide only an indication of the reality of popular practice. However, it will be shown that the coherence of the sources indicate a broad Anglican position. The sources cited are mainly ecclesiastical and predominantly clerical. Whether these clergy were functioning at a parish level, or as chaplains, or at a diocesan level, they were at the forefront of implementing Anglican practice and understanding. They could write about the realities of parish life, their goals and the obstacles to their ambitions. So that the authors whose works are cited do not echo as disembodied voices some key biographical information is included, either in the text or in the endnotes.

This study has been flavoured by the pragmatic approach to the life of the Church in much of Anglican writing. However, caution has had to be used in handling the considerable volume of source material to ensure that the theology of the practice in the Church of England is explored and articulated. An inadvertently partial selection of sources could highlight a misleading range of issues and thus risk the distortion of the results of investigation.

These dangers can be seen in Spurr's wide-ranging thesis that was prepared on the Restoration Church of England and which included a chapter on 'Anglican Piety'.[2] Whilst this chapter emphasised that people were expected to pray and to worship, there was no extended exploration of the printed sources to show how this was understood. The necessary restriction of sources imposed by such brief treatment gave undue weight to sacramental worship. A third of Spurr's chapter on 'Anglican Piety' was given specifically to the Holy Communion, which the author acknowledged to reflect the ideals of the sources that he had used rather than the practice of the Church. However, a sparsity of occasions for receiving communion in the Anglican Church had become a feature of the Elizabethan era,[3] and this characteristic endured into the seventeenth century.[4] The complexity of the factors that led people either to decline to receive communion or to be excluded from communion was a running sore in many communities.[5] Within the margins of this study, it is sobering to note the advice of the Bishop of Lincoln to his clergy, in which he referred uncritically to the Lord's Supper as an 'Occasional Office'.[6] It should be noted also that the text of a letter is extant in which John Fell, the Bishop of Oxford, discouraged the Archdeacon of Durham, Denis Granville, from contemplating the desirability of a weekly Communion service.[7] Further evidence rests in a document of 1692 entitled *The Hours of Daily Prayer in and about the City of London* which only listed eight churches as having a celebration of the Lord's Supper every Sunday, out of 123 parishes. In a land where generalisation has always been hazardous, it nevertheless appears that regular sacramental observance was more of an ideal than a practice.

Familiar issues about defining terms are present in the background of any consideration of this era. So many writings about the life of the Church have sought to facilitate their task by using polarities for the purpose of analysis, e.g., 'High Church', 'Low Church'; 'Arminian', 'Calvinist'; but there is a further risk of distorting the evidence on this subject of prayer by such patterns of analysis. Whilst the word 'Anglican' has been noted to be a term of contemporary usage,[8] the word 'prayer' covered too wide a range of activities to be a matter for definition. Prayer could be explained and encouraged, but prayer was an activity to be practised more than a subject to be defined. Thus, prayer did not figure as an article of the Prayer Book Catechism, but had to be learnt by example and shared congregational experience. It has been established that although the wider and very considerable catechetic literature of the time did offer some teaching on prayer, teaching about the liturgy was a rare exception rather than the rule.[9] Whilst definitions of prayer were offered in the sources that will be explored in this study, this teaching tended to be drawn in pictorial outlines rather than in analytical terms.

The Church of England attempted to lead and sustain the nation through the process of historical change. The problems of analysis and synthesis which have been encountered in dealing with this wide range of material have been tackled by imitating the approach of the sources. This pattern starts from a recommended or compulsory practice, and then gleans theological reflection based on the experience of usage. Thus, the Book of Common Prayer came first and then the reflection followed. This study explores Anglican practice and then charts the understanding of prayer that developed. Two basic historical facts were in operation for most of the years covered by this study: there was an establishment and there was a prayer book. Across the Church of England there was a general acquiescence in these facts. This study seeks to discern the broad pattern of Anglican usage and its theology. To seek to draw this outline it is necessary to look for the fundamentals across the great range of printed sources, perhaps responding to the evident truth in the assertion that "Historians ... have largely ignored the conformist element within the established Church".[10]

Some Previous Opinions and Research

The period 1641-1700 invites closer study because of the conflicting evaluations which historians and scholars have made of the piety of England. Two different overviews of this period may be offered:

> The Spirit of the Age was not conducive to worship in general, and was peculiarly opposed to liturgical forms. The dominating intellectual interest from the foundation of the Royal Society in 1660 to the French Revolution in 1789 ... was mathematical science.... A consequence of this interest was a tendency to omit all those mystical and aesthetic elements of experience which are incapable of being displayed in the lucid, consecutive, and convincing form which is proper to mathematical demonstration. Such an age will inevitably relegate to the background whatever is paradoxical and remote from the ordinary ways of thinking.[11]

> It must ever be remembered that the Seventeenth Century was an age of Anglican Piety, and remains a standing contradiction to those controversialists who have argued that the Church of England has produced no saints since the Reformation.[12]

The contradiction between these two opinions is so emphatic that neither can be taken to be any more than an indicator of possible conclusions. The implication arises that there is so much surviving material that these contrasting opinions reflect the effects of a particular selection of sources rather than a comprehensive survey. A more restricted selection of sources leads to almost predictable results. Thus one writer who surveyed the whole output of Royalist literature 1641-1660 acclaimed the popularity of Anglican rites:

> Probably the greatest failure of the Parliamentary and Commonwealth leaders was their inability to find a satisfactory replacement for those aspects of popular culture which were linked with Church of England practice.[13]

On the other hand a musical historian, disappointed at the failure of the excellent music that was available to penetrate popular appetites, wrote of the same period:

> The interregnum had completed a process of alienation between the liturgy and the people which was probably well advanced

even before 1640. Increasingly, they would be mere spectators to a performance by the minister, assisted by the parish clerk; and a service which was originally designed to take full advantage of the possibilities of variety and of congregational participation would become a monotonous and tedious duty, fully open to charges of empty formality.... [14]

It is significant that these different evaluations of Anglican devotional practice turn on attributions of popularity. Again there is a polarity of opinion, and an appeal to the inferred views of a silent and long-dead populace. There is always a risk in drawing conclusions but one definite view has been recorded that:

> Beneath the near-universal rejection of Archbishop Laud and his ecclesiastical aspirations, lay an enormous commitment to the hybrid religious forms and observances created in the mid-sixteenth century and now part of the daily and weekly experience of millions of Englishmen.[15]

The analysis of the piety of the seventeenth century in England has been characterised as being polarised between the 'Caroline Divines' and the 'Puritans', and these labels can be set in opposition.[16] Those who may be tabulated as 'Caroline Divines' include Lancelot Andrewes, Richard Montague, John Cosin, Thomas Fuller, Jeremy Taylor, George Herbert, Nicholas Ferrar, William Laud, Anthony Sparrow, Herbert Thorndike, and Thomas Ken.[17] However, such a list includes too few people to actually offer a comprehensive picture of Anglicanism in the seventeenth century. The list includes an archbishop who was executed (Laud), a non-juror (Ken) and a zealous man whose ambitions to remould the liturgy were repudiated by his peers (Cosin). Ferrar was a monastic figure rather than a representative of the English parochial system, and, even when the saintliness of Andrewes and Herbert is acknowledged, the remainder are too few in number to be more than an indication of possibilities within Anglicanism.

Whilst there may be grounds for drawing a dichotomy between 'Caroline Divines' and 'Puritans', this does not necessarily mean that the same opposition should be drawn between 'Puritans' and 'Anglicans'. Those who espoused the rule of Scripture can be called 'Puritans', whether they may be labelled 'Presbyterians' or 'Independents' or 'Anglicans', for Puritans were not necessarily separatists. It has been affirmed that categories of 'Anglican' and 'Puritan' only became meaningful after the Act for the Uniformity of Publick Prayers of 1662 created a definite division between those who attended parish churches and dissenters.[18] However, the matter of definition is far more obtuse, and more recently two writers have operated from the premise of accepting a contemporary definition of 'Puritan' which shows Puritanism to have overlapped with Anglicanism as much as to have been opposed to it.[19] This study offers a different perspective on the matter of the opposition between regulated and de-regulated prayer and its implications in the politics of local community and the nation.

The devotional life of Puritans has been investigated.[20] Williams has explored the doctrinal roots of the Puritan practice of prayer in their perception of the being of God and of the work of the Holy Spirit. Williams used the phrase 'experiential piety' to typify the distinctive quality of Puritan prayer as the primary locus of encounter with God. However, the sheer volume of Anglican literary remains has deterred some researchers from doing more than trying to find representatives who can act as spokesmen for the age, whilst other volumes overlook this period altogether.[21] One scholar summarily dismissed the value of the literary output of the Church of England in these years:

> The period of the later Caroline divines, from 1660-1700, has no conspicuous literary merit: it is a period of learning and commonsense rather than of conspicuous originality. Moreover, it may be observed how little it was associated with European culture or indebted to foreign influence.[22]

Such a disparaging comment could be a disincentive to investigate an allegedly unattractive and insular body of literature. But another writer has commended the literary facility of Anglicans and their theological awareness.[23] One may be deflected from even considering bishops as a source of serious matter for study; their literary efforts have been deemed to be insignificant,[24] but a survey of their surviving sermons has shown that their role as preachers has to be respected.[25]

It should be noted that a preliminary general survey of prayer in sixteenth century England has been undertaken[26] and many significant themes were identified. It was suggested that prayer could be categorised as:

Prayer as petition for help	Prayer as a duty or service to God
Prayer as protection against danger	Mystical prayer
Prayer as thanksgiving	Prayers of salvation

But these categories were treated so as to elucidate popular culture and provide material for research into drama. This work has been neither developed nor systematised. An underlying flaw in the usefulness of this particular work was the lack of any real acknowledgement of the importance of the Book of Common Prayer. A long-standing work covering the first forty years of the seventeenth century[27] noted resemblances to continental teaching in English devotional writing, but the possibility of an authentic Anglican spiritual integrity was not explored. No developed consideration of the role of the Prayer Book was formulated and individual works were appraised without attempting an impression of any general appreciation of English devotional life or practice.

There is no deeply researched work on the Church of England at prayer in the second half of the seventeenth century, even though this was the national task of the Church. Indeed, the author of a work on 'popular religion' in Restoration England declined to even consider bibles, psalters and prayer books.[28] There is one often-quoted book covering the period 1603-1690 in this area of investigation,[29] but its main strength was as a survey of secondary writing.

The Parishes: Heterogeneity and Common Factors
Whilst generalisations about Christian devotional practice in the seventeenth century can be formulated, those generalisations have to be representative of life in roughly ten thousand parishes and amongst five million people. Liturgical life was centred on the local parish church buildings, but parish churches were in a very varied condition even though central regulatory procedures treated them as a standard local fixture. Analysis of the surviving reports of the 1662 Visitations has evoked a picture of random dilapidation in Church buildings and occasional ruin.[30] There has been some research on the clergy of the seventeenth century.[31] One matter of contemporary concern was the low level of pay for many clergy; their maintenance was viewed as a substantial burden on the country. In places where clergy income was totally insufficient to maintain a clergyman, ministers either had to be shared so that parishes were held in plurality, or else no appointment was made. Whichever solution was adopted, the result affected the pattern of devotional habits in local churches.

Altogether, there was little that was standardised about the parish churches of the land. Whatever central dictates of policy may have arisen, local circumstances entailed a hugely varied response due to matters of finance and maintenance, let alone the subtle blends of conscience and religiosity that affected the interpretation of and response to any particular matter. Consequently, to delineate any general configurations of its teaching and practice across the national spectrum contributes towards formulating the identity of the Church of England.

A further variable, which was of immense significance at a basic practical level, was the effects of illiteracy in congregations.[32] Concern for the quality of the devotional life of illiterates was expressed in the literature of this period. There is extensive evidence of the allowance that was made in Anglican practice for popular illiteracy. Anglican practice tried to incorporate the illiterate in both spoken prayers and music.

Whilst liturgy was a national activity, liturgy only existed in its inevitable local variations. Liturgy was not only prayer but also acted as a tutor. Accordingly, this investigation has to find whatever can be discerned of the way that this process of tuition worked. There were expectations, ideals and goals which included the ambitions that there should be universal participation in national prayer, in local prayer, in household prayer and in personal prayer. It will be necessary to explore the way that these different levels of prayer were thought to inter-relate. Although legislation failed to ensure the eventual comprehensiveness of the Church of England, Anglicanism did have its achievements and managed to secure a broad pattern of common life. This was a time when there was a genuine and deep concern for the spiritual life of the nation,[33] and an essential central concern in this process was the matter of teaching people to pray.

Exclusions

Various matters have had to be excluded from this study: two matters arise through the necessity of containing this study within manageable proportions; the third exclusion has a partial character that arises through historical circumstances:

Firstly, the investigation of concerns of Church government has not been pursued because, whilst these affairs were hotly contested, they were more to do with church discipline and ministerial accountability than with the understanding of devotion.

Secondly, the matters of eucharistic devotion and the occasional offices have not been pursued as these have already been the subject of research.[34]

Thirdly, it has proved impractical to do much to investigate the Nonconformist opinions of the 1662 Prayer Book because of the impact of the 1662 Act for Preventing the Frequent Abuses in Printing ..... This act, known as the Press Act, directed that: 'no person or persons whatsoever shall presume to print, or cause to be printed ... any heretical, seditious, schismatical, or offensive Books or pamphlets, wherein any Doctrine or Opinion shall be asserted or maintained which is contrary to Christian faith, or the Doctrine or Discipline of the Church of England.' The Act controlled the import of books and re-established a licensing procedure.[35] A flood of heterodox and anti-clerical literature poured on to the popular book market after the Toleration Act when the Press Act expired in 1695.[36] The literature absent by implication from the years 1662-1695 cannot be grounds for comment.

Method

The work underlying this study began with an initial selection of sources, followed by a rapid survey of these works and an exploration of what may be termed 'proximate' sources. These were usually short works bound in with items already identified as targets for research. Alternatively, the works of particular authors who appeared to be significant were pursued through standard catalogue procedures. The scrutiny of these books was based upon four deceptively simple questions:

A) How were people expected to learn to pray?
B) How were people expected to pray?
C) How did people pray?
D) What is prayer?

Notes were made as research progressed then, as notes were grouped together, themes emerged which allowed patterns of comment and analysis to be built. These themes were largely practical, relating to the unfolding of national events, or to the life of the parishes and to home life. Sources were re-visited as necessary. Unpublished theses and modern works were consulted, yielding the resulting interweaving of analysis, commentary and reflection.

This brief outline of the method of this study needs to be enlarged upon. The issues of 'prayer', 'worship', and 'liturgy' were all subjects that figured vigorously in the writings of these years. The size of the task taken in hand with this study can be gauged from a title search that was undertaken using the Retrospective Catalogue of the British Library. A search of the years 1641-1700 yielded the following numbers of titles containing the words 'prayer', 'worship', and 'liturgy'. Even allowing for multiple holdings and multiple editions, the breakdown of these raw figures by decades shows a sustained interest in these areas of writing:-

	'Prayer'	'Worship'	'Liturgy'
1641-1650	175	57	22
1651-1660	146	69	10
1661-1670	133	49	27
1671-1680	120	37	10
1681-1690	209	70	39
1691-1700	164	39	19
Total 1641-1700	947	321	127

A search of 'Early English Books Online' for these words in book titles produces a similar pattern of results:

Total 1641-1700	1329	547	126

It would have been less demanding simply to survey and to summarise this plethora of sources rather than pursuing the more rewarding path of trying to abstract a chronologically evolving understanding from this large body of writing. However, the principal area of research for this dissertation has been primary sources. The 'Wing' Catalogue[37] was read throughout, and all likely references that could be traced were checked. Sometimes the titles were explicitly involved with prayer and sometimes the relevance was cryptic. Advantage was also taken of an eighteenth century index[38] detailing all the sermons published after 1660, which was extremely helpful in tracing expositions of particular verses of scripture. The *Cathedral Libraries Catalogue*[39] proved to be a valuable supplement to the 'Wing' Catalogue in this enquiry. The bibliographies to this book only comprehend works to which reference is made either in the text or in the endnotes.

The formulation of a coherent impression of Anglican prayer in the period 1641-1700 has many problems. The array of material located posed considerable challenges of thematic correlation. However, the literature of the period 1641-1700 utilised the categories of nation, congregation, family/household, and private individual. These labels were familiar in the seventeenth century and are used in this study to provide a structure that reflects society. Thus, the teaching offered in Anglicanism would have been readily appropriated to everyday life and work, and different strata of teaching and reflection applied to these different foci. Whilst the Church of England was organised into dioceses, which were clearly important for administrative purposes, only occasionally was devotional material produced specific to any particular diocese. However, printed material did not remain exclusive to the locality from which it emerged, but could be appropriated for use anywhere in the kingdom.

The life of the Church of England was many-layered and multi-voiced. In searching for indications of a generality of practice and understanding one has to have recourse to basic questions, whilst trawling across a broad sea of literature. In order to make sense of the subject of this work in this period it is essential that this study also includes theological commentary and analysis, even if only because this was part of the self-understanding of seventeenth century England. It is not enough simply to describe prayer in all its different roles. This investigation therefore has to discharge an obligation of theological explanation in order for the material to be intelligible within its own context. The material of this study unfolds as the process of the many layers of perception within the realm interacted, seeking legitimation and advantage. The results can be claimed to suggest common factors across the life of the Church and the nation, albeit at the level of ordinary people caught up in a multifarious life, which both promised the struggles of an unmechanised and largely agricultural society, and which also proffered the threshold of glory.

1

THE SURVIVAL OF ANGLICANISM
1641-1660

Years of Upheaval

In 1641, the control mechanisms of Laud were unravelled as the Court of High Commission was abolished by Parliament[40] and the House of Commons passed resolutions for the suppression of 'innovations in or about the worship of God'. The House of Lords thereupon authorised the publication of its order: "that the divine service be performed as it is appointed by the Acts of Parliament", without allowing the introduction of any extraneous material.[41] Three months later, the King issued *A proclamation for obedience to the laws, ordained for the establishment of the true religion in this kingdom of England*[42] in very similar terms. These developments accorded with the groundswell of non-Laudian conformist support for the Prayer Book that has been identified in the years 1640-1642.[43] However, the pressures for change required more than the dismantling of Laudianism; it was not enough merely to reaffirm the core establishment.[44]

The Houses of Parliament declared their intention to engage in church reform in April 1642,[45] and eventually passed the Ordinance of 3rd January 1645 which banned the Book of Common Prayer and enjoined the use of the *Directory for the Publique Worship of God*. The Directory merely gave directions for the conduct of worship. The principal service was to consist of prayers, a pair of lessons, psalms and a sermon. Many writers have assumed that this Ordinance marked the end of the Prayer Book and that it received only vestigial use until the Restoration.[46] However, if there had been such respect for the dictates of Parliament there would have been no need for Parliament to pass another Ordinance on 23rd August 1645: 'for the more effectuall putting in execution the Directory for Publique Worship ... and for the dispersing of them in all places....' This Ordinance noted that the earlier Ordinance had not specified any penalties for continuing the use of the Prayer Book, and that 'there hath been, as yet little fruite of the said Ordinance'.[47]

The legislation that had been intended to terminate the Prayer Book had not had penalties attached. The compilers of the Directory had hoped that it would commend itself for use by the quality of its contents. The Westminster Assembly had mentioned in a letter to the General Assembly of the Kirk of Scotland that:

> We have not advised any imposition which might make it unlawfull to vary from it in anything; Yet we hope, all our Reverend Brethren in this Kingdom, ... will so far value and reverence that which upon so long debate and serious deliberation hath been agreed upon in this Assembly ... that it shall not be the lesse regarded and observed. And albeit we have not expressed in the Directory every minute particular, which is or might be either laid aside or retained among us, as comely and usefull in practice; yet we trust, that none will be so tenacious of old customs not expressely forbidden, or so averse from good examples although new, in matters of lesser consequence, as to insist upon their liberty of retaining the one, or refusing the other, because not specified in the Directory; but be studious to please others rather than themselves.[48]

The idealism with which the Directory was launched does not appear to have met with a matching response and hence the history of Anglican devotion did not suddenly end.

Legal Confusion

One of the problems faced by Parliament in attempting to abolish the Book of Common Prayer was the confusion as to the status of an Ordinance of Parliament. An Ordinance was, in effect, an Act of Parliament that had not received the Royal Assent. As a result there was doubt as to the proper legal significance of an Ordinance. The implications in the affairs of the Prayer Book were complicated because Charles I opposed the Parliamentary Ordinance with a Proclamation. The King's *Proclamation concerning the Book of Common-Prayer and the Directory for Publike Worship* was given at Oxford in November, 1645. This Proclamation insisted on the continued use of the Prayer Book, of which the King claimed:

... it containes in it an excellent forme of worship and service of God, grounded upon the holy Scriptures, is a singular meanes and help to devotion in all Congregations, and that, or some other of the like forme simply necessarie in those many Congregations which cannot otherwise be supplyed by learned and able men, and keeps a uniformitie in the Church of England.[49]

The King's verdict on the Directory was predictable:

... a means to open the way, and to give the libertie to all ignorant, factious, and evil men, to broach their own fancies and conceits....[50]

And the King reminded his subjects of wider issues:

And be the minister never so pious and religious, yet it will break that uniformitie which hitherto hath been held in Gods service, and be a means to raise factions and divisions in the Church, and those many Congregations in this Kingdome, where able and religious Ministers cannot be maintained, must be left destitute of all help and meanes for the publike worship and service of God.[51]

However, whilst there was uncertainty in the status of a Parliamentary Ordinance, there was also uncertainty in the comparative status of a Royal Proclamation. Consequently, when the House of Commons requested that their legislation was printed in a collected edition, their printer also included various Royal Proclamations and virtually implied an equivalence of importance with the Parliamentary material. Both the Ordinance of August, 1645, suppressing the Book of Common Prayer, and the King's Proclamation insisting on the continued use of the Book of Common Prayer were included in this compilation.[52] So when clergy were prosecuted for using the Book of Common Prayer they could appeal to statute of long-standing and to the King's Proclamation.[53]

Whilst the status that attached to an Ordinance was unclear, the implementation of an Ordinance was equally problematical. Very little has been established about this process[54] and the truth only appears to be discernible at a local level where one finds all manner of variations. One study relating to Hampshire for the years 1649-1660 suggested that there is no way of knowing to what extent the Prayer Book was being used in the Parishes, and that the central government of the time did not know either. This particular area of enquiry led the researcher to conclude that, during the Interregnum, central government had little impact on local religious practice.[55] Local variation and lack of centralised control seem to have become a standard feature of seventeenth century life during the years 1641-1660.[56] Statute law and its enforcement had to contend with local practice and custom.[57] Accordingly, Parliamentary ordinances may have elicited only selective obedience depending on local preference.

Another element which complicates research into the conflict of use between the Directory and the Prayer Book was the slow pace of Parliamentary response to the need to support its own legislation and protect the Directory. Thus it was recorded that on 19th October 1647, the House of Commons sitting in Committee wished that:

> ... all Statutes for the Common-Prayer booke, and for enforcing all to come to Church, whereby many religious and conscientious people are daily vexed and oppressed, be forthwith repealed and annulled.[58]

However, legislation expressing the wishes of Parliament did not pass until 27th September 1650.[59] The eventual passage of this legislation reflects the discovery of evidence that in various places in the years 1645-1648 clergy had been successfully prosecuted for not using the Book of Common Prayer.[60] Morrill noted that this was still a problem for the authorities in 1658, further underlining the ineffectiveness of Parliamentary Ordinances.[61]

Another indication of confusion may be recognised in that the Directory specifically required that prayers be offered: 'for all in Authority, especially for the Kings Majesty....'[62] amongst the devotions before the sermon. However, despite the *Resolves of the Commons assembled in Parliament, Concerning such Ministers as shall Preach or Pray against the present Government established by Parliament* of 9 July 1649 which recorded their decision to apply sequestration to any minister who: 'shall directly or indirectly, in preaching or praying, make mention of Charles Stuart or James Stuart, Sons to the late King...', the Directory was not amended. Consequently, subsequent editions of the Directory continued to require prayers for the King, despite the wishes of Parliament.

Only armed with their Ordinances, Parliament surrendered any possibility of implementing a national policy for public worship.

Furthermore there is evidence that the Ordinances against the Book of Common Prayer became the pretext for continuing to use the Prayer Book, but in variations at the discretion of the minister. As the Directory of Public Worship did not set out any particular form of prayer, it did not preclude the use of material drawn from the Prayer Book, provided that it was not obviously read from the Prayer Book.[63]

The difficulties resulting from confusions in legislation and practice can be exemplified in the publication, probably in 1645, of a small pamphlet entitled: *A Supply of Prayer for the Ships of this Kingdom that want Ministers to pray with them; agreeable to the Directory established by Parliament (Published by Authority).* The preface is significant for describing the reasons for this attempt to solve a national problem by issuing a set form of prayer, which was supposed to be in accord with a Directory that had been intended to dispense with prescribed prayers:

> Whereas there are thousands of ships belonging to this Kingdom, which have not ministers with them to guide them in Prayer, and therefore either use the old Form of Common-Prayer, or no prayer at all; The former whereof for many weighty Reasons hath been abolished, and the latter is likely to make them rather Heathens then Christians (the Lords day being left without any mark of Piety or Devotion). Therefore, to avoid these Inconveniences, It hath been thought fit to frame some Prayers, agreeing with the Directory established by Parliament....

Without the Prayer Book guidance was still needed. Those who could not find words to pray without a book still needed a form of words.

Persistence in Anglican Practice

There is a considerable accumulation of evidence as to the widespread use of the Prayer Book, despite its proscription. Reports of the use of the Prayer Book have been cited from Evelyn's Diary and the Calendar of State Papers Domestic, jointly drawn from the years 1649, 1653, 1657, and 1658.[64] A casual exploration of the Thomason Collection in the British Library yields reports of the use of the Book of Common Prayer, for example, at Oxford in 1647[65] and at Bath in the same year.[66] Morrill has inspected surviving Churchwardens Accounts and Church Inventories for this period and he found that these documents suggest that copies of the Prayer Book were retained in more than one-third of all English parishes. Whilst this could be interpreted to mean that the

Prayer Book was retained but not used, this information could also imply that the Prayer Book was used in many parishes but not recorded with other parish effects, bearing in mind that its possession was an offence.[67] Morrill's investigations have definitely established that, according to the surviving records, more churches possessed the Prayer Book than the Directory. His research showed that the Directory was generally held only where the classical system was set up or where county committees enforced the ordinance of August 1645.[68] Whilst statistics cannot prove popularity, Morrill's findings nevertheless demonstrate the power of survival of the Book of Common Prayer, and imply its usage. In London, in the late 1640's, unemployed Anglican clergy were engaged by some London churches that could not recruit anyone else. The use of Anglican formularies was certainly linked to this development.[69] Indeed, it would be possible to suggest a widespread popular loyalty to Prayer Book tradition and even an aversion to the Directory.[70] These factors help to create the impression that the use of the Book of Common Prayer could be counted as a vehicle of protest.

Anglican continuity can be demonstrated further by the fact that the Book of Common Prayer continued to be printed after 1645, despite its prohibition. It does not seem to have been noted previously that there are copies of the Prayer Book in the Bodleian Library that date from these years:

The first copy to which reference should be made is dated 1645; it is in tiny print, with no printer or publisher mentioned; it omits the texts of the epistles, the gospels, and the ordinal; the edition appears to have been prepared with a view to being easily concealed.[71] The recent bibliographer of the Book of Common Prayer has suggested a clandestine origin of circa 1650 for this edition,[72] but as this bibliography is based on British Library holdings there is no mention of the next item.

The second copy from this period lacks a title page and carries the name of neither printer nor publisher; it was printed mostly in black letter, possibly to make it appear much older than the date of 1647, which is given in the colophon.[73]

The third copy would not immediately appear to have been printed in the years when the Prayer Book was supposed to be under suspension, as the title page is dated 1642. This particular edition omits the epistles, gospels, psalter, and ordinal, but is bound contiguously with a copy of the Bible, which bears the Royal Arms printed opposite the title page, and which is dated 1650. The volume ends with a copy of the Sternhold & Hopkins metrical psalter, dated 1651.[74]

These three survivors point to the continued demand for the literature necessary for Anglican observances. The transparently false dating of the last item alerts one to the possibility that there may be other survivors from this age, similarly misdated, awaiting identification.[75] Meanwhile, the bibliographer of the Book of Common Prayer has identified two versions of the Prayer Book dated 1641 that he suggests to have been printed abroad after 1646.[76]

The continuity of the Anglican heritage across the Civil War and Interregnum was also maintained through the Church's personnel. Whilst three thousand six hundred Anglican clergy were sequestered in the early 1640's, 70% of the parishes were unaffected by the upheaval.[77] Then, in a land of roughly ten thousand parishes, less than 20% of the parochial ministry had to leave in the period 1660-1662.[78] The reputation of the years before 1660 as years of massive dislocation may have been true at many levels of society, but may well be a misleading picture of many local parish churches. It has been noted that the social radical Gerrard Winstanley complained in 1652 about the continuing Anglican ministry:

In many parishes there are old formal ignorant episcopal priests established; and some ministers who are bitter enemies to Commonwealth's freedom and friends to monarchy are established preachers.[79]

One interesting statistic that would help to emphasise the continuity of the Church of England during this period would be to know how many of the beneficed clergy of 1641 were still at their posts in 1660, or back at their 1641 posts by the end of 1662. This information does not appear to be available nationally. However, Pruett's survey of Leicestershire may be representative.[80] He showed that one fifth of the Leicestershire clergy of 1642 were still at their posts in 1659. In two fifths of the County's parishes new incumbents had been necessary due to normal attrition. After the Restoration about one third of the parishes went through ejections and restorations. Accordingly, allowing for clerical movements, it may be reasonable to suggest that one half of the clergy of 1642 were still serving within the County in 1662, and, further, that a substantial proportion of these clergy were still in their old parishes.[81] Whilst there may have been significant local variations, the evidence from Leicestershire would strongly support the impression that continuity was as marked a feature of the 1640's and 1650's as disruption.

Criticisms of the Prayer Book

Whilst it was a commonplace that the Book of Common Prayer was merely the 'Mass-Book' in disguise, and whilst such an accusation was easily refuted, there were more substantial arguments against the Prayer Book. These criticisms are set out in two anonymous tracts from the early 1640's: *A Triall of the English Lyturgie* (1643), and *LIX Exceptions against the Book of Common Prayer* (1644). The earlier of these two tracts specifically aimed to answer the defence of set forms of prayer; the later tract challenged the inner consistency of the Prayer Book. Between them, these tracts represent a powerful body of argument that the Prayer Book was beyond revision and should be abolished. Both tracts complained that the Prayer Book legitimated a non-preaching ministry. A more moderate stance is illustrated by two further anonymous tracts, advocating the revision of the Prayer Book.[82] Any wish to re-order Anglicanism, however, never came to fruition; there was no movement for a compromise by which the Prayer Book could have been rescued.[83]

The virulence that it is possible to find in opposition to the Book of Common Prayer can be gauged from the title of the pamphlet: *The First Search after One Grand Cause of the wrath of God yet against his people, in the use of the so much Idolized Liturgie, or Common Prayer* (1644). However, material from the period 1641-1660 suggests that a critique of the Prayer Book failed to develop. The lack of development in the critique of the Book of Common Prayer is illustrated by such pamphlets as *The Old Non-Conformist Touching the Book of Common Prayer, and Ceremonies* (1660), which admitted that it was an abridgement of *The Lincolnshire Ministers Apology* (1605) and repeated the arguments that the Book of Common Prayer was the 'Mass-Book' in disguise. Equally, *The Anatomy of the Service Book* (1642), was merely reprinted with a different preface as *The Common Prayer-Book Unmasked, Wherein is declared the Unlawfulnesse and Sinfulnesse of it ....* (1660). Its contents, made up of invective rather than argument, were then re-incarnated as *The Anatomie of the Common Prayer-Book....* (1661). The balance of material suggests that the proponents of Anglicanism gradually developed arguments and found new enthusiasm for the Prayer Book, whilst the arguments against the Prayer Book were repeated until they became stale.

Anglican Apologetic

The resilience of the Church of England in the two decades before the Restoration is illustrated by the apology that was developed for the practice of the liturgy of the Church of England. Not having been prepared for the imposition of the Directory and the abolition of the Prayer Book, apologists had to substantiate their case despite official disapproval. Anglican apologists had to break away from appearing to argue that what had gone before was right simply because that was what had happened. The writer of an anonymous tract of 1641 called *The Use of Daily Publick Prayers* had thought it quite sufficient to insist that:

> ... daily publick Prayers have been in use among Christians from the beginning ... and were accounted a principall part of Gods worship. ...these prayers were at set houres, in a prescript form, not arbitrarie in either.   ... the peace and prosperity of the publike Weal, in the long life and happy preservation of Pious Princes, and other particulars; and the good successe of Armies in times of warre; have been thought by ancient Christians, of purest times, the fruit and effect, in part, of these publike Prayers, and daily Service of the Church.[84]

Another anonymous tract of 1641 rested under the title: *A Confutation of M. Lewes Hewes his dialogue: Or, an Answer to a Dialogue or Conference betweene a Country Gentleman and a Minister of Gods Word, about the Booke of Common Prayer Set forth for the Satisfying of those who clamour against the said Booke, and maliciously revile them that are serious in the use thereof.* Such bland opinions now required substantiation. Herbert Thorndike (1598-1672) was a dedicated high church student of theology who specialised in oriental languages and rabbinical literature. Whilst his whereabouts during the Civil War and Interregnum are largely unknown, he was a Fellow of Trinity College, Cambridge, and was appointed a Prebendary of Westminster in 1661, in recognition of his services to the Church of England. Thorndike's *Of Religious Assemblies, and the Publick Service of God....* (Cambridge 1642) was a lengthy work drawing together insights from patristic writings and rabbinical works. He legitimated the Anglican pattern of services as deriving from the early Church, and showed that the traditional daily, weekly and annual cycle of services were in themselves a development of synagogue practice. This lengthy work did not command the field; the scholarly style of Thorndike did not have a wide appeal.

An effort was made to engage the issues of the day rather than relishing the historical antecedents of the practice of Anglicanism. Daniel Whitby, described on the title page of his work as the Rector of Thoyden-Mount in Essex, had a sermon published as *The Vindication of the Forme of Common Prayers Used in the Church of England....* (Oxford, 1644). Whitby warned against innovation in prayers:

> ... Its fond to think that Almightie God loatheth prayers that come often in the same words, or likes one that hath a daily new Edition corrected or amended, or rather corrupted by the Author.... He is no Athenian Auditor, Acts 17.21, that delights daily to heare some new thing, and spends his time in expectation of thy invention: He doth not listen after noveltie and varietie of words; to heare the soule in a new tune, no more than to see the body in a new dresse: If we come every day in the same cloathes to Church we are as welcome. So if we apparell our thoughts in the same language.[85]

When the Directory arrived the lack of direct Anglican attack was remarkable. It has only been possible to trace two Anglican sources from 1645 that were specifically directed against the Directory.[86] The absence of a prompt concerted Anglican assault on the Directory may imply disorganisation or even that the Directory was widely ignored. In any case, the Directory itself was merely an outline with little content and therefore would have been difficult to target.

Henry Hammond (1605-1660) was a distinguished biblical scholar who, having proved himself to be an assiduous pastor, was appointed Archdeacon of Chichester in 1643. He was nominated to the Westminster Assembly, but he refused to attend. In 1644, Hammond fled to Oxford to join the King and, in 1645, was appointed a Canon of Christ Church and a Royal Chaplain. He was often in attendance on the King in the next few years. As a conscientious Anglican, Hammond wrote his *View of the New Directory and a Vindication of the Ancient Liturgy of the Church of England* (Oxford, 1645) in which he tried to persuade his readers that because people had died for the Prayer Book, therefore the Book of Common Prayer was the people's book. In this work a link was affirmed between the Prayer Book and the nation's identity, and the Book of Common Prayer was envisioned as a significant defence against any imposed tyranny. This was not a rigorous argument, but rather illustrated the same deliberate patriotism that led Hammond to use English rather than Latin for his scholarly writings.[87] Whilst Hammond's reputation continued to grow as a Biblical scholar and as a catechist,[88] the proliferation of his other writings and the prolixity of his style lead to his comments on the Directory being largely overlooked. The lack of substance that he was capable of offering in argument can be illustrated by his reaction when he was challenged on a reference to the fundamental matter of 'uniformity' in his *View of the New Directory*. He responded with a work entitled: *Ευσχημονως και Κατα Ταξιν: or, The Grounds of Uniformity From I Cor. 14.40* (1657) in which his basic arguments were practical rather than theological. Whilst Hammond acknowledged ceremony to be a matter of determining which local customs were eloquent of reverence and could rightly be used in public worship,[89] he justified uniformity by affirming that worship was impossible without some ceremony, and any size of gathering required some measure of uniformity if chaos was to be avoided.[90] Hammond received a reply in the year of his death which went without response. His antagonist dismissed Hammond's arguments by saying that:

> ... the pretence of reverence in Gods worship, hath oftentimes been an inlet unto many superstitious practices. ... you may affirm, but can never prove, that there is no possibility of worshipping God externally, and publickly without such ceremonies, for it is manifest that such Ceremonies are not necessary....[91]

Clearly, the Church of England had to refine its arguments if its claims to offer the proper path for national devotion were ever to be accepted. Accordingly, two strands can be seen to emerge: firstly, the frustration of having inadequate arguments to buttress claims, and, secondly, a great level of pastoral concern. Both these factors are exemplified in *A Dirge for the Directory*, where ending common prayers evoked the reaction:

> ... but to take them quite away, I am humbly of opinion you greatly sin against God and this poore Island of England; and I thinke as long as you keepe the Arke of God from us, I meane the Service Booke, you will ever have swellings and Emrods among you. I am no Prophet, nor the sonne of a Prophet, but I pray God in his mercy keep you from these plagues which hang over your heads, for leaving so many poore distressed soules in want, not having the known will of God taught among them, who

lye and languish for his knowne Lawes, and are kept short of them by force.[92]

The proponents of Anglicanism were forced to develop positive arguments for the merits of the Prayer Book. The apologist to be credited with breaking new ground in the discussion was Jeremy Taylor (1613-1667). He had been a protégé of Laud and had been made a chaplain both to Laud and to the King in 1636. After a short period of service in a parish, when war came, Taylor went to Oxford to join the King. In 1645, Taylor went to work at a school in Wales and to act as Chaplain to the Earl of Carbery. During the following years he wrote many books and his frequent visits to his publishers in London ensured that he did not become isolated from current issues. Taylor recognised the need for a fresh approach and brought a new tool to the task. He adopted the method of accepting all authorities and construing them as evidence and then using 'reason' as an arbiter to determine the relative force of the, sometimes competing, strands of material.   When he produced *An Apology for Authorized and Set Forms of Liturgie* (1649), he identified two particular characteristics of the use of the Prayer Book that made it necessary. Firstly, he determined that:

It is in the very nature of publike prayer that it be made by a publike spirit, & performed by a publike consent.[93]

That is, he felt it to be essential to public worship that there should be a consensus as to the content of the prayers and that such a consensus was impossible without a generally known and predetermined order of worship. Secondly, Taylor noted the role of the liturgy in the national life and in personal life:

Publike formes of Liturgy are ... the great securities and basis to the religion and piety of the people....[94] It is all that ... many men know of their Religion, for they cannot any way know it better, then by those Formes of prayer which publish their faith, and their devotion to God, ... and places their Religion in their understanding and affections.[95]

Thus, Taylor gave credibility to the liturgy as both a national and a personal tutor. In his hands the arguments about the Prayer Book passed out of the region of personal preference and into the realm of national necessity.

Taylor's approach was reflected in the *Velitationes Polemicae* (1652) of John Doughty (1598-1672), a section of which considered 'Solemne Set Prayers in Publique'. Having been chaplain to the Earl of Northumberland, Doughty joined the King's forces at Oxford at the start of the Civil War. Eventually, he had to shelter until the Restoration, when he became a Prebendary of Westminster Abbey. Doughty recognised the pastoral value of set patterns of worship. He felt that the practical matter of being able to say 'Amen' to a prayer depended on the congregation being able to give their heartfelt assent to the contents of the prayer, which became difficult if they had no previous knowledge of the words.[96]

However, whatever arguments were developed by Anglicans, there was no discernible impact on those who held the reins of power. Increasingly desperate clergy expressed their immovable adulation of the Prayer Book,[97] but the frustration that was felt by some clergy became the challenge of others. Anthony Sparrow (1612-1685) had been ejected from his fellowship at Queens College, Cambridge, as a royalist in 1644. When he secured a Suffolk living in 1648, he was promptly ejected for reading the Book of Common Prayer. The Restoration brought him the Archdeaconry of Sudbury, then a prebendal stall at Ely, and he was successively appointed as President of Queens College, Vice-Chancellor of the University, then Bishop of Exeter, and finally Bishop of Norwich. In *A Rationale upon the Book of Common Prayer....* (1655; 8th edition 1684), Sparrow affirmed that the reasons for using the Prayer Book were overwhelming. He demonstrated the way that set forms are present in the Bible, and that the liturgy was drawn from scripture itself. Sparrow extolled the desirability of unity in forms of worship as a symbol of national unity and he was convinced of the Prayer Book as a pastoral necessity:

> How many Millions of poor souls are in the world, ignorant, infirm by nature, age, accidents, (as blindness, deafness, loss of speech, &c.) which respectively may receive help by Set Forms, but cannot so well (or not at all) by extemporary voluntary effusions .... [98]

Sparrow surveyed the whole content of the Prayer Book and relentlessly insisted on its antiquity and its faithfulness to the Bible. It was significant that the problem of ignorance came first in his list. The general pastoral concern for those who had neither educational achievement nor intellectual ability, in a time characterised by probably widespread semi illiteracy, was symptomatic of Anglicanism. Sparrow's

Rationale was the first Anglican apologetic from these years that became popular and which ran into multiple editions. Whilst Anglican advocacy may now have become acceptable, Sparrow brought together both argument and scholarly rigour.

Another work, by a writer with an instinct for acrimonious controversy, was the *Ecclesia Vindicata: Or, the Church of England Justified....* (1657). Peter Heylyn (1600-1662) had come to Laud's attention in 1630. He soon became a Royal Chaplain and a Prebendary at Westminster. His significance fell with Laud and, after joining the King at Oxford, he wandered for some years until he became settled, and then he instinctively re-engaged in controversy. In his work he traced set forms of worship back to Abraham, denounced any attempt to try to organise public worship without set forms and took account of rabbinical and patristic writings to substantiate the claims of the Church of England. Heylyn suffered the decimation of his estate for this work, but he was re-instated at Westminster in 1660 and his final years were devoted to study in the midst of declining health.

The above evidence demonstrates a developing effort of teaching about the merits of the Prayer Book and its use. Ultimately, however, the re-establishment of the Prayer Book did not depend upon the quality of Anglican apologetic but upon the restoration of the monarchy. Some of the advocacy of the Prayer Book, re-published in 1660, was soon (deservedly) lost to oblivion with the 35 polite pages in *A True and Briefe Narrative of all the Several parts of the Common Prayer book, cleered from aspersions which some men cast upon it*, and the rather more pungently entitled item: *An Anti-Brekekekex-Coax-Coax. Or a Throat-Hapse for the Frogges and Toades that lately Crept abroad, Croaking against the Common-Prayer-book and Episcopacy*. The Restoration rendered such works superfluous.

The 'Εικων Βασιλικη'

The King and his execution were of great significance and Charles I has to be considered at this point because of the work which was associated with him - the *Εικων Βασιλικη* of 1649. Mystery surrounded its origins, even if credit for its compilation has been settled upon John Gauden (1605-1662)[99] rather than Charles I.[100] Typical of the confusion surrounding this work is the statement:

> The admiration for the 'Eikon Basilike', which resulted in thirty-five English editions and twenty-five foreign ones in the year 1649..., is one of the most important facts of the period.[101]

There is no reason to suppose that all these editions were produced in 1649, even if they were dated 1649. The dating most probably refers directly to the year of the King's 'martyrdom', especially as the title pages of some editions carry the words: "Reprinted in Regis Memoriam Anno 1649". If it is accepted that these many editions were not dated conventionally, that would explain why 1681 is the next date recorded for an English edition after 1649. That 35 English editions should be published over 32 years is more credible than having 35 editions in one year and then a gap of 32 years. Even if a huge stock of printed copies had been generated in 1649, it is arguable that the bulk of the pages would have been lost in the Great Fire of 1665 and reprints would have been necessary. Despite these considerations, the assertion about all these editions being produced in one year is recited and perpetuated.[102]

The text of the hopes and inner wrestlings attributed to the dead King has been held to be enormously influential on the basis of all these symbolically dated editions, but no evidence has emerged to link this reputation with Anglican apologetic. The laudatory remarks contained in the Εικων Βασιλικη about the Prayer Book were neither original nor remarkable and were only a part of a work whose overall polemical interest lay in matters of state rather than patterns of devotion. Even though the Εικων Βασιλικη was reprinted so often and was cited so much,[103] there was no significant input from this work to the area of concern of this study. Thus, whilst Sparrow in the preface to his Rationale quoted from Meditation 16 upon the Ordinance against the Book of Common Prayer, the quotation only added respectability, not argument. By contrast, the prayers that were published associated with the personal use of Charles I or his son did not catch the public imagination and remained in obscurity.[104] A more likely significance for the Εικων Βασιλικη was as a literary counterpart to the annual service for King Charles Martyr after the Restoration. The first collect for the ante-communion in the 1662 Prayer Book for the service for King Charles I included the words: "Let his memory, O Lord, be ever blessed among us, that we may follow the example of his patience and charity". The Εικων Βασιλικη certainly enabled this aspiration to be realised.[105]

Review

Morrill has written that:

> ... historians have been so dazzled by the emergence of the radical sects ... that they have failed to recognise that the greatest challenge to the respectable Puritanism of the Parliamentarian

majority came from the passive strength of Anglican survivalism.[106]

The suspension of the Prayer Book did not prevent it from being printed and its use being advocated and sometimes even protected by judicial process. Moreover, the arguments for the Book of Common Prayer continued to be developed during the years before the Restoration. By contrast, the arguments against the Prayer Book became repetitive and did not mature in the same way. During the years 1641-1660, an Anglican apologetic had been founded that could be developed in the remaining years of the century. Theological motifs had been identified which would assist the future self-understanding of the Church of England. These motifs were appeals to Biblical antiquity and to patristic studies, pastoral concern at the reality of widespread ignorance and the need for consensus and unanimity.

2

ANGLICAN UNDERSTANDINGS OF FREE PRAYER IN PUBLIC WORSHIP 1641-1660

Custom versus 'Strangeness' in Public Prayer

Very little has been written on the subject of the offering of unscripted public prayer. There could be a temptation to characterise the Anglican view of free public prayer as straightforward denigration. Such an approach, however, would miss out on the importance that should be attached to the Anglican response to the use of free prayer. The Anglican effort to understand free public prayer carried implications for the Anglican vision of its own patterns of prayer. The difficulty of writing about free prayer lies in its ephemeral character - it is only of the moment and therefore cannot be subjected to analysis as a text. However, the practice could be appraised as a tendency or movement.[107]

Unscripted prayer had its own dynamic, but for Anglicans there was both frustration and incomprehension at the proliferation of this practice. If there was something of ecclesiastical self-definition in an authorised liturgy, the deliberate choice to forego some or all of the liturgy led into a new world where other factors had to determine a Church's identity. Anglican bewilderment was underlined by the awareness of the importance of the Prayer Book for the identity of the Church of England. The avoidance of a set liturgy by a section of the ministry in some congregations made comparison between devotional material impossible.

There was alarm at a situation of growing disorder:

> None can ... deny ... that they present to God rude, and undigested extemporall evaporations of their desires; yea, such

tautologies, battologies and reiterations, as no hearer can truly joyne with them in these their prayers; for (though they often licke them over in one sermocination) they are no fitter then to Beares whelps, without forme, without fashion.[108]

The arrival of the Directory, in 1645, made the choice between conformity to the old and sharing in the new even more graphic. The fact that the principal service under the Directory only had a minimum list of ingredients made each experience of worship variable. The text of a letter survives in which Lady Verney described the experience of attending a church where the Directory was in use:

...one heares a very strange kind of sarvis, and in such a tone that most people doe noething but laugh at itt. And everybody that receaves must be examined before the elders, whoe they all swere asketh them such questions that would make one blush to relate.[109]

This letter, whilst a solitary item, gives a valuable indication that Anglican clergy were not the only ones who were baffled by this alternative culture. It is tempting to try to introduce an analytical tool in order to facilitate understanding in this enquiry. One suggestion has been that those who favoured set forms on the one hand, and those who favoured free prayer on the other hand, were locked in a disagreement as to what constituted authentic speech.[110] According to this analysis, those who favoured set forms felt that, for prayer to be authentic, the words had to be written down first, whereas those who favoured free prayer felt that the spoken word came first, and it was only when a word had been spoken that it could be written down. Set prayer was authenticated by its written precedent, whilst free prayer of itself authenticated any transcription. On this basis, free prayer became a protest against the mechanism of repetition in a customary society, in which the Prayer Book functioned as the printed pattern for corporate worship. Whilst this pattern of analysis has its own attractions, it does not utilise concepts that would have been recognised at the time. Furthermore, if free prayer is to be regarded as a form of cultural protest, or as a quest for some sort of emancipation, then such a line of enquiry does not actually disclose anything of the Anglican understanding of free prayer. In the absence of recorded texts of the free prayers that were offered, it is difficult to develop this line of discussion. The Verney letter quoted above emphasises the need to consider auditory experience as well as suggesting tensions in the area of the control and regulation of a local community in the context of a breakdown of centralised authority.

The Disruption of Aural Community

Part of church attendance was involvement in an aural community. When Lady Verney commented that '...one heares a very strange kind of sarvis, and in such a tone that most people doe noething but laugh at itt', the hearing was more important for the purposes of this segment of this study than the oral performance. Careful work has been done on the aural experience of sermons in the Early Modern period and on the way that people could be trained to relate to sermons and to absorb sermons. Literature aimed at facilitating the appreciation of sermons has been studied[111] and this type of literature continued into the second part of the seventeenth century. However, whilst people may have been taught how to listen to and appropriate the contents of sermons, there was a need of equivalent material for the appreciation of the liturgy.

If there is little modern study of 'free prayer', the aural experience of a community appears to be even more recherché. Helpfully, some basic key indicators have been determined regarding the features of shared aural experiences. These renderings have been characterised as having formulaic beginnings and endings, between which the aural experience moves forwards in recognisable sequences. The aural experience is given structure by the pairings or patterns that can be recognised as having the nature of structural repetition. Aural experience, by its very nature, is linear or sequential and mono-dimensional, but the arrangement of aurally perceived features yields the effect of a multi-dimensional landscape with its own sense of structure and architecture.[112] The rendering of conventional Prayer Book services was susceptible of such an analytical approach. The aural community found in attending Church services may be suggested to be a locus of religious experience. Any disruption entailed by the introduction of free prayer would have meant that there was neither shared aural landscape nor shared aural journey.

John Prideaux (1578-1650) had been in poor health when he wrote *The Doctrine of Prayer*, published posthumously in 1655. Prideaux had become Bishop of Worcester in 1641. Whilst being a moderate Calvinist with a reputation for impartiality, he was respected by Laud and was not dependent upon him. Prideaux was nominated to the Westminster Assembly but never sat. In his book, he included a section: 'Of prayers in public assemblies', in which he wrote that the set forms of prayer of the Bible were:

> ... so transmitted by the Apostles to all posterity, that no settled Church can be noted, that had not some public liturgy; wherein the people might join with the minister in God's service. Children, and the simpler sort, might thus be instructed by hearing the same words constantly repeated, and not come only as spectators to a Theatre, to hear much, learn little, and do nothing; as though all had not an interest in God's service, according to their abilities and callings, and that out of the mouth of babes and sucklings, Hosannas were not to be endured.[113]

Prideaux was anxious to emphasise the role of liturgy as tutor. His criticism of the vacuity of worship without a set form of prayer was part of the Anglican critique of free public prayer. The passivity of the congregation without a liturgy also disturbed him and was regarded as being inimical to worship. It is especially noteworthy that children were felt to be excluded from proper participation in free public prayer, bearing in mind the demographic structure of the population, of which children may well have comprised over 10%.[114] This estimate can be augmented by whatever numbers may be attributed to those whom Prideaux referred to as 'the simpler sort', as well as the 'babes and sucklings'. Consequently, Prideaux's comment points to a matter of great pastoral concern and it is reasonable to suggest that the failure to use a regular pattern of worship excluded possibly more than 25% of the population from a role in public worship. Children were often treated jointly with servants, and both categories could find church attendance problematic for the simple reason that because they were neither householders nor ratepayers they had no right to a seat in a parish church. Whilst some churches made a point of providing room for children and servants at Sunday services, others merely provided mats on the floor.[115] To be excluded from sharing in the communal function of worship on the basis of an absence of any auditory pattern, as well as being denied a physical place in the communal function by not being entitled to a seat, may have been grounds for alienation.

In an age when the learning of economic and life skills was often achieved by sharing in a repeated work process, it was very difficult for people to learn to pray unless words of prayer were repeated as a shared activity.[116] In re-issuing his previously anonymous tract, one royalist observer repeated his comment:

... if you tell them of Praying by the spirit, you may as well tell them a tale of the man in the Moone.[117]

Generally, it has been suggested that for successful audience appreciation, hearers should be capable of following a recited text and finding that its patterns and resolutions fulfil their expectations. A special kind of archaic or conventional language has also been suggested as being appropriate. However, a key feature of an aural community is the inter-relationship between its present experience and previous experiences, so that there is a sense of the accumulation of layers of shared corporate life.[118] Measured against these criteria, it can be appreciated that free prayer required a different mechanism of congregational involvement from customary prayer. The experiment may have started well in many places but then drifted into failure, because in an aural community continual spontaneity could be disruptive and even destructive.

Inspiration or Infatuation?
There was deep concern at the theological implications of the use of free public prayer:

> ... the fashion of Extemporary conceptions, in Praying and Preaching, insinuateth, and needs must insinuate to the people, the pretence of immediate inspirations, which to men of judgement they are constrained to disavow.[119]

Joseph Hall (1574-1656) had a distinguished record as an Anglican apologist and had already suffered sequestration as Bishop of Norwich when his book *The Devout Soul....* was published in 1644:

> If you tell me ... that there is a gift of prayer, and that the Spirit of God is not tyed to rules; I yeeld both these; but withall, I must say there are also helps of prayer, and that we must not expect immediate inspirations: I find the world much mistaken in both: They think that man hath the gift of prayer, that can utter the thoughts of his heart roundly unto God, that can expresse himself smoothly in the phrase of the holy Ghost, and presse God with most proper words, and passionate vehemence: and surely this is a commendable faculty, wheresoever it is: but this is not the gift of prayer; you may call it, if you will, the gift of Elocution.[120]

Hall had offered an alternative explanation of the ability of some people to declaim in prayer at length. He suggested that, rather than being a sign of divine inspiration, it was a sign of a natural endowment of eloquent speech. Consequently, Hall asserted that the gift of prayer not to be held by the person:

> ... that hath the most rennible tongue, (for prayer is not so much a matter of the lips, as of the heart) but he, that hath the most illuminated apprehension of the God to whom he speaks, the deepest sense of his own wants, the most eager longings after grace, the ferventest desires of supplies from heaven; and in a word, whose heart sends up the strongest groans and cries to the Father of mercies.[121]

Hall also felt that in addition to mistaking the source of their facility, exponents of free public prayer were misrepresenting the essential nature of prayer:

> There is commonly much mistaking of Devotion, as it were nothing but an art of vocall prayer, expiring with that holy breath, and revived with the next task of our invocation; which is usually measured by many, by frequence, length, smoothnesse of expression, lowdnesse, vehemence; whereas, indeed, it is rather an habituall disposition of an holy soul, sweetly conversing with God, in all the forms of an heavenly (yet awfull) familiarity.... [122]

It was natural for Anglican curiosity to be aroused as to why influential people held free public prayer to be important and so to try to understand this practice.

Méric Casaubon (1599-1671) was a classical scholar who had been made a Prebendary at Christ Church, Canterbury, under Laud's patronage. He was deprived of his livings by Parliament in 1644, and in his rural retreat, whilst he awaited the restoration, he had time for reflection and writing. His book, *A Treatise Concerning Enthusiasme, As It is an Effect of Nature: but is mistaken by many for either Divine Inspiration, or Diabolical Possession* (1655), was remarkable for its study and analysis of specific case histories, and also for the context of those histories, noting the reactions and opinions of those involved with various unusual phenomena. The many claims to a special religious experience, that were often a feature of free public prayer in these years, were approached on the basis of the pattern of analysis that Casaubon developed. As a Christian minister, he was anxious to affirm the value of prayer, asserting that it was impossible to: "pour out our Souls or spirits unto God in prayer, but by the spirit of God".[123] However, Casaubon drew a distinction: "between a general concurrence, and immediate inspiration or possession".[124] Casaubon set out his position as follows:

> The cause of naturall Enthusiasme in point of Prayer, may be referred either to a vehement and continued intention of the mind, or to the power of the language, or to the naturall temper of the person. [125]

He wrote of the spoken word:

> ... that it hath the same power, to raise the same passions and affections upon the speakers, or bare utterers, as it hath upon the Auditors .... All writers of Rhetorick insist upon it largely, and conclude generally, that he can never be a perfect Oratour, whose speech hath not the same, or greater power upon himself, as he would have it to have upon others.[126]

Casaubon related the practice of rhetoric to prayer as follows:

> But that which giveth most advantage, as to all Rhetorick in generall, so to prayer particularly, is, that naturall ardor or fervency, wherewith nature hath endowed some men above others.[127]

He, like Hall, developed the view that free public prayer could be merely an exercise in the gift of eloquent speech. Casaubon had no hesitation in declaring:

> The ignorance of this advantage of nature, being unhappily mistaken for true Christian Zeal, hath been the occasion of much mischief in the world, and a great stumbling-block to simple people ....[128]

He reached the position in his recital of evidence and argument where he could assert that those who claimed a special gift of prayer, which they could exercise in free public ministry, were themselves deceived and were deceiving others.

The saintly academic, Henry More, drew together some of the threads of the Anglican appraisal of the self-regard of those who had the temerity to offer unscripted public prayer:

... Enthusiasme is nothing else but a misconceit of being inspired. Now to be inspired, is to be moved in an extraordinary manner by the power or Spirit of God to act, speak, or think what is holy, just, and true. From hence it will be easily understood what Enthusiasme is, viz. A full, but false perswasion in a man that he is inspired.[129]

Concerning Praying, it is an Epidemical mistake, That men think extemporary Prayers are by the Spirit, and that the Spirit is not in a Set Form....[130]

... the Spirit of Praier does not consist in the invention of words and phrases ... but in a firm belief in God through Christ, and in a hearty liking and sincere desire of having those holy things communicated to us that we pray for. And ... he that reads, or hears a publick Liturgy read, in such a frame of minde as I have described, does as truly pray by the Spirit as he that invents words and phrases of his own. For there is nothing Divine but this holy Faith and Desire, the rest is mere Nature.[131]

The analysis of feelings of inspiration in the offering of prayer was evidently incisive, but may not have reached a wide audience.

The Emergence of an Anglican Critique

Jeremy Taylor had no hesitation in decrying the practice of free public prayer. In *A Discourse concerning Prayer Ex tempore....* (1646), Taylor chose to resort to questions bordering on sarcasm to expose the position of those with whom he disagreed:

... I would faine know what the difference is betweene deliberate and extempore Prayers, save onely that there is lesse consideration and prudence....[132]

He used this approach to reveal inconsistencies in his opponents' claims:

If they can pray with the spirit, why also do they not preach with the spirit? & if praying with the spirit be praying ex tempore, why shall they not preach ex tempore too, or else confesse that they preach without the spirit, or that they have not the gift of preaching? For to say that the gift of prayer, is a gift ex tempore, but the gift of preaching is with study and deliberation, is to become vaine and impertinent.[133]

Taylor continued with the implications of these arguments in a later work:

The summe is this. Whatsoever this gift is, or this spirit of prayer, it is to be acquired by humane industry, by learning of the Scriptures, by reading, by conference, and by whatsoever else faculties are improved, and habits enlarged. Gods Spirit hath done his worke sufficiently this way, and he loves not either in nature or grace ... to multiply miracles when there is no need.[134]

Taylor was quite uncompromising:

No man can assure me that the words of his ex tempore prayer are the words of the holy Spirit: it is not reason nor modesty to expect such immediate assistances to so little purpose, he having supplied us with abilities more than enough to express our desires aliunde, otherwise than by immediate dictate; But if we will take Davids Psalter, or the other Hymnes of holy Scripture, or any of the Prayers which are respersed over the Bible, we are sure enough that they are the words of Gods spirit....[135]

Doughty was certain that free prayer was a hindrance; he felt that the will and the understanding of hearers could not keep pace with the minister.[136] Doughty also maintained that: "the true and warrantable sole sense of using extempory prayer" had been confined to the early Church.[137] Doughty took up one of Taylor's arguments and extended it trenchantly:

I see not ... how the same Spirit which furnisheth them, as they pretend, with such extraordinary abilities in the work of Prayer, should not be also as extraordinarily assistant to them in the duty of preaching (thus Acts 2.4,14) of disputing (Acts 6.9,10) which neverthelesse for the one commonly they do not, and for the other they dare not lay claim unto.[138]

Heylyn added a further note of concern to the criticism of free public prayer. He was puzzled by the inconsistency of the minister's position in a congregation where he claimed to exercise a gift of prayer:

> For being that the ability ... of powring out extemporary prayers, doth come by gifts, and not by study; in which regard themselves entitle it most commonly the gift of prayer: why may not other men pretend unto that gift, as much as he; or on opinion that they have it, may not make use thereof in the Congregation? ... Assuredly, the gift of prayer is as much restrained in the people, by hearkening only to those expressions which are delivered by their Ministers, as that of the Minister can be, ... by tying up his spirit to those formes, which are prescribed by the Church.[139]

Furthermore, Thorndike noted that the practitioners of free public prayer were not holding to their claims:

> ... though they exclude the service of God out of the Church, upon pretense of praying as the spirit indites, yet are indeed no lesse provided aforehand, then the prayers of the Church, varying a little from time to time, as occasion may require, to make the people believe that they are extempore dictates of the spirit.[140]

Thorndike indicated that the practice of extempore prayer had tended to become routine or stale and that supposedly spontaneous utterances were finding stable forms.

Henry Leslie (1580-1661) had been made Bishop of Down & Connor in 1635 and became recognised as an opponent of the Presbyterian enthusiasts in his diocese who had abandoned the Book of Common Prayer. After some years of poverty and obscurity, he preached two sermons in 1659 that were used to form: *A Discourse of Praying with the Spirit and with the Understanding* (1660). A preface by the successor to his see, Jeremy Taylor, reminded readers that:

> Hasty and unstudied prayers are against Scripture; expressely I say against the word of God whose spirit hath commanded thus: 'Be not rash with thy mouth, and be not hasty to utter anything before God' (Eccles 5.2).

Referring to his text from I Corinthians 14.15, Leslie declared:

> This Text is much abused, in this age, to justifie praying ex tempore, whereby they have destroyed the right use of Prayer, and, indeed, have left us nothing which can truely and properly be called the publick worship of God. And it is the highest pitch of sacriledg to make the scripture itself patronize impiety....[141]

Leslie felt substantial reservations about contemporary practice and succinctly said:

> As they who pray without study and deliberation cannot follow the direction of the word; so neither can they promise unto themselves the assistance of the spirit....[142]

Review

The pre-Restoration Anglican critique of free public prayer came to regard this approach to prayer as revealing more about human nature than divine truth, by showing eloquence in free prayer to be a product of human gifts rather than divine inspiration. The congregation could not assimilate an understanding of the prayers offered, and subscribe to them, if they had no prior knowledge of what those prayers would be. There was anxiety that free prayer excluded all those who could only learn to pray by hearing set forms repeatedly. As Henry More declared:

> ... the end of ministry is not the Ostentation of any mans particular Gifts, but the Edification of the People....[143]

On the one hand the ambition of those who sought to exclude the Prayer Book from the life of the nation had been to unleash the powers of godliness that they felt had been stifled. On the other hand the Church of England regarded itself as having to care for everybody, not only those with a facility in vocal prayer.

Richard Sherlock[144] was a devoted Anglican who went to join the King at Oxford in 1644. He felt strongly that:

> For the maintenance of unity in the Faith, 'tis necessary that there should be one common form of sound words, which all should hold fast, and stick close unto; that as we are all members of one Church, (or should be so at least-wise) so we should all stand upon one ground, be built upon one foundation, and steer our course towards the land of Promise in one and the same bottome.[145]

The de-regulation of prayer was held to be the prelude to chaos rather than liberty. So long as the practice of free public prayer was officially sanctioned, there was the risk that many people who could not pray without a form would be alienated from the life of prayer. The results of all this reflection lead to a deeper appreciation of the value of the set prayers within Anglicanism and gave the Church of England confidence for the next episode in its history. Whilst Anglican writers were clearly capable of thinking along similar lines, there is little sign that these opinions were the product of shared debate and the writers do not appear to refer to each other. The broad thrust of the Anglican critique had revealed a category mistake on the part of the advocates of free prayer - that the prized gift of free utterance in public prayer was in reality a faculty of eloquent speech. The Anglican critique had further revealed inherent inconsistencies in the practice of free prayer that made it desirable to return to the settled use of the Prayer Book.

3

RESTORATION AND REVISION

The Return to Establishment

In many places the restoration did not mark the re-introduction of the Prayer Book, but rather the official recognition of its continued usage. Whilst the framework of Church government was re-assembled, the Book of Common Prayer only had to be re-printed. Legally, the regime of 1642 was restored, but the Bishops remained excluded from the House of Lords until the passing of the Act restoring the temporal authority of the Clergy in 1661.[146] The minutiae of the post-Restoration discussion of the liturgy are very extensive and the facts have received meticulous attention.[147] The details of the changes to the Prayer Book have also received close scrutiny, from the lists of these details that were circulated in 1662[148] to the standard commentaries on the history of the Book of Common Prayer. The revision of the Prayer Book has also been examined in the context of the Restoration.[149]

It may be felt that nothing can be added to the scholarship which has already sifted through this information and its interpretation. However, the data of the revision of the Book of Common Prayer have been consistently interpreted in the light of one major assumption - that the Prayer Book had been generally suppressed during the years 1645-1660.[150] There have also been a series of minor assumptions based on the idea that, before 1660, Anglicanism had been reduced to the status of a minor eccentricity and that the Church of England was only able to recapture its prestigious position by the manoeuvres of its adherents and supporters in the Restoration years. For example, Bosher described the tactics of Anglicans in the Restoration process as 'feigned conciliation'.[151] The latent presumption of Anglican disingenuity and duplicity has coloured the general appraisal of the revision of the liturgy.

The procedures leading up to the finalised text of the Caroline Prayer

Book acknowledged Dissent rather than debated common ground. This was unavoidable given the structures within which debate was held and the persistent reality of a Book of Common Prayer that had proved impossible to suppress. There is good reason to suppose that the revision of the Prayer Book and its imposition, attached to the new Act for the Uniformity of Publick Prayers, may be more successfully construed starting from a demonstrated position of Anglican strength rather than a presumed Anglican weakness. Accordingly, as the discussion of a religious settlement unfolded, those who favoured non-Anglican usage already found themselves facing an establishment conformity.

Such an approach demands corroboration and is congruent with the few statistics that are available. Even before the Restoration John Gauden reckoned that there was a ratio of Anglicans to nonconformists in the country of twenty to one.[152] Various authorities have been cited elsewhere debating the value of the attempted religious census of 1676. The appraisal of their comments inclined towards a similar ratio of Anglicans to protestant nonconformists, which implied a fairly stable nonconformist constituency within the population in this era.[153] Whatever the procedural weaknesses of the census of 1676, it has been affirmed that the investigation showed incontrovertibly that the population was overwhelmingly Anglican.[154] The results of the 1676 census have been shown to complement information about the geographical distribution of licences issued under the Declaration of Indulgence of 1672.[155] A more recent article noted that, whilst the 1676 census has to be treated as not offering exact figures, its results confirm other evidence.[156] A realistic estimate of 5% committed nonconformists in this period, of course, did not imply that the remaining 95% of the population were committed Anglicans. Anglicans may have had a more passive regard for Church membership, but it is clear that they were in an overwhelming numerical superiority throughout the period under review in this study.

The role of the Book of Common Prayer had been summarised in the Book of Homilies:

... the church ... is the due and appointed place for common and public prayer.[157]

... as a people willing to receive at God's hand such good things as in the common prayer of the church are craved, let us join ourselves together in the place of common prayer, and with one

voice and one heart beg at our heavenly father all those things
which he knoweth to be necessary for us.[158]

However, the simplicity of such statements on the role of the Prayer
Book was also extremely subtle, containing many presuppositions and
ideas. The notion of a settled form of Church service was linked to an
assurance that the Prayer Book was specifically designed to entreat God
for the gifts that he wished to bestow. This meant that any departure
from the practice required by the Prayer Book would be a departure
from seeking the revealed will of God for his people, as understood by
the compilers of the Prayer Book. Therefore, any revision of the Book
of Common Prayer was unlikely to break the mould that already existed,
as this would imply that the original perception of the will of God had
been flawed. The Book of Common Prayer functioned as a compendium
of the interpretation of the Bible; the forms of common prayer selected
material from the scriptures and therefore interpreted holy writ. Any
revision of the Prayer Book was expected to perpetuate the mind of the
Church. The failure of the non-conformist representatives to anticipate
this pattern of thought may explain some of the disappointments of the
coming years.

Revision - The King, Savoy, Convocation and Parliament
The Declaration of Charles II of 25th October 1660 *Concerning
Ecclesiasticall Affaires* had offered an interim compromise of toleration
pending the outcome of a conference that the King would summon:

> We are very glad to find, that all with whom we have conferred,
> do in their Judgements approve a Liturgy, or set form of Publick
> Worship, to be lawful; which in Our Judgment, for the
> preservation of Unity, and Uniformity, We conceive to be very
> necessary: And though We do esteem the Liturgy of the Church
> of England, conteined in the Book of Common Prayer, and by
> Law established, to be the best We have seen ...; yet since We
> find some exceptions made against several things therein, We
> will appoint an equal number of Learned Divines of both
> perswasions, to review the same, and to make such alterations as
> shall be thought most necessary; and some additional forms ...
> suited unto the nature of the several parts of Worship, and that it
> be left to the Ministers choice to use one or other at his
> discretion. In the meantime, ... we do heartily wish and desire,
> that the Ministers ... would not totally lay aside the use of the

Book of Common Prayer, but read those parts against which there can be no exception; ... until it be reviewed, and effectually reformed, as aforesaid.[159]

Whilst theologians were indeed appointed to confer, issues including the possibility of identifying potential alterations, of preparing additional forms and of allowing ministers to use their discretion in worship, never became part of the remit of the Savoy Conference. The King's Letters Patent initiating the Savoy Conference gave only a limited brief. Those deputed were required:

... to advise upon and review the said Book of Common prayer, comparing the same with the most ancient liturgies which have been used in the Church in the primitive and purest times.[160]

Such a commission could not lead to the formulation of any major innovations, especially as the Book of Common Prayer functioned as a well-established pattern of theological interpretation. Whilst there was an Anglican appetite for the Prayer Book to be 'bettered',[161] this has to be seen in the context of an expectation of a perpetuation of the contours of Anglican devotion.

The discussion of the revision of the liturgy can be analysed in terms of three diverging tendencies: the desire to alter the liturgy radically, the desire to elaborate it and the desire to keep it as it had been. These three approaches can be characterised as the radical, the elaborative and the conservative. Each of these approaches is represented by a document: respectively, the Savoy Liturgy, the Durham Book and the 1604 Prayer Book.

The surviving documents relating to the Savoy Conference have been scrupulously examined.[162] Whilst it has been claimed that the Savoy Conference was the occasion when the Book of Common Prayer was more thoroughly examined than at any other time in the seventeenth century,[163] a great deal of the effort that participants contributed to the Conference bore no fruit. Perhaps the real achievement of the Conference was to give a detailed briefing to the Anglican representatives on the perceived problems with the service book. The confrontational style of the Conference rapidly became clear. The chief concerns that were expressed concerning the Prayer Book were that repetitions, responses and the alternate readings of canticles and psalms should be omitted, and that the litany should be formed into one long prayer to be read by the minister alone. Furthermore, saints' days and

Lent should be abolished, free prayer allowed and parts of the liturgy omitted on occasion at the discretion of the minister. It was requested that only the Authorised Version of the Bible should be used and that no portions of the Apocrypha should be included in the lectionary. It was further sought that various other details of wording and rubric should be amended. The Presbyterian side of the Savoy Conference listed dozens of 'Exceptions ... Against some Passages in the Present Liturgy', and added:

> Thus have we in all humble pursuance of his Majesties most gracious endeavours for the publick weal of this Church, drawn up our thoughts and desires in this weighty affair, which we most humbly offer to his Majesties Commissioners for their serious and grave consideration: wherein we have not the least thoughts of depraving or reproaching the Book of Common-Prayer, but a sincere desire to contribute our endeavours towards ... reconciling the mindes of Brethren.[164]

The Anglicans replied that they thought that the Presbyterians had totally misunderstood the nature of the King's commission. Indeed, the Presbyterians were suspected of trying to impose their own agenda on the discussions.

The Divines ranged as opponents to the episcopal party at the Savoy Conference then produced a *Petition for Peace: with the Reformation of the Liturgy....* (1661). Baxter's draft liturgy was included, but his efforts were not as concise as the Book of Common Prayer. With the time allowed by the King's commission running out, Baxter's alternative form of liturgy for use by those who disliked the Book of Common Prayer was not welcomed. The result was that the Anglicans refused nearly every detail requested by the Radicals. However, it was nevertheless evident from the final piece that they produced that the Presbyterian divines were still hoping for a different agenda to the Savoy Conference. Their final document appeared as: *The Grand Debate between the most Reverend the Bishops, and the Presbyterian Divines, appointed by His Sacred Majesty, as Commissioners for the Review and Alteration of the Book Of Common Prayer, &c....* (1661). The inclusion of the word 'alteration' reflected their persistent desire to adjust the terms of reference of the Savoy Conference, but it was inconsistent with the terms of the King's commission and at odds with the Anglican theology of prayer, which could only accommodate refinement. The final expostulation from the episcopal side was entitled: *Pulpit-*

Conceptions, Popular-Deceptions: or The Grand Debate resumed, in the point of Prayer: Wherein it appears that those free Prayers so earnestly contented for have no advantage above the Prescribed Liturgie in publick Administration.... (1662)

The detailed study of the Savoy Conference is inevitably inconclusive; its outcome only re-affirmed the existing Prayer Book. If the Conference had been meant to pacify non-conformist opinion by giving it an outlet, it failed. However, the Conference had distracted attention from the proceedings of the House of Commons, where a Bill for the Uniformity of the Publick Prayers with the 1604 Prayer Book annexed was given three readings and sent to the House of Lords while the Conference was in progress.

When the Anglicans came to consider the revision of the Prayer Book in Convocation in late 1661, they were further confronted with the Durham Book. This book was a Jacobean Prayer Book, with many draft alterations in manuscript. It was chiefly the product of Bishops Cosin and Wren, both of whom had been linked to Laud. Particularly, the Durham Book included the main changes that had been incorporated in the Scottish Prayer Book of 1637, which had caused enormous controversy at that time. Thus, the Durham Book elaborated the Communion Service beyond the received doctrinal compromise, but the Durham Book was not accepted. Even though the Durham Book was presented by Cosin, its innovations were not regarded as a proper path for the refinement of Anglican worship. The Durham Book, like the Savoy Liturgy, would have signalled a development of Anglican practice rather than a refinement and had to be abandoned in the search for stability. The reviewers of the Prayer Book had to work for 'the preservation of Peace and Unity in the Church' (Preface to the 1662 Prayer Book).

The proceedings of Convocation in dealing with the revision have been criticised as being 'rapid and superficial'.[165] However, the sheer pressure on the Convocations to conclude this business can be gauged from surviving correspondence relating to the affairs of the Convocation of the Province of York. The Proctors of the Northern Convocation were constrained to appoint proxies to represent them at the Convocation of the Province of Canterbury:

... His Majestie requires all possible expedition. His Grace and ourselves sitt in consultation with the bishops of the province of Canterbury: and because time allotted for the despatch of these things is so short, and an Act of Parliament for confirmation of them ready to pass, the ordinary course for concluding them here first, then sending of them downe for your concurrence, and returning them up againe is soe delatory, that it will not be consistent with His Majesties expectation.[166]

Not surprisingly, when the predominantly conservative representatives of Convocation successively considered the claims of radicals and elaborators, the result was a sober revision which incorporated helpful points from both the other groups in order to widen the appeal and the usefulness of the Prayer Book.[167] Consequently, the Caroline Prayer Book acknowledged the King's instructions, the radical requests for the Prayer Book to be consistent and intelligible, and the elaborative tendency to respect ecclesiastical dignities. All that was done could be claimed to have brought Anglican usage closer to the use of the Church 'in the primitive and purest times'. Thus, at the request of the radicals, the Authorised Version of the Bible was adopted for the text of the Epistles and Gospels, and a rubric was included requiring those intending to receive the Holy Communion to give due notice. Meanwhile, on behalf of the elaborators, the offices of bishops, priests and deacons were acknowledged as such, and the word 'congregation' was altered to 'church' in some places. Only one substantial item was introduced to the Book of Common Prayer which eventually affected Sunday worship in Parish Churches - the General Thanksgiving - the felicitous phrasing of which aroused no exceptions.

The revisers themselves thought that the changes to the Book of Common Prayer were more in the nature of common sense.[168] The amended Prayer Book was ratified by Convocation before Christmas 1661 and became attached to the Bill for the Uniformity of Publick Prayers in the House of Lords in February the following year. Meanwhile, a level of official satisfaction with the progress in the restoration of the Church of England was reflected in a prayer included in the Litany in *A Form of Common Prayer, to be Used upon the Thirtieth of January*. This service was issued in time to be used in 1662, but was omitted when the service for King Charles Martyr was attached to the revised Prayer Book. The prayer was worded:

O Lord God, who out of thine infinite mercy and goodnesse hast brought back the captivity of Sion, and in good part restored this late afflicted Church, perfect (we beseech thee) this thy great deliverance. Hedge it about with thy continual protection, with the custody of Angels, with the patronage of Kings and Princes, with the hearts and hands of Nobles, with the defence of the whole secular arm, and with the affection of all good people. Reunite all our remaining divisions, reconcile our differences, and change all our spirit into a sweet Christian temper of gentleness and peace, that with one heart and voice we may serve and praise thee in thy holy Church....

The Bill for the Uniformity of Publick Prayers returned to the Commons in April and received the Royal Assent in May 1662. Whilst the Book of Common Prayer that was appended to the Act contained over 600 changes to the book of 1604, there were few alterations of any significance. One distinguished commentator was convinced that if any major changes had been proposed to Parliament, the 1604 book would have been kept without any alterations.[169]

The revision of the Prayer Book was almost incidental to the life of the Church of England in the parishes. The result was that the life of many parishes continued for the most part without great dislocation, except inasmuch as some parishes were subjected to a change of clergy. The actual liturgy prescribed went largely untouched and such changes as there were may well have passed largely unnoticed. The Act for the Uniformity of the Publick Prayers perhaps had more impact upon the matter of retaining control of local pulpits than upon the substance of the worship that was offered. A theological principle of continuity of usage allowed the text of the Book of Common Prayer to be refined. This principle was understood to enable the Church of England to relate directly back to the early Church, as was echoed by the terms of the King's Letters Patent cited above. Continuity was at the heart of the distinctive position of Anglicanism and can be suggested to be a defining characteristic. As will be shown below, the wealth of Anglican reflection on prayer and worship was ultimately co-ordinated and moulded by this principle in the debates of the early Restoration years.

Contemporaneous Discussion of the Revision of the Prayer Book
The process of the revision of the Book of Common Prayer was conducted in an atmosphere of open contention. Anglicans found enormous resources of disdain for:

> ... the new Gospel of the Long Parliament, that set up the pretense of praying by the Spirit; the Gift whereof is now claimed for every Ministers privilege, in bar to Gods Church.[170]

Lines of attack can be identified from both the supporters of the Prayer Book and its opponents.[171]

In 1661, a very significant work of Anglican apology was published by John Gauden, who was designated on the title-page as 'Bishop-Elect of Exceter'. Gauden had become Dean of Bocking in 1641 and had shifted his convictions from being in favour of the Parliamentary cause to being a Royalist. He had maintained his position by conforming to Presbyterianism whilst writing books in support of the Church of England.[172] His new work, *Considerations touching the Liturgy of the Church of England,* was even more resolutely Anglican. This book generated substantial controversy, perhaps because of Gauden's definite and uncompromising approach. Gauden was an experienced author who knew how to engage the mind of the discerning public and whose confidence may reasonably be suggested to have been augmented by the fact that his covert project, the *Εικων Βασιλικη,* was in demand by an international readership.

In the *Considerations touching the Liturgy,* Gauden firstly affirmed that a Prayer Book both protected and preserved the Church by insisting that a Prayer Book promoted reverence in worship. Secondly, he felt that the Book of Common Prayer helped to maintain true Reformed doctrine, and, thirdly, he regarded the Prayer Book as being an instrument for maintaining Church unity.[173] Gauden's fourth point emphasised that the Prayer Book met the need for careful expression in liturgy.[174] Gauden's fifth and sixth points bear extensive quotation, both because they recapitulate the pre-Restoration Anglican critique of non-liturgical public prayer, and also because they give an impression of Gauden's vision for the future of the Church of England and the crucial role of public liturgy in that future:

> 5. But above all, a constant and compleat Liturgy mightily conduceth to the edification and salvation as well as unanimity and peace of the meaner sort of people; to whom daily variety of expressions in prayer, or sacraments, is much at one with Latin Service; little understood, and lesse remembred by them.
>
> ... Alas (as I have oft observed) when poor Boys and Girls, (who have no institution of Religion from their ignorant Parents, or Masters and Dames,) when these (whose souls are precious) begin to gape upon the Minister in Religious duties, and to see, as well as hear a Sermon; which way can they in populous places be brought to or built up in Christian principles of Religion, without some easy, clear, and constant summary or set forme of

wholesome words, and sound doctrine, in the Catechisme and Liturgy, or Common-prayer; frequently repeated to them, and so inculcated in their minds and memories.[175]

6. In summe, as not the Christian Religion can easily be planted or thrive among the country and common-people, without a settled constant Liturgy, well composed, strictly imposed, and duly used by Ministers; so nor can the Reformed part of Religion be preserved in England, to any flourishing and uniform state, unless such a Liturgy be autoritatively enjoyned, and constantly maintained, as the daily, firme, and most impregnable bulwark, against both Romish superstitions and other Fanatick Innovations.[176]

Gauden's statement of Anglican policy was promptly challenged by John Owen's *A Discourse concerning Liturgies and their Imposition* (1661). Owen denounced Gauden's whole approach, which Owen sensed would undo his work and the congregational life that he had come to know. Owen took the view that an imposed liturgy was in principle opposed to true Christian freedom and he roundly insisted that there were no set forms of liturgy in the first three centuries. Owen, therefore, directly countered two key Anglican principles: firstly that liturgy could function as a national spiritual tutor and, secondly, that there could be continuity of usage with the early Church. These two issues continued to be debated for many years, as will be explored in the pages that follow below.

Review

When the Jacobean Prayer Book was finally superseded in 1662, the revised Book of Common Prayer represented national continuity and a conservative consensus of practice. The constriction of religious freedom that supplemented the revised Prayer Book can be viewed as a distinct political issue. There was a real anxiety to preclude any further devotional irregularities and a pattern of set forms was felt to be the way to achieve national solidarity. The two principles upon which the Anglican theology of prayer was based were: continuity of usage, and the conviction of the efficacy of liturgy as a national tutor.

These reflections on the strength of Anglican conformity suggest that Anglican worship related to the great majority of the English people. Whether dedicated nonconformists amounted to 5%, or even 10%, of the population, the status and practice of the Anglican teaching on prayer was linked to most of the people of the realm and was therefore of national significance. Against this background, the assertion that, by virtue of the 1662 Act for the Uniformity of Publick Prayers 'nonconformists became a substantial minority in English life.'[177] is plainly misleading. Equally, to claim that this Act was: 'The basis on which the Church of England contracted from its previous national comprehensiveness....',[178] does not acknowledge the small size of Dissent in the national equation. Instead, in the context of the Restoration, it could be said that the Act for the Uniformity of Publick Prayers only confirmed the national significance of Anglicanism. Accordingly, in examining the politics of the Anglican theology of prayer at this time, one is investigating a national position rather than an administrative backlash in a Parliament dominated by vengeful Cavaliers. The reactionary approach to the possibility of toleration did not compromise the patterns of teaching about prayer and worship that appear to have been tolerable to at least 90% of the population. The revision of the Prayer Book and the re-establishment of the Church of England was not, from this point of view, an exercise in acquiring power or status. However, just as the use of the Prayer Book had been a vehicle of protest in the years 1645-1660, so the avoidance of the Prayer Book could become a form of protest after 1662.

4

THE FELT CONTINUITY OF USAGE
WITH THE EARLY CHURCH
1660-1700

The Context of the Appeal to the Past

This was an era when there was great antiquarian interest and accessible collections were being formed of materials from earlier ages.[179] There was a great energy for classical study[180] and the investigation of the relationship of the Church of England to the early Church was a characteristic contemporaneous concern. The past was often used to legitimate present practice. The distant past and its interpretation was of great political significance. In matters of law, historical enquiries were expected to resolve questions of jurisdiction and precedence.[181] The principles of law and the constitution itself were subject to this pattern of investigation.[182] Common law was based on custom and precedent. Lawyers defined custom in a way which emphasised its immemorial nature and intensified the tendency to read existing law into an increasingly remote past.[183]

While the pattern of the English constitution was legitimated by being discerned in a remote past, the same approach was adopted in the matter of legitimating the liturgy. Accordingly, clerics could take advantage of contemporary rabbinical scholarship to draw on information on the use of set forms in the time of Jesus and to trace forms of prayer back through Ezra and David to Moses. It could thus be asserted of Christ, as a Jew, that in the Lord's Prayer he used:

... known Phrases and Forms of Speech; so far was he from affecting any unnecessary novelty.[184]

Against this background the patristic enquiries of both the Anglicans and the Nonconformists can be seen as typical of the culture of their age. The Anglicans wished to legitimate the liturgy; the Nonconformists tried to prove their contention that there had been no early liturgy. Thus, when Bishop Joseph Hall found his *Humble Remonstrance to the High Court of Parliament* (1640), answered by 'Smectymnuus',[185] the exchanges that followed inevitably invoked patristic authority. Bishop Hall attempted to vindicate liturgy; 'Smectymnuus' strove to denounce liturgy. So, when Bishop Hall issued his *Defence of the Humble Remonstrance....* (1641), he appealed to Tertullian, Augustine, Justin Martyr and ancient conciliar canons in support of liturgy.[186] When 'Smectymnuus' replied, the combined authors used the same evidence to oppose a settled liturgy.[187] Bishop Hall's response was to redouble the evidence in favour of liturgy to include Cyprian, Origen and Clement.[188] Although Hall may have had the final word, the argument was swept up into the turmoil of the times and Bishop Hall's difficulties following his translation to the see of Norwich. However, this brief exchange illustrates the process of seeking validation from the remote past.

Even when the patristic knowledge of the time is seen out of its cultural context, this learning is still immensely impressive.[189] However, there can be a variety of shades of emphasis in the interpretation of the significance of this scholarship. Thus, one writer has credited Jeremy Taylor with holding that the Fathers were, '... next to the Bible, ... indisputable authorities on religious matters',[190] whilst another writer has maintained that for Jeremy Taylor, '... any appeal to the Fathers had to be discriminating and directed to the elucidation and ordering of exegesis'.[191] Yet another writer has written even more circumspectly that: '... the fallibility of the Fathers is no serious obstacle to their use, if we believe, with Jeremy Taylor, that they are not our masters but our good instructors.'[192] Such differing views indicate the possibility of an underlying uncertainty about the programmatic significance of patristic study in these years. The recognition of the study of the remote past as a means of giving validity to, and conferring authority upon, the life and teaching of the Church of England may help to clarify this area of investigation.

There can be no doubt about the important place of prayer in the early Church, nor that the reality of prayer was freely acknowledged in patristic sources.[193] Patristic piety can be characterised as exhibiting a sense of utter dependence upon God and as emphasising the community of believers. Whilst patristic study had been a major ingredient in the process of the Reformation, it has been suggested that only three documents had particular influence on the general shape of reformed worship: Pliny's letter to Trajan, Tertullian's Apology and the Divine Institutes of Lactantius.[194] By 1660, patristic scholarship had made enormous advances; for example, the genuine epistles of Ignatius had been almost determined. The result was that the understanding of worship had to be re-authenticated from patristic sources.

Anglican Confidence and Nonconforming Scepticism
The assurance that the Church of England had achieved in its Reformation the form of liturgy closest to the practice of the early centuries was important for the confidence of Anglicanism. This was not a process by which the use of liturgy became an essay in antiquarianism, but rather a matter of relishing the life that was felt to flow through the Church of England. Thus, Gauden asserted that:

> ... the ancient Churches, from the very first century did use such publick, wholesome formes of sound words in their sacramental celebrations especially, and afterward in other holy Administrations or publick duties, as made up their ... Liturgies: which paterns all modern and reformed Churches of any renown have followed, according to the many Scriptural examples and expressions in set forms of Prayers, Praises, Psalms, Confessions and Benedictions, commended to us by holy men in all ages, and by Christ himself....[195]

To worship in what was understood to be the purest pattern became a spiritual experience, which was understood to be a way of sharing in the life of the apostolic community. Therefore, those who joined in Anglican public worship enjoyed the privilege of being as close as possible to the life that flowed from the ministry of Jesus Christ. Thus it was that the value of the Book of Common Prayer was heavily emphasised and its role was both acclaimed and defended. It is necessary to enquire how the Church of England handled the issue of the re-authentication of the Prayer Book and how the accord that was felt to exist between the Prayer Book and the usage of Christian antiquity was understood. The Anglican view of the patristic anchorage of the Prayer Book had been challenged and needed to be re-affirmed within the current debate. Against the background of the Restoration and the revision of the Prayer Book there was considerable argument about the claims made for the Prayer Book. Casaubon felt forced to reply to a tract of 1660 entitled: *The Common Prayer-Book Unmasked,*

Wherein is declared the Unlawfulnesse and Sinfulnesse of it...., and summarised the position of his target as follows:

> The Masse-Book, Breviaries, &c. are idolatrous popish-Books; therefore whatsoever is taken out of them, (or may be supposed to be taken out of them, because to be found there) is popish, and idolatrous.[196]

Casaubon ridiculed this approach by adding:

> Now a good part of both of the Old and New Testament, besides the whole Book of Psalmes, is to be found in Mass-Books, and Breviaries: Is any man so blind that dooh not see what will follow? And is not the same reason for many godly prayers and forms ... that were in use in time of purest Christianity, long before Popery was heard of; yet to be found in Mass-books and Breviaries?[197]

One can discern here the basic Anglican conviction that the form and content of the devotional life of the early church was accessible and could be used without subsequent accretions and distortions. Anglican convictions, however, did not go unchallenged; the pressures of the time appear to have been responsible for John Owen's *Discourse concerning Liturgies and their Imposition* (1661) being issued anonymously. Owen insisted that:

> ... neither did the Apostles of Our Lord Jesus Christ use any Liturgies..., nor did they Prescribe or Command any such to the Churches, or their Officers that were planted in them; nor by any thing intimate the usefulness of any such Liturgy, or Form of Publick Worship as after ages found out and used.[198]

Owen felt that the two main reasons advocated for liturgies were the inability of ministers to lead worship without liturgies and the importance attached to uniformity. However, Owen maintained that if Christ had promised gifts to enable his Bishops and Pastors to minister, then:

> is not the pretended necessity derogatory to the glory of the faithfulnesse of Jesus Christ, as plainly intimating that he doth not continue to fulfil his Promise....[199]

Owen also insisted that no expectation of uniformity could be deduced from the Apostles. He roundly insisted that there were no set forms of liturgy in the first three centuries, and that:

> ... the Introduction of Liturgies was ... the principal means of increasing and carrying on that sad desertion & Apostacie, in the guilt whereof most Churches in the World had enwrapped themselves.[200]

Owen continued to expound these views in his subsequent writings. It was not surprising that Parliament sought to protect the 1662 Act for the Uniformity of Publick Prayers with the Press Act, but that did not prevent Owen's views from being printed and circulated.

Anthony Sparrow had contended that it was a 'Fundamental Consideration' that the Prayer Book was 'agreeable to Primitive Usage',[201] but assertion was not the same as demonstration. The conviction that prescribed forms were used in the first three centuries was repeated by many writers, all of whom used the same limited stock of evidence.[202] In the same way, William Cave's *Primitive Christianity* (1673)[203] reflected contemporary confidence that the outline of the Book of Common Prayer was right, even if the detail could not be substantiated. Edward Pelling (?-1718) had been Vicar of St Martin's Ludgate since 1678. He was also Chaplain to the Duke of Somerset when his book of 1680 appeared entitled: *The Good Old Way, or a Discourse offer'd to all True-hearted Protestants Concerning the Ancient Way of the Church, and the Conformity of the Church of England Thereunto....* Pelling was a stout defender of the Anglican Church and affirmed that:

> ... no Church in Christendom this day can shew a more lively Monument of Antiquity, than our Common-Prayer Book.[204]

Pelling cited a series of evidences going back to Tertullian and Origen affirming the rightful place of set-forms in Christian worship, but he did not get any further than Cave in supporting the details of the Prayer Book.[205]

The Patristic Authentication of Prayer Book Material
The material considered up to this point in this chapter indicates a problem that was becoming more significant for the apology of the Anglican Church: the lack of ancient substantiation for the details of the

Prayer Book. Faced with the need to advocate the use of the Prayer Book, Anglican writers found themselves in need of a detailed justification of its text. It was not enough to claim that there were set forms of prayer in the early centuries; the alleged continuity of Prayer Book usage with the pattern of the life of worship in the early Church had to be substantiated. They could not persuade assent to the overall value of the services contained in the Prayer Book without being able to demonstrate the merits of the particles of each service. The scholar who met this need was Thomas Comber (1645-1699), who rose from being Precentor of York Minster to become Dean of Durham in 1691. After publishing various preliminary essays on Anglican services, in 1684 he produced a folio work entitled: *A Companion to the Temple: or, a Help to Devotion in the Use of the Common Prayer....* This work was so urgently needed that despite its considerable size it reached its third edition in 1688. Comber's meticulous approach and his devotional savouring of the Prayer Book text have not endeared him to modern commentators. Modern judgements such as: 'laborious and diffuse'[206] or 'deadly dull'[207] have masked the significance of this work. Comber gave the detailed derivation of the text of the Prayer Book from the text of the Bible, and expounded the meaning of each clause of the Prayer Book, both in its context in its order of service and in sectional paraphrases. The result of Comber's efforts was that any uncertainty in Anglicanism about the value of the Prayer Book was dispelled. Comber demonstrated that Anglican liturgy was anchored in Scripture and that there was significant patristic attestation of the framework of the prayers, of many of the phrases that they contained and also of the meaning attached to these phrases in their context in Anglican worship. However, as a vindication of the details of the Book of Common Prayer this book intensified a different problem. If the details of the biblical origin and the value of the text of the Prayer Book were proven, then controversy was now concentrated on whether it was legitimate to claim that there were recognisable patterns of liturgy in the early Church. It would not have been too difficult for this dispute to have been minimised and for the whole issue to have been regarded as having arisen from differing interpretations of the same stock of evidence, had it not been for the implications of this controversy for the validity of the practice of the Church of England.

The effort to disavow Anglican claims intensified. David Clarkson (1622-86) became a colleague to John Owen at Leadenhall Street in 1682, and succeeded to Owen's position in 1683. He and Owen held the same views regarding all set forms of worship. The more congenial climate of the Toleration Act of 1689 allowed his arguments on this subject to be published posthumously as his *Discourse Concerning Liturgies* (1689). Clarkson had ransacked the whole available patristic corpus to try to find evidence for the use of liturgies. Instead he produced a connected sequence of material that pointed against the use of liturgies. He did not specifically target the Church of England or the Prayer Book in drawing implications from his researches but, within the context of the times, Clarkson raised questions that had to be answered for Anglicanism to retain its credibility. He surmised that if liturgies had been known before the seventh century, then:

1. Certainly there would have been some mention of them, by some Fathers, Councils, or other Writers....
2. Undoubtedly they would have been generally admitted, as other Apostolical Writings were. None would have seen reason, to have composed other Liturgies, nor would any other have been preferred before them.
3. Finally, none would have presumed, or would have been suffered without controul, to have inlarged, curtailed, inverted them, and made all kinds of alterations therein....[208]

There was only one prayer in the Book of Common Prayer that Clarkson acknowledged could 'pretend to any footsteps of antiquity': the prayer from the order for the Lord's Supper for the whole state of Christ's Church. But the only evidence that Clarkson admitted was from a letter of Epiphanius to the Bishop of Jerusalem[209] and he chose to entirely overlook the patristic support marshalled by Comber.[210] This comparison raises the possibility that Clarkson was guardedly selective in his use of evidence. However, it is difficult to develop the contrast between Clarkson and Comber on the treatment of the contents of the Prayer Book because Clarkson did not offer a detailed critique of the Prayer Book. Apart from his comments on this one prayer, he held to his purpose of trying to build a general argument for the absence of liturgies in the early Church. When Clarkson did incorporate patristic mention that prayers had been offered, he harnessed this evidence to emphasise the lack of any uniformity in prayer in the early Church. He specifically linked the rise of the use of liturgies to the decline in the calibre of ministers, leaving the innuendo unsaid that the Church of England was dependent upon set liturgies because her ministers were gravely inadequate for their duties.[211]

Comber replied promptly and comprehensively, compiling a digest of patristic evidence supporting his position century by century.[212] William Cave, the distinguished patristic scholar, described the historical section of this work by Comber as 'the best of the kind'.[213] Comber reviewed the same extensive patristic corpus as had been surveyed by Clarkson and reached the opposite conclusions. Comber then turned Clarkson's arguments around:

> He argues, there were no Liturgies in the first Four or Five Ages at least, because no Writers of that Time have any such Phrase, as Reading of Prayers, though they do speak of Reading the Lessons and the Passions of the Martyrs. (Disc. of Lit. p7). I Reply, ... the force of this Argument turns upon himself: For I may Argue, There were no Extempore Prayers in all that time (at least after the miraculous Gift of Prayer ceased) because in all that Space, he (who hath so diligently searched Antiquity) cannot produce any Writer who speaks plainly of Extempore Prayers.[214]

Whilst Clarkson was not alive to reply, another writer using the initials 'S.B.' entered into the debate.[215] The general thrust of his argument was that the word 'liturgy' had changed its significance over the years and that Clarkson had misled Comber into following him into a category mistake. S.B. felt that they had both investigated the use of liturgy in the narrow sense of Forms of Prayer, and declared that: 'this is not the proper signification of a Liturgy as used and enjoined in the Church of England'.[216]

Comber's reply[217] showed himself to be rather irritated by S.B., and protested that what he had set out to do was:

> ... to collect in every Century such Testimonies of the Original, Use and Antiquity of Liturgies, as the Argument needed.[218]

and insisted on identifying liturgies as verbal formulae. S.B. promptly replied in print,[219] and abandoned the argument with the conclusion:

> ... hitherto I think we have not had any substantial proof of such a Liturgy, as is the point in debate betwixt Mr Clarkson and Dr Comber. And if this be so, we may have some reason to think, that neither the ceasing of pretended miraculous Gifts, nor the settling of the Church under Christian Magistrates, gave birth to

prescribed Liturgies; but that prescribed Liturgies are of a later Date, and owe their Original to something else than the Doctor hath alledged.[220]

The gravity of the issues that were involved in this debate over the felt continuity of usage with the early church was immense. Comber even went to the trouble of obtaining the approval of William Beveridge before he released his second reply called *The Examiner Briefly Examined....* (1691) for publication.[221]

However, the leading Anglican apologist, having answered the grounds of the debate over the pedigree of the Prayer Book and the ancient use of liturgies as forms of prayer, had then found yet a further question arising: the question as to the nature of liturgy. At the end of the century, the evidence above suggests that debate was moving away from factual questions concerning liturgy towards conceptual questions. Perhaps the debate had grown stale. An indication of this torpor was the way in which one Royal Chaplain dismissed the whole area of contention with the advice that no claims for inspiration in prayer should be accepted unless that person could also heal the sick and cure the lame.[222]

As in any living debate, the ground of contention shifted. This further demonstrates that there was not a monotypic Anglican theology of prayer in this era, but an evolving organism revealing different aspects in different contexts.

Review

Up to now in this enquiry, no discussion of the Book of Common Prayer itself has been offered because it is necessary first to establish the matrix of understanding within which the Prayer Book was held. These contextual matters can only illuminate the Prayer Book and clarify any examination of the Prayer Book. Such an essay can be made after the role of the Prayer Book has been explored.

The Book of Common Prayer was given an intellectual anchorage in the early Church. The evidence suggests that Comber was the only writer capable of handling the details of the connections felt to exist between Biblical and patristic studies on the one hand, and the contemporary usage of the Prayer Book on the other. Comber held of the Book of Common Prayer that:

... most of the Words and Phrases being taken out of Holy Scripture, ... the rest are the expressions of the first and best

Ages: so that whoever takes exceptions at these must quarrel with the Language of the Holy Ghost, or fall out with the Church in her greatest Innocence. Indeed, the greatest part of these prayers are primitive, or a second Edition of the most ancient Liturgies of the Eastern and Western Churches corrected and amended.[223]

In hindsight, Comber's work was clearly anachronistic as he did not attempt either to recreate or to understand the process of the compilation of the Prayer Book. Comber wrote as though the Book of Common Prayer had been drawn directly from Biblical and patristic sources. However, Comber's work did express his enthusiasm for Anglican worship. He encouraged people to share his conviction that, in the Prayer Book services, people were sharing in the worship of the early Church and also that, through the pages of the Book of Common Prayer, they were as close as was possible to the apostolic community and to the direct presence of Jesus Christ.

5

THE VOICE OF THE PRAYER
BOOK - IN THE NATION

The Prayer Book as an Instrument for National Education
General opinion in the Church of England in this period recognised that
the Church faced one particular problem in its role in the life of the
nation. This problem was the fact of popular ignorance. Whilst there
was no expectation that there should be universal literacy, let alone a
well-informed populace, the ignorance that disturbed the clergy was an
ignorance about how to pray and the alienation of people from the
process of prayer with all its implications. Clergy who ventured into
print were deeply concerned for those to whom they ministered and
looked on them with compassion. If people were helpless in their efforts
to pray it was, in part, because they had no comprehension as to what
prayer might be. 'Common and ordinary people' were described by a
parson of extended parochial experience as:

> ... not only ignorant, but very dull and lumpish in the
> performance of Divine Service: They do it without Reverence or
> Fear, need often stirring up and quickning. Many of them think it
> is enough if they come to Church and be there with their bodies,
> wheresoever their hearts be....[224]

Carr, who served as Rector of West Chiltington, near Pulborough in
Sussex, from 1628 until 1668, had the ambition:

> ... to raise up their attention and Devotion, to mind them of the
> business they are about, and to bring them to some measure of
> Knowledge and Understanding.[225]

George Bright, the Rector of Loughborough in Leicestershire from 1669 to 1696, felt the practice of prayer to be at risk nationally, as though it were a dying craft. He was anxious that the future of prayer as a national habit was at risk from three segments of the population: the 'ignorant and vulgar', those 'addicted to speculation' and 'vicious and debauched persons'. Bright claimed that for these three groups: '... Religious and Godly are become the most ordinary words of scorn.'[226] Bright saw the problem as a contagion in social attitudes:

> Nor is this humour but too much among the rich and great only, but (as is usual), the fashion is followed by the inferiour sort. And it is ordinary enough for them to think that they have wit and worth enough to despise Religion and the Priest.[227]

Bright acknowledged that the Church itself had contributed to these problems with inadequate scrutiny of candidates for ordination, but nevertheless felt that the practice of prayer in England was under considerable threat. Bright had a very clear impression of the national need of tuition in the matter of prayer. The massive base of popular ignorance, especially when coupled with the effects of upper class disdain, caused great concern. Such a widespread problem could only be dealt with by a universal solution which had to be uniform, otherwise the result would be confusion rather than elucidation. The solution was the Book of Common Prayer. As Jeremy Taylor had enthused about the Prayer Book:

> It is all that ... many men know of their Religion, for they cannot know it better then by those Formes of prayer which publish their faith, and their devotion to God, ... and which by an admirable expedient reduces their faith into practice, and places their Religion in their understanding, and affections.[228]

At the same time it was recognised that the solution required exemplary practice; it would not be enough to merely issue prayer books. The vision for this work of example and education can be traced principally in printed visitation sermons. Visitations were very important to the self-regulation of the Church of England. Whilst they were part of the mechanism of official coercion,[229] visitations were also occasions when the clergy could be exhorted to their tasks and reminded of the standards that were expected of them. As the incumbent of Earls Colne, Essex, recorded:

At visitacon, where I received admonicon to use all the prayers alwayes....[230]

At least one printed visitation sermon was normally issued every year from 1663 to 1700. Examined as a specific body of literature they provided a running commentary on church affairs and also articulated the ideals of the ministry of the Church of England as they unfolded through these years. The sincere conscientiousness that was reflected in these sermons continually reverted to the themes of pastoral care and ministerial responsibility. The clergy were felt to be in a leading role of offering an example, 'an Illustrative Holynesse'[231] and were encouraged accordingly:

Let the Sanctity of God's House, wherein we daily minister, and the Majesty of the living God we serve, awaken and keep alive in us a constant gravity, and quick sense of piety. And then the most Sceptical men will be ashamed to blaspheme Religion, and call it a meer Juggle of the Priests, when they see us live under the power of it. And then shall the Divine Glory descend upon us and our Church, as it was wont to doe upon the Ark of God.[232]

The actual practice of public prayer was not only regarded as setting an important example, but was also held to be an effective instrument of pastoral nurture:

But how are they to Feed them? I answer, First by Prayer for their respective charges both in Public and in Private. This is the First thing belonging to the Pastoral Office.[233]

Indeed, the perceived imitation of Jesus Christ in the life of a minister was claimed to authenticate the example of that minister:

This is that, which will convey such a might, and swaying Majesty into all our discomposed, and unruly people into a better, and more kindly compliance; yea, this is that, which will give life and spirits to our Liturgy; and make our Common Prayer, to come with an extraordinary power upon the hearts of the people.... [234]

It was from the practical basis of national usage that the Prayer Book was expected to tutor the nation. The minimal revision of the Prayer Book in 1662 did not disrupt this vision. Alan Carr was most anxious that: '... all ought to joyn in the Common-prayers of the Church'.[235] The ambition for the Prayer Book to provide spiritual nurture for the bulk of the population was earnestly held by the Church of England. Accordingly, the priority of the Prayer Book was ardently defended. Edward Kemp felt that ministers who used anything that was not in the Book of Common Prayer had chosen to give the people 'empty husks of prayer'.[236] The lingering antagonism towards anything that did not emanate from the Prayer Book can be illustrated from a Cathedral sermon of 1672:

> ... praying by the Spirit, (as they call it), hath prayed all into Confusions; It hath prayed off the head of Charles the First, it hath prayed Peace and Truth out of the Church, and the People out of their wits....[237]

The Quest for Unanimity

Symon Patrick, Royal Chaplain, Dean of Peterborough and future Bishop of Chichester and Ely, insisted that the benefits of sharing in public worship were simply summarised:

> ... the Blessings we enjoy in common together, are far greater than those we enjoy singly and distinct one from another.[238]

Common prayer was understood to be the key to a genuine corporate life in the faith and to the future well-being of the Church and nation. The problem of a fundamental ignorance in the matter of prayer had been recognised, and Common Prayer was regarded as the solution through personal example and through popular participation in the liturgy.

There was much discussion of 'conformity' and 'dissent' in these years, but the matter was not merely a divergence of attitudes. One commentator discerned a middle course in the discussion:

> All the possible unity ... that is to be held in matters of Religion amongst men, is either Internal, or External. The Internal unity is that which is held in respect to Inward Acts of the mind; and ... as respecting Doctrines and Worship in matters of Religion as their object, are either Assent, or Dissent, or the middle thing, doubting about them.[239]

However, whilst it was noted that external conformity was immediately measurable and verifiable:

> Nothing Internal can possibly be of itself, and immediately, a medium or means for the procuring a Charitative Communion amongst men in any matter whatsoever; And so then, not in matters of Religion: And that because inward Acts of themselves come not under the cognizance of men: they not affecting their sense, and so cannot affect them.[240]

These strictures did not prevent a substantial discussion developing on the internal aspects of public prayers. One anonymous writer commented particularly on the matter of 'unanimity':

> The publique prayers require Unanimity, so we read of the first Christians. They were altogether with one accord in one place, the multitude of them that believed were of one heart and one soul: and St Paul severely chides the Corinthians for discord in their assemblies....[241]

This particular source alluded to Cyprian's *De Unitate Ecclesiae* and noted on the basis of Cyprian's treatment of the dominical saying 'I say unto you, that if two of you shall agree on earth as touching any thing that they shall ask ...' (Matthew 18 v. 19) that much was ascribed not to the multitude, but to the unanimity of those that pray. Anglican reflection reached beyond the mere demand for uniformity in order to consider the inner dynamism of congregations and of the inner life of the whole Church:

> ... in Publick Services we must put on Publick Spirits, and mind the Condition of others as well as our selves, praying and praising God for others as well as our selves.[242]

It was held that the quest for unanimity could only proceed from the basis of uniform Prayer Book usage. Departures from the Book of Common Prayer were decried as threatening the coherence of the Church and the realm. Establishment figures embraced the implications of unanimity in the life of the Church. Thomas Pittis (1636-1687) was a Royal Chaplain and became Rector of St Botolph without Bishopsgate in 1678. Whilst he argued for the prescribed use of the Prayer Book, he felt that there was more to uniformity than conformity:

> Unity of affection and consent in prayer is that which renders
> our publick devotions so acceptable to God. ... Now there cannot
> ... in my opinion, be this consent, and unity of affection in
> prayer, but where there is an uniformity in calling upon
> God....[243]

An Anglican theology of prayer was being developed which argued that
God expected the people of the land to speak with one voice from a
united heart. In order for everybody to share in that one voice it was
essential that the ordinary people recognised the value of the Prayer
Book. Not surprisingly, someone of the status of Kettlewell could plead
that 'Dissenting Brethren':

> ... must not break the Publick Unity and Peace to carry on their
> own Profiting in Private Graces.[244]

The quest for unanimity, however, reinforced the expectation for an
exact observance of the Prayer Book. Any elaboration of, or deviation
from, the printed text of the services was held to undermine the
unanimity of the Church. Richard Sherlock served as Rector of
Winwick in Lancashire from 1662 to 1689. He had been ordained
before the Civil War and had been chaplain to the Governor of the
royalist garrison at Oxford in 1644. His remarks were the fruit of the
convictions of experience:

> ... private prayer, whether before Sermon, or at any other time in
> the Congregation, doth not onely secretly imply a defect in the
> Publick Prayers of the Church, which must (forsooth) be
> supplyed by mens private conceived prayers: but also, 'tis a
> disorder and confusion in the service of God....[245]

It was possible for those committed to the Anglican devotional
programme to be baffled at the failure to accept something that had so
much value, as another incumbent wrote:

> ... if the same confession of Faith be to the Glory of God and
> Christian Religion, why not the same publick confession of sins,
> the same public oblations of Praise and Thanksgiving? If to have
> one minde and one Tongue, be commendable, and highly
> desirable in the Christian Church; why not one Form of Prayer,
> why not one publick worship? [246]

National Stability

A great deal of the credit for the long-term stability of the Church after the Restoration has been accorded to Gilbert Sheldon (1598-1677), who became Bishop of London in 1660 and then Archbishop of Canterbury in 1663.[247] Sheldon emphasised properly enforced order and unity of belief, but he integrated the Church of England with the common law so as to affirm the authority of statute rather than emphasising the Church's independence in jurisdiction.

The Anglican apologia of these years ensured that the nation was not allowed to forget what had followed when the Prayer Book had been abolished. Anglican authors and preachers could rely on a common awareness of the contortions that the nation had suffered:

> We may all know what ensued the abolishing Common-prayer among us; Let us sin no more, lest a worse thing come upon us.[248]

> If you regard the Common Safety and the Publique Peace, or your Private Interest therein involv'd; ... break not our Parish-bounds; forsake not, sleight not, our Publique Worship and Assemblies.[249]

Symon Patrick was sensitive to the social dimension of the Church, and its place in building up the nation through national prayer:

> ... the Blessings we most want, as we are sociable Creatures, being public Blessings; they ought, in all reason, to be sought in our Common Prayers, as most generally needful for us all.[250]

Patrick directly linked social disorder and confusion to the neglect of public prayers.[251] According to Patrick, the practice of common prayer affected the whole of society:

> ... we may by the common Offices of Religion, keep ourselves the closer knit together, in firm Love and Unity, in the same Society.[252]

Against the background of the brief and troubled reign of James II, with the looming instability in central religious affiliation, this theme of the effects on the nation of the national observance of Anglican set prayers had particular significance:

... Publick Prayers ... are the proper Instrument for the obtaining and continuing Publick Peace, and Tranquility; or the Establishment, and Prosperity of a Church and State.[253]

It was possible at that difficult time to look back and to conclude:

... That as the neglect, and dis-use of our Common-Prayer was the beginning of those Confusions, and Miseries which ruined both our Church and State; so the most probable means to secure our Religion, as it is now Established, and to engage Almighty Power on our side, is, for us all to unite ourselves ... in the same daily Publick Worship of our great Lord.[254]

Thus, the practice of Common Prayer was embraced as a means of securing the preservation of the nation. People were reminded to pray for the sovereign, especially when the passage: I Timothy 2 v. 1,2 was selected for exposition:

We are to pray for Kings, because it is the only way the generality can do them service in. Those that cannot help them by their counsel, nor their Purses, may by their prayers. This way the charity and kindness of the poorest Cottage may visit and relieve the Court itself, and the greatest King may be indebted for his preservation, his life, his health, the success of his affairs, to the prayers of his meanest Vassal.[255]

National Prayer

Three annual services were directed to be annexed to the Book of Common Prayer by Royal Warrant in 1662. These were the services for the Deliverance from the Gunpowder Treason (5th November), the Martyrdom of King Charles I (30th January), and the Thanksgiving for the King's Birth and Return (29th May). These services were full of significance for the state and for the stability of the realm. Whilst using the familiar format of Morning Prayer, Litany and Ante-Communion, these extra services provided special readings, responses and prayers.

The deliverance celebrated on 5th November was ascribed to Almighty God, as was the Restoration of Charles II. However, the service for King Charles Martyr could be viewed as a pattern of manipulating congregations into being dependent upon the national church to secure national forgiveness. The gospel readings appointed for 30th January were about the death of Christ - implying that the heinous death of Charles I was typologically linked to the death of Jesus Christ - which, in turn, implied that the monarchy participated in divine status. The full title of the service when it was first issued explained the anxieties of this service:

> *A form of Common Prayer, to be Used upon the Thirtieth of January, Being the Anniversary Day, Appointed by Act of Parliament For Fasting and Humiliation, To implore the Mercy of God, That neither the Guilt of that Sacred and Innocent Blood, nor those other sins by which God was provoked to deliver up both us and our KING, into the hands of Cruel and Unreasonable men, may at any time hereafter be visited upon us or our Posterity*

Over the years 1660-1700 there were many special services issued for national use. Usually, they were issued for use in London and Westminster on one Sunday and then for the rest of the country for a following Sunday, so as to allow time for distribution. The response to major disasters acknowledged them to be the judgement of God. Thus the torrential rain of 1661 led to a special service for 12th June which featured the flood narrative of Genesis 8 as the first reading. The following January, the threat of hunger arising from the terrible weather led to the formulation of a service for 15th January and the use in the first collect of the words:

> O Eternal God, and most gracious Father, who by this strange and unseasonable Weather, causest us to fear, that Scarcity and Famine, Sicknesses and Diseases may ensue, and justly fall upon us for our iniquities: We humbly here confess, there can fall nothing so heavy upon us, but we have deserved, even whatever thy Law hath threatned against perverse and obstinate sinners. Our contempt of thy Divine Service is great, and we hear thy Word, but obey it not: Our charity to our Neighbours is cold, and our devotion to thee is frozen: Our unthankfulness to thee is very great.... [256]

The plague service of 1665 picked up the tradition of services focussed on this horror and after the Prayer for the Church Militant the words were set to be offered that:

> We, the sinful people of this land, whom for our iniquities and

manifold transgressions thou hast in many places most justly
visited with the noisom Plague, and Pestilence, come now before
the throne of thy grace.... [257]

These sentiments of national contrition were echoed in the Litany in the
service for 10th October 1666 to mark the Great Fire of London:

> Look down, O Lord, in the bowels of thy mercy, upon the
> sorrows and distresses of thy servants, who in the deepest sense
> of thy amazing judgements, and our own manifold provocations,
> lie prostrate in the dust before thee. To thee O God holy and
> true, belong mercy and forgiveness, But unto us confusion of
> face as it is this day. For we are that incorrigible Nation who
> have resisted thy Judgements, and abused thy Mercies.... [258]

The annual services for King Charles Martyr and the King's Birth and
Return ensured that there was a latent royal cult, meaning that any
significant threat to the king's person was an occasion for a service for
the defeat of treason and conspiracy. The accession of James II led to
profound changes in the services for King Charles Martyr and the
Restoration. In the 1662 Prayer Book text for the service of King
Charles Martyr, the prayer after the Prayer for the Church Militant had
included the words:

> ... but by thy gracious providence didst miraculously preserve
> the undoubted heir of his Crown, our most gracious Soveraign
> King Charles the Second, from his bloody enemies, hiding him
> under the shadow of thy wings, until their tyranny was overpast,
> and bringing him back in thy good appointed time to sit in peace
> upon the throne of his Father, and to exercise that authority over
> us, which of thy special grace thou hadst committed unto him.

However, in 1685 this sentence was revised to read:

> ... but by thy gracious Providence didst miraculously preserve
> the undoubted heir of his Crowns, our then gracious Sovereign
> King Charles the Second from his bloudy Enemies, hiding him
> under the shadow of thy Wings, until their Tyranny was
> overpast; and then didst bring him back in thy good appointed
> Time, together with his Royal Brother King James, to sit
> successively in peace upon the Throne of their Father, and to

Exercise that Supream Authority over us, (one after the other) which of thy special Grace thou hadst designed for them.[259]

The assertion of supreme authority as the design of God was echoed as an obligation of allegiance to the sovereign in the service for the Restoration. The second collect in the Ante-Communion in the 1662 text for 29th May read:

Grant, we beseech thee, Almighty God, that our Soveraign Lord the King, whom thou didst this day happily bring home, and restore to us, may be a mighty protector of his people, a religious defender of thy sacred Faith, and of thy holy Church among us, a glorious conqueror over all his enemies, a gracious governour unto all his subjects....

The revision of 1685 ignored this precedent and included the words:

Vowing all holy Obedience in Thought, Word, and Work unto thy Divine Majesty; and promising in thee and for thee all loyal and dutiful Allegiance to thine Anointed Servant now set over us, and to his Heirs after him....[260]

The shift of emphasis so that the obligation of the monarch to his people was turned into the obligation of the people to the monarch was remarkable.

The Queen's pregnancy was marked by a national service for 15th January 1688, in which the first lesson was the promise of a child to Abraham and Sarah (Genesis 17 v 1-17).[261] The birth of a prince was celebrated by another service for use on 17th June and included the words in the special collects:

Grant the Princely Infant health, strength, and long life, that he may grow up to live in thy fear, and to thy glory, and to excell in all virtues becoming his high Birth, and the Royal Dignity to which thou hast ordained him.[262]

The change of tone following the accession of William and Mary must be noted. The *Form of prayer and thanksgiving to Almighty God, for having made His Highness the Prince of Orange the glorious instrument of the great deliverance of this kingdom from popery and arbitrary power....* for use on 31st January 1689 included the words for use after the General Thanksgiving: '... our Laws and Liberties are rescued from the Hands of Violence and Oppression.' A further prayer for use after the Prayer for the Church Militant declared: 'It is of Thy Mercy, O Lord, that we are not utterly consumed, that our Religion was not destroyed, nor our Liberty subverted....'

The ensuing wars in which King William took such a leading role spawned a large number of services and published prayers. These services particularly carried the intention of the safety and preservation of the King and the success and well-being of the army and navy. In addition to regular prayers for the King there were also prayers for the Reformed Churches and a prayer that was often directed to be used after the Prayer for the Church Militant that was eloquent both of the ambitions of Anglicanism and also the aspirations of peace:

> O God the Father of our Lord Jesus Christ our only Saviour, the Prince of Peace, look down in much pity and compassion upon this Church and Nation, now seeking unto thee in Fasting and Prayer; and grant, we beseech thee, that our humiliation and Repentance may have that blessed effect, that we may all cleanse our selves from all filthiness of flesh and spirit, perfecting holiness in the fear of God. Give us grace, O Lord, seriously to lay to heart the great Dangers we are in, by our unhappy divisions. Take away all hatred and prejudice, and whatsoever else may hinder us from godly Union and Concord: That as there is but one Body, and one Spirit, and one Hope of our Calling, one Lord, one Faith, one Baptism, one God and Father of us all; so we may henceforth be all of one Heart and of one Soul, united in one holy Bond of Truth and Peace, of Faith and Charity, and may with one mind and one mouth glorifie thee, O God, through Jesus Christ our Lord. Amen.[263]

When the 30th Anniversary of the Fire of London was marked in 1696, a special format of service was issued which included these words to follow the Prayer for the Church Militant:

> O Almighty Lord God, thou governest all things in Heaven and Earth. Thou commandest the flames, and all the powers of the creation, and they obey thee.[264]

All these forms of prayer shared in an insistence upon the sovereign will of God, and a sense of God's involvement in the affairs of the nation.

The Failure of Ambitions for the Prayer Book

The capacity to make good use of the Prayer Book was an acquired art and it was noted that people had to be taught how to become involved in Church services. There was almost an element of shock early in the reign of William and Mary when it was realised that people could prefer non-Anglican approaches to prayer:

> For I know some that have constantly attended at the Publick Prayers of the Church ...; yet because they knew not how to use them as they should, they have not at any time found that inward content which they now think to receive from new Modes of Prayer; and at last have totally forsaken them, crying out most bitterly against their Formality, luke-warmness, and indifferency in Prayer. As if that unfit temper proceeded from the Prayers, and not from the ignorance of their minds....[265]

The only educational methodology that has been detected in this period to accommodate the Book of Common Prayer to the mass of the people was example and repetition. This process, however, did not necessarily engender popular imitation, even though Anglican enthusiasm for its national task precluded complacency in its establishment:

> If the Lives of the Sons of the Church of England, were as Holy as its Doctrine, as Divine as its Discipline, and as much Reformed as its Liturgie, This, This would bring our Way of Worship into Credit. This would put to silence the Evil-speaking of Foolish men, yea and This would make Converts flie to our Churches as Doves to their Windows....[266]

Confidence was broadly maintained in the Prayer Book, and the problems associated with the liturgy were understood to devolve upon its use and the lack of popular education. John Templer summarised the Anglican consensus of the period when he listed three things as the ends of public worship:

> The Glory of God, The Salvation of the Soul, The Preservation of the Community.[267]

In all this, a conviction of the importance of public worship consisting exclusively of the prescribed contents of the Prayer Book was maintained. However, the high expectations that were attached to the

Prayer Book by the consensus of Anglican thought were impossible to fulfil. The Anglican church had no educational techniques available to reach the mass of the population beyond example and repetition. Catechism may have taught the language of Christian belief, but did not necessarily teach the life of devotion. Consequently, the outline of the contents of the Prayer Book became more important and the contemporary understanding of their use became critical. The theological ambition of unanimity may have been very attractive, but the Prayer Book itself was not an adequate resource to secure these goals. The execution of the Prayer Book services became the pivot on which it was felt popular feeling turned: whether to become involved in or alienated from the life of the Church. It is to the voice of the Prayer Book as it was heard in the parishes that the next chapter must turn.

6

THE VOICE OF THE PRAYER
BOOK - IN THE PARISHES

The Restoration Printing of the Book of Common Prayer
The Restoration of the Monarchy in 1660 was linked to a revived
official presumption in favour of the Book of Common Prayer. The
Jacobean Prayer Book was promptly reprinted. The previous folio
edition had been issued in 1639, but four discrete folio editions of the
Prayer Book have been traced that were issued in 1660 and 1661.[268]
The fact that the unrevised Prayer Book was printed four times in folio
in these two years reflects its restored position as the national liturgy.
The folio editions of the Prayer Book were used on the minister's desk
as he led public worship,[269] and these were the only size that were
legally acceptable for the use of the minister.[270] The four new editions
of the Book of Common Prayer in folio, even in an age when printing
runs were usually limited to two thousand copies for a large book,[271]
meant that the unrevised book was immediately available for purchase
and that sufficient copies were available for many of the parish churches
of the land to acquire a copy.
    The revised book only received two folio editions in 1662, and then
it was not reprinted again in folio until 1669. Whilst there had been
considerable public demand for the unrevised prayer book in folio at the
time of the Restoration, the revised prayer book in folio was only
spasmodically reprinted. This continued until the need for a second
folio copy in each parish church for the use of the Parish Clerk came to
feature more and more in Visitation Articles of Enquiry after 1680.[272]
However, the thirst for editions of the Prayer Book in 1660 and 1661
left little market for the revised editions of 1662. One diarist recorded
that his churchwarden would not buy the revised service book in 1662
at the exorbitant price of eight shillings.[273] This lack of potential

demand may also explain the dilatory approach of the printers towards producing the revised Prayer Book.[274]

The Prayer Book as a Standard Text

William Beveridge (1637-1708), the future Bishop of St Asaph, was Rector of Cornhill when he delivered his 1681 sermon entitled *The Excellency and Usefulness of the Common Prayer*. This sermon was based on I Corinthians 14 v. 26 'Let all things be done unto edifying', and was reprinted nine times before the end of the century. Beveridge was very much an establishment figure. He had been ordained in 1661 and appointed to St Peter's Cornhill in 1672, when he was made a Prebendary of St Paul's. He received a Cambridge DD in 1679 and became Archdeacon of Colchester in 1681, shortly before offering this sermon. His comments emphasised that prayer must be common:

> ... a set form of prayer is an extraordinary help to us; for if I hear another pray, and know not beforehand what he will say, I must first listen to what he will say next; then I am to consider, whether what he saith be agreeable to sound doctrine, and whether it be proper and lawful for me to join with him in the petitions he puts up to God Almighty; and if I think it is so, then I am to do it: but before I can well do that, he is got to another thing....[275]

Beveridge was used to paying detailed attention to language, having specialised in the study of languages at Cambridge, and he was not alone in offering this particular argument.[276] At best Beveridge considered shared prayer without the Book of Common Prayer to be a halting exercise in frustration:

> ... if we hear another praying a prayer of his own private composition or voluntary effusion, our minds are wholly bound up and confined to his words and expressions, and to his requests and petitions, be they what they will: so that, at the best, we can but pray his prayer. Whereas, when we pray by a form prescribed by the Church, we pray the prayers of the whole Church we live in ...; which cannot, surely, but be more effectual for the edifying, not only of ourselves in particular, but of the Church in general, than any private prayers can be.[277]

Beveridge had said far more than that 'the practice of prayer affects the people who are praying'. Instead he affirmed participation in the prescribed prayers of the Church to build up both the individuals involved and the Church as a whole. A prescribed national offering of prayer was integral to the life of the Church of England.

John Scott (1639-1695) ministered in London parishes for many years and was made a Canon of St Paul's in 1685. He offered some lengthy writings connected with practical Christian living and encouraged people to see the value of standardised forms of prayer. Scott was confident in the value of immersing oneself in the meaning of pre-formed prayers before offering them.

> ... if the mind be truly devout and doth affect the matter of prayer for itself and not for the sake of the words, I cannot imagin how new words should any way advantage its devotion, unless they were to express new matter. Since therefore the matter of publick Prayer neither is nor ought to be new, unless it be upon extraordinary publick emergencies, what colour of reason can there be assign'd, why the devotion of the hearers should be more affected with it in new words than in old.[278]

Matthew Hole, another incumbent, had no hesitation in insisting on the uselessness of supposed alternatives to Anglican worship. Hole had been appointed Vicar of Stogursey, Somerset, and a Prebendary of Wells Cathedral in 1688. He affirmed:

> ... the gift of Prayer now remaining in the Church, consists not in pouring out many and new words, but in the pious Motions, and good Affections of the Heart.... [279]

The essential Anglican confidence in the Book of Common Prayer enabled a future non-juror, when preaching in his own parish church, to claim that the Prayer Book had, by implication, been prescribed by God and that therefore there was no legitimate alternative to Anglicanism. John Kettlewell (1653-1695) was a deeply conscientious incumbent who, having been ordained in 1677, was Vicar of Coleshill in Warwickshire from 1682 until he was deprived in 1690. He had an enduring reputation as a devotional writer:

> A second thing in Religion due to God, is worshipping him according to his own Rules. This is another of Gods Rights. For his adorable Excellencies, and Soveraignty over us, claim our

Worship; and he himself alone can prescribe it. The end of it is
to honour and please him; and what will do that is best known to
himself; so that his Worship must be of his own prescribing....[280]

The depth of confidence in the Prayer Book was quite remarkable and
precedence was claimed for the format of the Book of Common Prayer
over variations or alternatives:

Forms of Prayer are not to be excepted against. There never was
any solid cogent argument brought against them, nor, I believe,
ever will be. Nor are our Publick Prayers to be disliked. Those
many aspersions heretofore cast upon our Liturgie, have in the
issue proved rather beauty spots, to adorn and commend it, than
blemishes to disguise and disgrace it.[281]

Difficulties of the Parish System

The regulation of parish life had been considered at the Convocation of
1661. Reference has already been made to the significance and impact
of the process of Visitation. Discussions were held in the Upper House
to consider the issue of a standardised book of Visitation Articles of
Enquiry. However, there is no record of this proposal ever getting
further than a draft prepared by Bishop Cosin.[282] The inconclusiveness
of the attempt to reform the internal regulation of Church life did more
than just secure the variety of Diocesan life; the result was latitude and
flexibility in Church life rather than any precise pattern of official
expectations. Furthermore, this approach allowed local custom to be
maintained within the broad spectrum of Anglicanism, for custom could
only be amended by statute, not by canon. As was affirmed in
connection with local church practice:

Custome of the Realm cannot be taken away but by Act of
Parliament.[283]

It has been observed that: "Custom was both a way of doing things and
knowing things".[284] It was a considerable challenge for the Church of
England to engage contemporary culture with a written liturgy, and
inevitably there was a wide range of outcomes. However, the only
common ground that the Church could offer to the variety of cultures of
the day was the set liturgy. Anglicans could have a naïf pride that in the
Prayer Book the Church had:

... sufficiently provided for the simplicity of the plainest, and the devotion of the most intelligent....[285]

A layman who was enthusiastic for Anglican worship was bewildered by the tensions generated by using the psalter; he could not understand how the psalter could fail to unite people of different levels of comprehension:

> ... our praising God ... is so accomodate to the capacity of all, descending to the very meanest, without abating the delights of the greatest, that it is strange any should not like it.[286]

Whilst the opposing extremes of literary scholarship and illiteracy are easily distinguished, the gradations of literacy are not readily discerned after 300 years. The context of the Book of Common Prayer was a complex cultural matrix which included the 'grey area' of the cultural overlap where there was both partial literacy and partial illiteracy. However, whilst it may be convenient for the purposes of analysis to contrast these factors in opposition, it would be a mistake to regard these elements as diverging cultural forces. This is because, in the era under discussion, it was hoped that these varied cultural currents would inter-react so that they would be complementary:

> ... although you cannot read, yet your heart may join with them that do read; and your Mouth also may shew forth the Praise of God, by saying after every Psalm, Glory be to the Father, &c.[287]

> ... if every one spake as loud and plain in repeating his Verse, as the Minister doth in repeating his, ... there would be no cause for this Complaint ... by those that cannot read, who might be helped by the next by-stander to perform their part without it, or at least understand as much as if the Minister read all, and be more edified in that holy Joy which this manner of reading is apt to beget.[288]

Considering the Prayer Book in its context gives the prospect of a national system with a stated ideal but accompanied by huge variations of attainment. One also considers the frustration of dedicated souls who could not understand why the parish system was not producing the anticipated results. Clergy were ready to blame many influences in the society of their time as undermining the work of the Church. While many people were ready to blame the clergy, no comment has been noted regarding the inadequacy of the parochial system to its task. The Church itself was probably not in a position to make such an objective assessment. Consequently, in appraising the comments about the operation of the Book of Common Prayer, one is often dealing with aspirations born of idealism rather than practical achievements and sometimes with unbridled enthusiasm:

> ... who can behold the Pious and Devout Soul prostrate before God, repeating the Prayers of the Church with Fervency and Devotion, and a Congregation united together both in Heart and Voice, but he must needs be affected with it.... How often have prophane and wicked Wretches, who came to the Publick Worship of God; either out of Fashion, or Custom, to look and gaze about them, or on some worse Design, been touch'd by a Coal from the Altar? how often have their Hearts glow'd within them, and they have taken up serious and Solemn Resolutions, of serving and worshipping God better for the future? [289]

Legally, the Church of England had to use its Prayer Book. Theologically, there was an overwhelming tide of opinion and argument in favour of using the Prayer Book. Individually, clergy were sworn to use the Book. And the population of England were required to attend Common Prayer by royal command[290] and by statute.[291] The identity of the public face of the Church of England was totally bound up with the use of this book. However, even the low level of complexity of the worship in parish churches was too much for too many people.

The expectation that people would learn by repetition may be inferred to have been largely unfulfilled; no trace has been found of any acknowledgement of a general competence in the popular contribution to common prayer having been achieved. The ambitions of the Church to encompass the whole of the nation were thwarted by the Book that had to be used. Had it not been for the popular use of the metrical psalter, a considerable proportion of the population would have been alienated altogether from sharing in any form of corporate praise. Meanwhile, the life of the Church of England had a curious circularity and the inherent tendency of Anglicanism to fail in its ambitions was fed by the intensity of the insistence on the use of the Prayer Book. The pressure to use the Book of Common Prayer may itself have generated a tradition of non-participation. If the Church of England located its identity in the process of parochial worship, and in the utilisation of the

Prayer Book, then there was an effectual exclusion of those who did not have the competence to participate.

Non-Attendance and Inattention

It would be possible to accuse the Church of England as having failed to harness the popularity of the Prayer Book at the Restoration, but it was impractical to sustain the adulation of the old order for any long period of time. Popular disregard for Church attendance was often commented upon by Anglican writers, with varying degrees of incomprehension. Thus it was remarked that:

> The gross neglects, and contempts of some, with the disorders of others, as to the Common Service of the Church now injoyned, arise principally (as farr as my observation reaches) from the not understanding and weighing aright these two things. First, the great necessity, worth, and benefit of publique worship ...; and Secondly, the sutable and excellent provision made for that performance by our present establishments....[292]

> ... there is utterly a fault amongst us; In that ... that ancient and Constant way of Gods worship in Publick, is by many too much slighted and neglected....[293]

Disregard for public worship was even officially claimed to be a contributory cause to the unleashing of the Great Plague in 1665.[294] The self-reinforcing popular indifference to the Book of Common Prayer was noticed by writers commenting on the lack of interest in the Prayer Book amongst some of those who did attend Church:

> This Church receives no small injury from the careless and remiss attendance of many of her professed admirers, upon her publick Devotions and Instructions.[295]

> ... some Men think, they worship God sufficiently, if they come time enough to Church to join in the Pulpit Prayers, I would desire them to consider, that Church-Communion principally consists in joining in the Publick Prayers of the Church.[296]

Contemporary guidance emphasised the importance of learning how to give attention in prayer:

... If you will have your Prayers acceptable to God, you must offer them with that attention and intention of the mind, that so weighty an action, and the greatness of God's Majesty require: For to what purpose is it to attend, and be present in a praying Congregation, if we be no more concerned in the Devotion, than the Timber and Stones of the Fabrick; if our Bodies be present without our Souls? [297]

Note has already been taken of George Bright's anxiety that the disdain for the Prayer Book held by the upper classes was transmitted to the lower classes. Bright's was not a solitary voice:

... The publick behaviour of many of the Nobility, Gentry, and persons whose Examples are regarded, is another cause of the Peoples disesteem of our Liturgy. When Men of Learning, of Wealth, and of Honour, assist at the Devotions of their Brethren, without expressing any respect for them, and without bearing any part in the Service of the Church, others are discouraged from the use of it. This we see almost in every Congregation, some of the Chief are commonly distasted at some part of our praying or praising of God, in which, they will shew no sign of devotion; or, it may be, the Gentlemen of the Parish are not so religious as they should be, therefore they think it sufficient for them, if they bring their Bodies to the Publick Prayers, though they remain there in God's presence, as so many Stooks or Brutes, without expressing any Devotion for the Prayers, or any Worship to their Creator.[298]

These lines illustrate that the problems of education faced by the Church of England were not merely confined to those related to illiteracy and cultural diversity. Even in intellectual milieux difficulties were noted with the use of religious language:

Similitudes and Metaphors in Religion are those clouds of Incense wherewith at the same time we both enter and obscure the Sanctum Sanctorum.[299]

It was also necessary to teach those who were educated how to pray. Teaching was available, although it is impossible to discern the level of success. Earnestness in prayer was encouraged, but encouragement and exhortation seem only to have emphasised the problem.

The Execution of Prayer Book Worship

It is furthermore necessary to look into the ways in which the Prayer Book was recommended to be used in these years and to consider surviving indicators of the ways in which services were executed. Anglican worship comprehended considerable local variations in practice and a chasm between the ideal and the reality of what was practically possible.

The Sunday services of Morning Prayer were conducted by a Clerk in Holy Orders and the people were usually led in their responses by the Parish Clerk. These responses often extended to creating a pattern of offering alternate verses of the appointed psalms and canticles. A person appointed to be Parish Clerk was required, in the terms of Canon 91 of 1604, to be "of honest conversation, and sufficient for his reading, writing, and also competent for his skill in singing, if it may be". Although the Canon required the Clerk to be appointed by the Incumbent, actual practice was not so straightforward:

> ... since the making of this Canon, the Right [of appointment] hath often been contested between Incumbents and Parishioners, and Prohibitions prayed, and always obtained, where there has been a Custom contrary to Canon.[300]

The right of appointment of the Parish Clerk, therefore, often lay with the Vestry Meeting in each parish. This procedure gave the people of the parish control over who led them in church services and guided them in the offering of metrical psalms, as will be explored below. Rural Parish Clerks were not necessarily literate.[301] There were training and resources provided in London by the 'Company of Parish Clerks', which had particular value in the use of the metrical psalter. However, there were probably not many direct benefits from the Company for those living away from London. Contemporaneous expectations of the Parish Clerk were that he was:

> ... only appointed to answer as the Guide and Leader of the people and Congregation, to draw them on, and to encourage them to follow him; for what he says, all should say with him in the confession of sins, the Lords prayer, in the Letany, repeating of the ten Commandments or elsewhere, yea all, Minister, Clerk, and Congregation should joyn with their hearts (and may sometimes with their voices) in all the prayers of the Church, for deliverance, for Mercy, for Grace, for Peace, &c. what is uttered

by one, should be seconded with the Mouths, or at least with the hearts of all the Congregation, especially in saying (Amen) to all, because all ought to joyn in the Common-prayers of the Church.[302]

There are indications that the level of competence expected of Parish Clerks rose during the period 1660-1700. In Visitation Articles of Enquiry, there was a development from a question of 1662:

Is he ... sufficient or able to perform his duty in reading, writing and singing? [303]

to a question of 1686:

And doth he diligently attend him [i.e. the Minister] in all Divine Offices; audibly making, and repeating the Responses and Suffrages, as in the Liturgy he is directed? [304]

High standards were expected of the Clerk's example in public worship. One can also surmise that there may have been a development in the role of the Parish Clerk, from being the leader and encourager of the congregation towards a more professional approach. The Clerk was expected to compensate for any lack in the audible offering of the congregation, so that he and the congregation would complement each other. The two quotations that follow illustrate the practical differences between countryside and London congregations, as well as the tasks of Parish Clerks:

... some as soon as they are setled in their seats, hold down their heads and fall asleep; other gaze about, and some are slugging and slumbring, little minding the service of God, so that they need quickning and stirring up. Now if they would joyn and say with the Clerk (as they ought) it would be a means to put life into them, to shake off drowsiness, to raise up their attention and Devotion, to mind them of the business they are about, and to bring them to some measure of Knowledge and Understanding.[305]

By responding, by standing up, by bowing, and by Genuflections proper to all parts of the Holy Offices as is directed in the Rubrick: by all which he more than intimates the Duty of every individual person in the Congregation, particularly by saying Amen to all the Prayers throughout the whole Service; which if the Clerk were not obliged, ex Officio, to say Amen, ... the carelessness, and lukewarmness of the generality of people is such, that (as experience sheweth) there would be few or none oftentimes to perform that part, or say Amen to the Prayers. Therefore tis well the Church is provided of a proper Officer to supply the defects of others in the Worship of God.[306]

The contribution of the Clerk to proceedings was often crucial to the intelligibility of public worship:

... the people generally answer the Minister, especially in the Responses and Psalmody, with too soft a voice; and are so little heard, that it hath seemed to me ... as if the Minister read a Verse, and then stop'd a while and read again, the people being so little heard; especially if the Clerk be absent....[307]

Against this background it is not surprising that it has been noted that in country churches the parson often read the whole allocation of psalms.[308] No service could make sense when half the words of some sections were inaudible. Participation in common prayer was evidently beyond the ability of many people and so there was a flexibility in the responsorial treatment of Morning Prayer:

... the People should recite the Psalms and other Hymns with the Minister by way of Answering in turns, as the custom is with us, more or less in most places. ... by the way, this method of reading the Psalms is not commanded, but every Parish Church is left at liberty to observe her own Custom about it.[309]

There are other indications of a more radical flexibility in the execution of Morning Prayer, but this material on diversity in Anglicanism is very difficult to assemble. However, there is evidence for the selective usage of extracts from Prayer Book services, rather than the full liturgy, in the Dioceses of Exeter (1671) and Peterborough (1683).[310] One can also note the comment from Lancashire (1669) that the liturgy was:

by many irreverently and indevoutly celebrated, by many mangled and maim'd, curtail'd, abbreviated, and by the Additions of others implicitly vilified....[311]

This complaint was also echoed in Lincolnshire (1697), when the Bishop remarked upon misfeasors who read:

> ... the Common Prayer very seldom, or not in order, or not the whole, but only some parts and peices [sic]....[312]

Consequently, it is difficult to maintain a tidy picture of Anglican practice, especially when one considers the evidence of an extraordinary letter from London, dated 1683, addressed to the Dean of Durham. A law student who was trying to find a service which simply conformed to the Prayer Book, wrote that it was:

> ... a felicity which I cannot yet discover in all London, tho' blessed bee God, London is metamorphised exceedingly for the better in point of conformity both of Priest and People. We have yet as many separate wayes of worship as wee have ministers, and every one that I could discove, offends in something....[313]

This letter even detailed the variations found in the execution of the liturgy:

> To bee a little more particular. One cuts of the preparatory Exhortation, Dearly beloved brethren, &c. Another the Benedictus, and Jubilate, and satisfieth himself with a psalme in meeter instead out of Sternald and Hopkins, which, all know, is no part of your Office, and a bad translation.... A third brings in part of the Visitation Office ... into the publick congregation.... A fourth adds very formally a preface of his own to the recitall of the Creed, tho' hee would not allow one of the Church's to the whole service. A fifth jumbles both first and second service together, cutting of not only the concluding prayer of St. Chrysostome, and the Grace of our Lord Jesus Christ, but allso our Lord's Prayer in the front of the Communion Office....[314]

The multiformity of Anglican practice alerts one to the importance of local custom in the execution of services and raises the suspicion that abridging services was a way of tailoring them to popular powers of participation. It must also be noted that the Commissioners appointed by Letters Patent of William and Mary[315] to prepare '... Alteracõns and Amendments of the Liturgy ...' '... for the good Order Edification and Unity of the Church of England ... and for the reconciling as much as is possible of all differences....' revealed a degree of dissatisfaction with the 1662 Prayer Book in their private discussions. For example, it was even said that the Litany should end at the Lord's Prayer, 'the latter part seeming now but a botch'.[316] This may go some way to explain the curious flexibility that seems to have been permitted in the offering of Anglican services. If senior clergy and Bishops were disenchanted with the text of the 1662 book, there would not necessarily have been any persecution of minor deviations.

After the Act of Toleration, the delivery of church services became of even more concern. The quality of the execution of Anglican worship naturally became part of the agenda for discussion in the Church. Concern that Prayer Book services suffered as much from the incompetence of ministers as from the incomprehension of the congregations gave rise to a considerable body of advice about how to conduct services. Until then, the only coherent reflection on the matter had been contributed by a layman.[317] When the Church of England found itself in legitimated competition for Church attendance then anxiety began to develop about the popular perception of the Sunday services. Thus the Bishop of Worcester, who had himself enjoyed popularity as a preacher in London, told his clergy that he wished them to offer the liturgy:

> ... in such manner as may most recommend it to the People. I mean with that Gravity, Seriousness, Attention, and Devotion, which becomes so solemn a Duty as Prayer to God is. It will give too just a cause of Prejudice to our Prayers, if the People observe you to be careless and negligent about them; or to run them over with so great haste, as if you minded nothing so much as to get to the end of them. If you mind them so little your selves, they will think themselves excused, if they mind them less.[318]

The advice available to clergy did not stop at the externals of performing their duty; they were further encouraged to think about the relationship between their inward life and their public functions. Clergy were told that each:

> ... must bring his Mind to an inward and feeling Sense of those things that are prayed for in our Offices: That will make him pronounce them with an equal measure of Gravity and Affection, and with a due Slowness and Emphasis.

... a light wandring of the Eyes, and a hasty running through the Prayers, are things highly unbecoming; they do very much lessen the Majesty of our Worship, and give our Enemies advantage to call it dead and formal, when they see plainly, that he who officiates is dead and formal in it. A deep sense of the things prayed for, a true Recollection and Attention of Spirit, and a holy Earnestness of Soul, will give a Composure to the Looks, and a weight to the Pronounciation, that will be tempered between affectation on the one hand, and levity on the other.[319]

Bishop Sprat of Rochester, who had also been a popular preacher, lectured his clergy at some length on this area of concern and urged his clergy in public worship to aspire to:

... such a grave, unaffected Delivery of the Words, as ... will, indeed, naturally flow from a right and serious consideration of their Sense.[320]

In his earlier years Sprat had been credited with being fond of satire and perhaps his awareness of how easily people could bring ridicule upon themselves led him to try to alert the clergy to their vulnerability. Sprat wanted the rendering of public worship to be of such a standard as to encourage people to hold the services of the Church in proper esteem. He hoped that those leading worship would reach beyond mediocrity:

... to an Excellency in this kind: Which in my small Judgement, can never be done, unless we shall make this Duty a Business by it self, and assign it a special Place among our other Ecclesiastical Studies.[321]

Sprat tried to awaken his clergy to the potential impact of the lines of the Prayer Book and would not let them forget that so much hung on the rendering of the words. He thought it possible that:

... a vigorous, effectual, fervent Delivery of the Words and Conceptions, put into his mouth by the Church it self, may give a new enlivening Breath, a new Soul, as it were, to every Prayer, every Petition in it....[322]

Bishop Sprat thought that the correct approach to liturgy would give the Church of England a total advantage over its rivals:

... nothing can be more grave, or moving, more lofty, or Divine, either in the confessing, petitioning, or praising part, than where the Thoughts and Expressions are strictly weigh'd, and prudently reduced into standing unalterable Forms: Provided also, those very Forms be not pronounced in a formal way; but that they may be assisted, inflamed, inspired as I may say, with such a present Ardour, and sprightly zeal in reading them, as will always make them seem to be extempore: Extempore, I mean, in the new, ready, vehement manner of their Pronounciation; but set Forms still, in the solid Ripeness of the Sense, and the due Choice, and deliberate ordering of their Phrases and Figures; Which are the peculiar Advantages of set Forms: And therefore, so spoken, they will in all Reason, produce a far more real, unfeigned, and durable Devotion, than all the other meer-extempore, raw, and indigested Effusions ought to pretend to.[323]

It would be possible to surmise that such strictures as these imply that the standard of execution of the services of the Church could, in places, have been execrable. There does not seem to be any evidence of continuity in practice with the Renaissance ideal of eloquence.[324] Sprat was more concerned to ensure that those who offered public worship did not settle into complacency. As an experienced preacher he knew the power of words and he was aware of the indifference that could be evoked by an indifferent offering of worship.

In the Diocese of Lincoln there was some detailed consideration as to the quality of voice that was used in worship. Their Bishop recognised that due to natural limitations:

There is indeed a natural Indisposition in some Men to all kind of vocal Harmony, even to that which consists only in the Elevation and Depression of the Voice in proper places and periods; I call them proper, not only with regard to the art of Music, but even to the sence of the Words; And I shall not urge this further than the natural capacity of men will bear; There is certainly a felicity in Voice and Accent, which they ought to make good use of to whom God has given it, and those that want it, can only use their Endeavour to attain to such a degree, as to avoid at least all gross, absurd, and ridiculous pronounciation.[325]

This material, addressed initially to the clergy of Lincoln Diocese, was reinforced by the sermon at Bishop Gardiner's Primary Visitation.[326]

The collective impact of this burst of instruction in the 1690's indicates that although the Book of Common Prayer continued to be the only service book of the Church there was concern about the way in which it was used. The way in which prayers were said was found to be connected with the credibility of the Church of England once it had lost its official monopoly of Protestant worship.

The jumble of local custom and official practice in the offering of worship implied that the Prayer Book was treated as much as a resource as a prescriptive standard text. The liturgy of the Book of Common Prayer may have been a national obligation, but its text became a tool of local identity. It is against this background of practice and usage that the text and the theology of the Prayer Book can begin to be examined.

7

THE VOICE OF THE PRAYER BOOK - ANALYSIS AND THEOLOGY

Prayer Book Style

The scheme of services in the Prayer Book provided for Morning and Evening Prayer daily; the Litany on Sundays, Wednesdays and Fridays; and Holy Communion on Sundays and Holy Days. Weekly collects were attached to set readings from the epistles and gospels for Holy Communion and a lectionary provided daily readings. Further occasional services were available which were linked to the recognition of the stages of human life: baptism, confirmation, marriage, childbirth and death. There was further provision for adult baptism and congregational penitence.

The structure of Prayer Book services included a daily repetition, with a litany to be used three times in the week, a collect for each week, a monthly pattern of psalms and an annual lectionary, all intertwined. The net effect was of a kaleidoscope of elements of accumulating familiarity, and yet these elements were held together in a framework which had the potential of yielding an endless sequence of new combinations. Whether hearers attended on a daily or on a weekly basis, or more occasionally, they could still expect a familiar framework and a shifting selection of prayer, psalms and readings.

Although there was a rich variety of dialect across England,[327] the Prayer Book was regarded as a national standard that could transcend the wide divergences of language and elocution. The population was expected to acquiesce in the idiom and metaphor of the Prayer Book, but the Book of Common Prayer could have been regarded as being handed down by a cultural élite. It may have been that 'standard' English was only 'standard' in a small number of places and, possibly, with a rather small percentage of the population. This difficulty may have distanced a significant proportion of the population from the phrases of the Prayer Book. However, there was the balancing factor that the Book of Common Prayer with the Sternhold and Hopkins metrical psalter, shared a vocabulary of about six thousand five hundred words, as against the Authorised Version's roughly eight thousand word vocabulary, as against the grand total for Shakespeare's plays of approximately twenty-one thousand.[328] The English of the Prayer Book may have been regarded as 'standard' by some, but the core vocabulary of Church of England services was not an impossible obstacle.

Whilst the style of the Book of Common Prayer was crucial to its success, for the great mass of people their normal experience of the Prayer Book was as an aural text as opposed to a visual text. Many who attended services in a largely rural nation were not fully literate and therefore what they heard took primacy over what they would have read. This is reflected in the collect for Advent 2 where it is petitioned of the scriptures that 'we may in such wise hear them, read, mark, learn, and inwardly digest them....' Here, the aural took precedence over the written. Equally, the introduction to the Offices exhorted people to 'hear his most holy Word'. The hearing of the service had a transformational power, as was noted in one of the optional collects for use when there was no communion:

> Grant, we beseech thee, Almighty God, that the words, which we have heard this day with our outward ears, may through thy grace be so grafted inwardly in our hearts, that they may bring forth in us the fruit of good living, to the honour and praise of thy Name; through Jesus Christ our Lord. Amen

The text of services was perceived as an aural reality and the living shared experience of hearing gave rise to a distinct form of community. The text of the Litany reinforced this understanding: 'O God, we have heard with our ears, and our fathers have declared unto us, the noble works that thou didst in their days and in the old time before them'. The auditory community telescoped the historical process and itself acted as a repository of faith. For those within that experience, it may be suggested that they shared in aural communities, within which there were levels of awareness and forms of knowing. The offering of worship was located somewhere in the speaking and the hearing of the text. An aural community functioned both as a tacit political embodiment in which local relationships were articulated visually in terms of where people sat and what functions they undertook, and also as an explicit political embodiment every time the royal supremacy was affirmed in the set prayers. The royal supremacy was, in part, validated by being recognised in the context of the ultimate supremacy of God. A particular problem that therefore needs investigation is the nature of the congregational apprehension of the Divine. If an encounter with the Divine presence is posited, then there is a need to underline this aspect of the awareness of the numinous in the writings that have been surveyed in this work.

The literary core of Anglican worship was totally dependent for its function and performance on being translated into an auditory experience. The Prayer Book had been drafted to meet this situation, which may explain why it served as well as it did. In the investigation of the use of the Prayer Book one could perhaps call upon modern work on oral tradition, but that would be an inappropriate resource because people did not go to Church to learn the text of prayers which they would then teach to others. Instead, every generation was expected to attend the service of the Church and thereby to learn the prayers. Repetition, epithet, rhythm, frequent lack of historical specificity and the requirement of being read aloud have been suggested to be characteristic of popular literature in the seventeenth century in that it was designed to engage people who were used to hearing things read out loud.[329] These features were also characteristic of the Prayer Book. The grounds for the success of the Prayer Book have been traced to the use of rhetorical devices in the wording, which have been surmised to have come naturally to a writer with a Renaissance training in the classics. A training in rhetoric gave attention to the use of individual words and the structure of sentences, as well as to the overall effect. Particular note has been taken of the use of devices such as alliteration (words in close succession beginning with the same sound - e.g. 'devices and desires'), anaphora (the beginning of successive sentences or clauses with the same word or phrase - e.g. 'Thou art the King of Glory, O Christ, Thou art the everlasting Son of the Father'), chiasmus (the contrast of parallel ideas in reverse order - e.g. 'desireth not the death of a sinner but rather that he may turn from his wickedness and live...'), climax (the arrangement of ideas in ascending degrees - e.g. 'thou only art holy; thou only art the Lord; thou only, O Christ, with the Holy Ghost, art most high in the glory of God the Father'), and parallelism (the meaning of one phrase being repeated in the next - e.g. 'to whom all hearts are open, all desires known, and from whom no secrets are hid').[330]

The prose style of the English of the Prayer Book has been examined minutely and the suggestion has been made that the language of the Book of Common Prayer derived its special quality from its pattern of cadences, which have been claimed to have derived from the cadences of Latin.[331] However, detailed examination of the collects has since demonstrated that the pattern of cadence in the Prayer Book relied for the most part upon the ordinary cadences of spoken English.[332]

The success of the Book of Common Prayer relied on its integrity as standard English. What have been called the basic rules of 'stress-prosody' have been formulated thus: firstly, that the stress governs the rhythm and, secondly, that the stresses must all be true speech-stresses.[333] The basic, perhaps instinctive, observance of these rules in the composition of the Prayer Book may help to explain its felicitous phrasing. Whilst the Prayer Book was commended for its phrasing in the seventeenth century, it was not subjected to literary analysis. More practically, it was held that a significant point in its favour was the shortness of the individual prayers:

> Our Prayers are framed, both according to a grave, modest, and serious manner; every one of them being moderately short, and all together not immoderately long; and so, more accomodate to render Devotion more earnest and intent: and properly intermitted by other parts of Divine Service, that by a moderate variety, the Devotions of Christians may be both entertained and advantaged.[334]

> Nor are those frequent breaks in Liturgy inconsiderable Helps to the common People, who are lost in a long-continued Service; whilst they are able to attend to that which is short....[335]

> ... Worship ought neither to be unreasonably long, nor excessively short. The length must be proportion'd to what the greater part of Mankind can bear; it ought also to to (sic) be so diversifi'd, that mens minds be not kept too long at any one part of it, or their bodies in any one posture....[336]

The Prayer Book on Prayer

In order to present the implicit structure of the understanding of the process of prayer in the Prayer Book, a catena of phrases from the Book of Common Prayer has been prepared and commented upon in sequence. To use this technique is not without precedent as a way of expounding prayer book doctrine.[337] Not surprisingly, the teaching in the Prayer Book about prayer permeates the text which, of course, includes the Psalms. The wealth of material that follows is drawn from the Offices, the collects, the occasional prayers and the Psalter. The references to the Psalms are annotated to show on which day they were designated for use in the month, and whether in the morning or the evening.

At base, people were dependent upon God for prayer to be possible. This was underlined in the response: 'O Lord, open thou our lips; And our mouth shall shew forth thy praise' (Morning Prayer & Evening Prayer). And whilst people were dependent upon God for prayer to be possible, they also needed God's help as they were praying: 'O God ... that despiseth not the sighing of a contrite heart ... mercifully assist our prayers that we make before thee....' (Litany). God was greeted as the source of the human ambition to pray: '... grant that we, to whom thou hast given an hearty desire to pray....' (Collect for Trinity 3); and also of guidance as to the content of prayer: '... that they may obtain their petitions, make them to ask such things as shall please thee' (Collect for Trinity 10).

The Prayer Book taught that God hears and answers prayer: '... when two or three are gathered together ... thou wilt grant their requests' (Chrysostom's Prayer, Morning Prayer, Litany, and Evening Prayer). The conviction ran very deep that God hears prayer: 'who art always more ready to hear than we to pray....' (Collect Trinity 12).

Key times in the day were identified as opportunities for prayer: 'O God, thou art my God, early will I seek thee' (Ps63v1 - Day12M); 'Early in the morning do I cry unto thee....' (Ps119v147 - Day26E); 'In the evening, and morning, and at noon-day will I pray, and that instantly: and he shall hear my voice' (Ps55v18 - Day10E).

Again and again the text contains prayers asking God to hear prayer: 'O Lord, we beseech thee mercifully to receive the prayers of thy people which call upon thee....' (Collect Epiphany 1); '... look upon the hearty desires of thy humble servants....' (Collect Lent 3); 'Mercifully hear the supplications of thy people....' (Collect Epiphany 2); '... Receive our supplications and prayers....' (Good Friday 2nd Collect); 'Let thy merciful ears, O Lord, be open to the prayers of thy humble servants' (Collect Trinity 10); '... Be ready ... to hear the devout prayers of thy Church ....' (Collect Trinity 23); 'we humbly beseech thee most mercifully ... to receive these our prayers....' (Prayer for Church Militant, Ante-Communion).

There was an undercurrent of desperation at the prospect of the awful possibility that God might not listen: 'Hear me when I call, O God ...' (Ps4v1 - Day1M); 'Ponder my words, O Lord ... O hearken thou unto the voice of my calling' (Ps5v1,2 - Day1M); 'Consider, and hear me, O Lord my God' (Ps13v3 - Day2E); 'Save, Lord, and hear us, O King of heaven when we call upon thee' (Ps 20v9 - Day4M)(cf. Ps27v8 - Day5E; Ps28v2 - Day5E; Ps39v13 - Day8M; Ps64v1 - Day12M; Ps141v1 - Day29M). Prayer could be born of anguish: 'Hear my prayer, O God ... how I mourn in my prayer' (Ps55v1,2 - Day10E); 'Hear my crying, O God ... when my heart is in heaviness'. (Ps61v1,2 - Day11E). Prayer could be born of a simple refrain to: 'Hear my prayer' (Ps54v2 - Day10E; Ps102v1 - Day20M). Equally, the practitioners of prayer could face the horrifying possibility that God was not listening: 'I cry in the day time, but thou hearest not: and in the night season also I take no rest' (Ps22v2 - Day4E). Mercifully, it was also possible to affirm in the morning that 'Thou hast proved and visited mine heart in the night-season' (Ps17v3 - Day3M).

God could be hailed as 'the author of peace' (Second Collect at Morning Prayer); but was also declared to have said: 'Unto whom I sware in my wrath that they should not enter my rest' (Venite). God was not to be taken as placid: 'Put me not to rebuke, O Lord, in thine anger' (Ps38v1 - Day8M); 'For we consume away in thy displeasure' (Ps90v7 - Day18M); and human mortality was linked to God's anger (Ps90v9 - Day18M). God was also characterised as a safe haven: 'Thou art my hope, and my strong hold' (Ps91v2 - Day18M). God was acknowledged as both scatterer and gatherer: 'O God, thou hast cast us out, and scattered us abroad' (Ps60v1 - Day11E); 'The Lord doth build up Jerusalem: and gather together the out-casts of Israel' (Ps147v2 - Day30E).

Another important aspect of the teaching of the Prayer Book was that there was a declared presence of God: 'Tremble, thou earth, at the presence of the Lord....' (Ps114v7 - Day23E); '... Under the shadow of thy wings will I rejoice.' (Ps63v8 - Day12M); 'I am alway by thee: for thou hast holden me by my right hand' (Ps73v22 - Day14E); 'O let my prayer enter into thy presence ... early shall my prayer come before thee' (Ps88v1,13 - Day17M). The awareness of a presence of God was also linked to a quest for that presence: 'My heart hath talked of thee, Seek ye my face: Thy face, Lord, will I seek' (Ps27v9 - Day5E); 'My soul is athirst for God, yea even for the living God: when shall I come to appear before the presence of God?' (Ps42v2 - Day8E); 'Let my prayer be set forth in thy sight as the incense: and let the lifting up of my hands be an evening sacrifice' (Ps141v2 - Day29M).

This sense of the presence of God could also, by virtue of the location of public worship, be interpreted as implying a localised presence at the Parish Church: ' ... come before his presence with a song' (Ps100v1 - Day19E & Morning Prayer); 'O praise the Lord, laud ye the Name of the Lord ... Ye that stand in the house of the Lord: in the courts of the house of our God' (Ps135v1,2 - Day28M); 'Ye that by night stand in the house of the Lord: even in the courts of the house of our God' (Ps134v2 - Day28M); 'O how amiable are thy dwellings ... Blessed are they that dwell in thy house ... I had rather be a doorkeeper in the house of my God ...' (Ps84v1,4,11 - Day16E; cf. Ps61v4 - Day11E; Ps23v6 - Day4E; Ps27v4 - Day5E; Ps28v2 - Day5E).

The suggestion that the presence of God could be located was strengthened by linkage with the references to the 'hill' of the Lord and ideals of personal holiness: 'O send out thy light and thy truth, that they may lead me: and bring me unto thy holy hill, and to thy dwelling' (Ps43v3 - Day8E); 'Lord, who shall dwell in thy tabernacle: or who shall rest upon thy holy hill?' (Ps15v1 - Day3M); 'Who shall ascend into the hill of the Lord: or who shall rise up in his holy place?' (Ps24v3 - Day5M).

Appeals in prayer were declared to be founded in the character of God: 'Hear my prayer, O Lord, and consider my desire: hearken unto me for thy truth and righteousness' sake' (Ps143v1 - Day29E). God was declared to hear prayer in response to the worshipper's personal dedication to him: 'I cried unto the Lord with my voice: yea, even unto the Lord did I make my supplication.... I cried unto thee, O Lord, and said: Thou art my hope, and my portion in the land of the living' (Ps142v1,6 - Day29E); 'I said unto the Lord, Thou art my God: hear the voice of my prayers, O Lord' (Ps140v6 - Day29M).

The Prayer Book also carried a doctrine of praise; there was a duty to praise God: 'Sing we merrily unto God our strength.... For this was made a statute for Israel....' (Ps81v1,4 - Day16M). There were almost as many directions to praise as there were to pray. God was to be praised every day (Ps68v19 - Day13M). God was to be praised because of his word (Ps56v4,10 - Day11M), because of his works (Ps66v1,2 - Day12E; Ps92v4 - Day18M; Ps107v8,15,21,31 - Day22M; Ps111v1,2,3,4 - Day23M; Ps98v1 - Day19E), because of his caring protection (Ps66v7,8 - Day12E), and for rescuing the social outcast (Ps71v6,7 - Day14M; Ps71v19,20 - Day14M).

Praise and thanksgiving were the appropriate response to God (Ps30v12,13 - Day6M; Ps68v32-35 - Day13M) and one was as dependent upon him for the content of praise as one was for prayer (Ps40v1,3 - Day8M). When people said that they would 'shew ourselves glad in him with psalms' (Morning Prayer - Venite) they declared that they were going to use something that God had already provided. Praise required personal commitment (Ps34v1-4 - Day6E; Ps9v1 - Day2M; Ps138v1 - Day28E) and even led to the harvest (Ps67v5,6 - Day12E). God was expected to take pleasure at the joy of worshippers in him (Ps104v34 - Day20E). Praise was also an act of witness to God's greatness (Ps96v1,3,4 - Day19M; Ps105v1 - Day21M), even though it was impossible to offer adequate praise of God (Ps106v1,2 - Day21E). God was to be praised for creating his people (Ps149v1,2 - Day30E) and for the pleasure that he took in his people (Ps149v3,4 - Day30E).

God was to be praised for his outstanding qualities: his forgiveness (Ps103v1,3 - Day20M), his redemption and deliverance (Ps107v1,2,6,7,8 - Day22M; Ps35v18 - Day7M; Ps57v2,3,10 - Day11M), his greatness (Ps145v3 - Day30M; Ps95v1,3 - Day19M; Ps150v2 - Day30E), his excellence (Ps148v12 - Day30E), his glory (Ps104v1 - Day20E), his holiness (Ps150v1 - Day30E; Ps30v4 - Day6M) and his mercy (Ps108v3,4 - Day22E; Ps118v1 - Day24M; Ps136v1 - Day28E).

There was a link between worshipping God and honouring God (Ps29v2 - Day5E; Ps50v23 - Day10M); indeed, it was declared that '... it is a good thing to sing praises unto our God: yea, a joyful and pleasant thing it is to be thankful.' (Ps147v1 - Day30E).

Prayer affected one personally: 'When I called upon thee, thou heardest me: and enduedst my soul with much strength.' (Ps138v3 - Day28E; cf. Ps42v6,7,14,15; Ps43v5,6 - Day8E). Prayer engaged the worshippers: 'Thou art my God, and I will thank thee' (Ps118v28 - Day24M); 'I will be glad and rejoice in thee' (Ps9v2 - Day2M). It was possible to express a personal dedication to the perpetual praise of God (Ps145v1,2 - Day30M; Ps146v1 - Day30M).

All this was the foundation of the vision of God that naturally led to ask God to be involved in the direction of national life: '... that we may henceforth obediently walk in thy holy commandments; and ... may continually offer unto thee our sacrifice of praise and thanksgiving....' (Thanksgiving for Restoring Publick Peace); '... religion and piety, may be established among us for all generations.' (Prayer for the High Court of Parliament).

Despite the occasional desperation, there was a great deal of confidence in prayer because of the overwhelming conviction that God heard prayer (Ps18v2,6 - Day3E; Ps28v7,10 - Day5E; Ps31v25 - Day6M; Ps65v2 - Day12E; Ps66v15,17,18 - Day12E; Ps107v6,13,19,28 - Day22M; Ps116v1 - Day24M). It was acknowledged that the Lord heard the prayers of the righteous (Ps34v15,17 - Day6E), but not the prayers of the wicked (Ps66v16 - Day12E).

A particular matter for confidence was the favour of God towards the poor (Ps34v6 - Day6E; Ps69v34 - Day13E; Ps86v1,6 - Day17M; Ps102v17 - Day20M; Ps113v1,6 - Day23M; Ps140v12 - Day29M). There was also reassurance for those in trouble (Ps30v2 - Day6M; Ps31v8 - Day6M; Ps50v15 - Day10M).

The teaching of the Prayer Book about prayer may have been implicit, but as these dispersed passages constituted the only major statement of the Church's doctrine on prayer they had to be set out at some length. The material of this teaching was delivered continually throughout each month with the result that attitudes were. There was the opportunity of a cumulative impact that informed people's awareness and built confidence in the work that they undertook in prayer.

The outlines of the teaching of the Prayer Book on prayer are taken from material used in services. Therefore these outlines are not detached observations. Inevitably, these outlines appear as a pastiche, but give shape to a perspective on prayer which recognises the human desire to pray as only being possible through the enabling of Almighty God. God hears appropriate prayer and is hailed for his response to prayer. God was also regarded as present to his worshippers, as must now be investigated.

The Agenda of Morning Prayer

There is a general pattern of address to God in the Prayer Book. The prayers are characterised by being cast in a direct address to God within the framework of a direct relationship. The metaphors within which this relationship is expressed are those such as: children ~ Father; sheep ~ Shepherd; subjects ~ King. Accordingly, common prayer is presented as a natural activity of the soul and as a proper facet of human association. This approach remedies any human uncertainty as to what words are suitable for prayer in the moments when inevitably unworthy people draw near to One of overwhelming greatness. The daily office of the Prayer Book was commended to clergy as:

... a powerful Means to preserve an awful Sense of God continually upon your Minds....[338]

Furthermore, prayer following the Prayer Book is a corporate activity, which incorporates participants in a common offering to God. Thus it was declared that:

> The Liturgy is the Churches Publick Sacrifice of Praise; and in that we are not onely to give thanks for blessings immediately conferred upon our persons, but upon us with the whole Church....[339]

The basic experience of attending the use of the Prayer Book on Sunday mornings was hearing the service of Morning Prayer. Whether this was inevitably followed by the Litany, as the Prayer Book rubric required, cannot be known. Equally, the frequency with which this combination was followed by Ante-Communion is beyond discovery, though one writer regarded the pattern of Morning Prayer then Litany and then Ante-Communion as 'the general Practice of our Church'.[340] One may suggest that variations of local custom prevailed and that visitation articles could not successfully probe into the exact details of how the Prayer Book was used. The sheer frustration of trying to control parish life through the Visitation process was admirably captured by the Vicar of Halstead in Essex in his remarks about the approach of Churchwardens to articles of enquiry:

> ... they can ... make a Return of Omnia bene ... the traditional use of it has made them expert in it; nay, may not some of them think that they are excused from their Duty in English, when they make a Return in Latin? [341]

However, if the lowest common denominator of prayer book usage was that of Morning Prayer, it is still possible to discern a basic theological structure in the service of Morning Prayer which is a very important part of the understanding of Anglican worship at this time. At first sight, clergy had to lead an intermingling of precept and prayer, of praise and lection, of social response and direct address to the Divine:

> ... we are the Ministers of God to men, for their Spiritual and Eternal Good; and by which the Communion between God and Men is maintained. For by Prayer Men make their Addresses unto God; and by his Word, God makes his Addresses unto Men.[342]

Whilst it would be possible to focus attention on the separate elements of Morning Prayer, the service is open to an analysis of its sequence in terms of a coherent theology of access to God. After due preparation, the Venite articulates a theology of approach to God, then the Te Deum offers a direct address to God, which is phrased on the pre-supposition of being in the divine presence, then the Jubilate envisions this invitation as being extended to the whole world, that all should come and share in the joy of the presence of God. The main elements of familiarity to the generality of churchgoers were in the sequence:

Preparation	(Confession, etc.),
Approach	(Venite),
Threshold	(Psalms)
Presence	(Te Deum),
Universal Invitation	(Jubilate),
Affirmation	(Creed),
Petition	(Responses, Collects).

In this pattern, the offering of the Psalms marked the threshold or limen that was crossed from the approach into the presence as people joined the traditional praises of the people of God. The readings were heard either side of the Te Deum, which implied that the readings were heard as God's Word in the presence of God.

The Psalter

The psalms were considered to be offered to the glory of God and were primarily regarded as an anthology of praise. Henry Hammond wrote of psalmody that people should expect to 'spend no unconsiderable part of our present lives in this most blessed and holy imployment' as part of the mortal preparation for the eternal work of praising God in heaven.[343] Part of the rigour of the daily prayer of the Church of England was the continual recital of the psalms. The Coverdale Psalter, which had long been printed with the Book of Common Prayer, was formally appended to the Prayer Book in 1662. The monthly recital of the psalter was more than a mere product of legal compulsion and more than an act of deference to the practices of antiquity. The duty of the recital of the psalter was accepted out of respect for the psalms and in turn evoked a very high estimate of the value of the psalms.

The use of the psalter was regarded as a specifically Christian act of worship; it was confidently affirmed that the Book of Psalms was:

> A Book never to be used enough, because it containeth the
> marrow and flour of holy Scripture, and is the Repository of
> Devotion.[344]

> ... the instrument of Vertue, the marrow of Divinity, the store-
> house of Devotion, the Epitome of Holy Scripture.[345]

With the 150 psalms divided into sixty monthly portions, the sequence
of services could be considered to have been dominated by the psalms,
but the psalms relied on the context in which they were heard for their
significance. It was held that the psalms should be construed in a
Christian pattern of interpretation and that it was no use to simply read
the text. A deliberate effort had to be made in the course of using the
psalms in order to engage the matter of the particular psalms and to
present an offering that was commensurate with the theme of each
psalm:

> But he that would make good use of them, must endeavour to
> form his Spirit according to the Affection of the Psalmist. If the
> Affection be of Love, that runs through the Psalm, it must be
> read with the same Affection; if of fear, the Spirit of Fear should
> be imprinted on the Soul; if of Desire, it should be carried on
> with the same Transportation; if of Gratitude unto God, the Soul
> should be lifted up in Praises, and come with Affections that way
> inflamed.[346]

> He who would make a right and good use of the Psalms, read
> over in private or publick, must endeavour to form his Spirit to
> the affection of the Psalm....[347]

There was evidently a felt need for a discriminatory approach to the
psalms so that their different characters could be recognised. Comber
thought that were four sorts of psalms: Psalms of Instruction, of
Exhortation, of Supplication and of Thanksgiving.[348] He taught that
preparation was required and set out the personal effort that he felt to be
needed. It is impossible to gauge the results of this teaching, and one
can only note that this approach to the Psalms made considerable
inward demands.

It was hope that reciting the psalms would become a genuinely
corporate action, develop the spiritual experience of the congregation,
and elevate worship to a new plane:

> For the plain End of reciting those Psalms in the Congregation is
> to Praise and Magnifie Gods Name, and to excite in our Hearts
> such like devout affections in doing so, as those Holy Men felt
> in themselves; who were assisted by God's Spirit in Composing
> them.[349]

The use of the psalms in worship inevitably entailed interpretation in the
process of their use. Yet pastoral concern was also displayed in the
unflinching expectation that the psalter should be used as directed.
Particular reference has been noted with regard to the difficulties of
those in distress being able to find the inward resources to offer praise:

> Many things in the Psalms may seem not to sute well with every
> Man's Condition at all times; so that the Spirit of the Reciter may
> meet with Contradiction, more than Advantage and Assistance:
> As for Example, A Man over-whelm'd with Grief, can't have a
> vigorous Spirit of Praise; or a Man in a prosperous Estate, can't
> have the Spirit of Humiliation. To this is answered That both
> Humiliation and Praise are things in no way improper, or
> impertinent to any Soul at any time; for in all Afflictions there is
> some Spring of Joy and Consolation ...; as also in all Prosperity
> and Consolation, there is matter and occasion enough of
> Humiliation for Sin.[350]

There was advice available as to how psalms could be understood to be
appropriate to people in differing circumstances[351] and there was advice
on how to construe the psalms rather than treating them literally.[352]
Besides Patrick's *Paraphrase on the Book of Psalms*,[353] there were
many other compendiums available as to how the psalms could be
interpreted. An anxiety to establish the Christian use of the psalms
contributed to so many versions of the psalter being produced in this
era.[354] The psalms were available in metre as well as in paraphrase, but
the Anglican theology of Morning Prayer must be surveyed before
attention is given to the principal metrical psalter of this era.

The Understanding of the Use of Morning Prayer
The Anglican service of Morning Prayer, on its own, could be construed
as a pattern of access to the Divine presence; a gateway to God:

> Come not to the Publick Prayers, as Spectators to a Theatre, to
> hear much, learn little, and do nothing; but come out of a sincere

Obedience to Gods Commands; and with full trust in his Promise, that he will be in the midst of those who are gathered together in his Name, to hear their Prayers, and to grant their Requests.[355]

The agenda of the Litany, the Lord's Supper and Evening Prayer presupposed the offering of Morning Prayer. Even Evening Prayer, with its readings gathered around the affirmation of the Incarnation in the Magnificat and the Nunc Dimittis, despite the fact that it mirrored Morning Prayer, could not be viewed as an independent unit. The evening canticles affirmed the presence of God in this world, the access to whose presence was to be found through Morning Prayer. When Patrick prepared prayers for people to use before they went to Church on Sundays, he recommended people to say before the morning service words that included:

> ... I most humbly desire leave to join myself with all those holy Ones, to worship thy most glorious Majesty, to express the due Sense I have of all thy Benefits ... to make thee the best Oblation I am able, and to devote myself intirely to thy Obedience.

Before evening service, the suggested prayer included the words:

> ... I am bold again to approach into thy Presence; to renew my Requests unto thee, to bless thy holy Name, to make Profession of my Love to thee, and Readiness in all Things to obey thee.[356]

These prayers reflected the view that Morning Prayer was a service in which one gained entry into the court of heaven and that evening prayer was an extension of that blessing.

The ideal of the Church of England was that there would be a daily offering of Morning and Evening Prayer in all the parish churches in the country. The reality was rather different, to the extent that, in 1692, a survey of London churches could only list 47 churches as having daily Morning and/or Evening Prayer out of 123 parishes.[357] Consequently, the Church was faced with the need for some theological understanding of its practice. The recipe for understanding was identified in the Anglican instinct for mutuality.

> ... our Service is a continual daily sacrifice, a Morning and Evening Prayer. And though the greatest benefit of this belongs

to those that daily attend it; yet because it is the Publick Sacrifice of the Church, all that are Members of that have their part and interest in it, though they be absent.... The present are intitled to the benefit as a Sacrifice offered by them; the absent as a Sacrifice offered for them. For this is our 'juge Sacrificium' that is perpetually burning upon the Altar, for the service of God, and in behalf of every member of the Church that doth not ... set a bar upon himself by his wilful neglect of it, and opposition to it.[358]

The vision of the Church of England to be the national Church remained intact, whether people were present or absent and almost regardless of the level at which people could participate. Thus the reality of local attendance at the services of the Book of Common Prayer was linked to the idealism of its national significance. The Archdeacon of Durham had no difficulty in embracing the idea that people could attend Church services in a representative capacity:

... It is without all doubt, that every Lay-man, of our Communion, is bound to assist at, as the Minister is to say, Divine Service daily, when God placeth him in such blessed Circumstances ... to enjoy the same, and the necessary and indispensable Affairs of his Life and Calling will permit; and when they will not (which is a just Impediment) on days of business to send, if possible, some Person of his Family to be a Representative, and keep up its Interest in that continual Sacrifice, appointed by God and the Church to be Offered up, in behalf of the whole Congregation, and which extends to the Faithful that are lawfully absent as well as the present.[359]

The working context of the Book of Common Prayer in the years 1660-1700 led to the Anglican theology of prayer having to accommodate the ineffectiveness of the ideal of universal usage at a local level. The theological pattern of representation related to both concept and practice.

8

THE 'STERNHOLD & HOPKINS' METRICAL PSALTER

A recent study[360] has emphasised the importance of the Psalter as a cultural resource. The images and phrases of the psalms formed part of the English collective cultural awareness and memory. The range of material generated in response to the Book of Psalms covered the whole gamut of society. Some translations and paraphrases of the psalms were only suitable for an intellectual élite. Other versions of the psalms appealed to those with less discerning palates. However, this chapter focuses on a version of the psalms that ordinary people could embrace and take to their hearts. The pages that follow recite and explain some of the characteristics of the affection in which this version was held.

Popularity
An integral part of seventeenth century devotional life revolved around the metrical psalms gathered under this title.[361] This Psalter had an enormous popular appeal; it has been claimed that it is possible that a million copies had been produced by 1640.[362] 162 editions of this version of the psalms have been recorded from the period 1641-1700.[363] These psalms had a distinct public role and enabled local aural communities, in all their multiplicity, to find a voice. It was quite usual for these metrical psalms to be bound up with a Bible or a Prayer Book.[364]

The popularity of this particular version of the metrical psalms had been inherited from an earlier time[365] and, just as 'Sternhold & Hopkins' outlasted the many competitors of the Elizabethan era, so its rivals in Stuart England fared no better in comparison. As a result of its long standing, 'Sternhold & Hopkins' came to be known in Stuart times as the 'Old Version'. Many alternatives were prepared and published, but none

displaced the Old Version from overall national use.[366] The dire modern
reputation of the Old Version obscures the value that was attached to it,
and its use has been presented simply as an absurdity rather than as
something to be explained. Thus Temperley[367] calculated that four
hundred thousand copies of the text of the Old Version were sold in the
period 1663-1696, but did not go much further than reciting the way
that the literary shortcomings of this version of the psalms were open to
ridicule. He analysed the way that the Old Version was rendered but
omitted to explain what merits the rendition may have carried for the
congregations. Instead, Temperley cited contemporary comment
scorning the actual performance of these psalms. Elsewhere the practice
of metrical psalm singing has been dismissed as earning a 'steady
scoffing' and any serious consideration of its merits has been avoided.[368]
Two twentieth century commentators treated the Old Version as
essentially awaiting replacement by something better and preferred to
contrast the comparative literary qualities of the other available versions
without any sustained attempt to analyse the popularity of the Old
Version.[369] Further writers have ignored the Old Version altogether
whilst writing in this subject area.[370] However, as the final decade of the
seventeenth century was reached, the singing of metrical psalms was
held in such importance as a matter of Christian practice that when the
leaders of some Baptist congregations vetoed the use of the Old
Version, or any other metrical psalter, one writer opined ruefully that
this decision had had a very adverse effect on recruitment.[371]

Performance

In considering the Old Version, the first matter is to clarify its pattern of
use, many details of which have been determined by Temperley on the
basis of surviving musicological evidence. It was possible to sing these
psalms before and after the Office and before and after the sermon. The
first factor to note is the significance of the Parish Clerk, as he chose the
psalm and the tune. The psalm could be chosen to relate to local needs,
or to any other matter that the Clerk felt appropriate. Guidelines were
available as to which psalms were suitable for any given occasion or
local event that needed recognition. There were flavours of joy and
sorrow, of thanksgiving and petition and lines appropriate for the
seasons of the year and the seasons of the Church calendar.[372] By the
end of this era there was even a concordance of the Old Version
available to Parish Clerks in order to facilitate the finding of significant
words and phrases.[373] The actual number of tunes that Parish Clerks
may have known varied widely from only one tune upwards, but the

important thing was that a man could actually cope with the expectations of his congregation. One contemporaneous record of parish life mentions that when a Parish Clerk was appointed who was incapable of discharging his duties, an assistant had to be provided.[374]

After the psalm was chosen and announced the rendition proceeded as follows: firstly, the Clerk read the first line; this was known as 'lining-out'. The practice of 'lining-out' may be traced back to the instructions 'Of Singing of Psalmes' in the Parliamentary *Directory for the Publique Worship of God* of 1645:

> ... the chief care must be, to sing with understanding, and with Grace in the heart, making melody unto the Lord. That the whole congregation may joyne herein, every one that can read is to have a Psalme book, and all others not disabled by age, or otherwise, are to be exhorted to learn to reade. But for the present, where many in the Congregation cannot read, it is convenient that the Minister, or some other fit person appointed by him and the other Ruling Officers, doe read the Psalm, line by line, before the singing thereof. [375]

These directions do not carry the appearance of being necessarily new instructions, but it has not proved possible to find any earlier reference to this pattern of proceeding in England, although 'lining-out' has been acknowledged as a continental practice.[376] More specifically, a suggestion has been made linking the origin of 'lining out' to the use of the 1552 Prayer Book amongst exiled Marian congregations in Europe. The 1552 Prayer Book directed that the congregation should join in the corporate prayers by repeating them 'after the minister', phrase by phrase.[377] Possibly, the practice of lining-out was given broad licence in the Injunctions of 1559, where permission was given for 'an himne, or suche like song' at the beginning or end of common prayer 'having respect that the sentence of the himne maie bee understanded and perceived.'[378] Bishop Wren thought that the 'uncouth and senseless custom' of lining out was attributable to the words 'saying after me' at the end of the introduction to the office.[379]

In considering congregational use of the metrical psalter, one can build a general impression sufficient to enable the devotional significance of this practice to be grasped. As the use of the Old Version was broadly of national practice in the life of Anglican churches, a further facet of the Anglican theology of prayer in these years can be constructed. Whilst there were recognised tunes available for the singing of the metrical psalms, in view of the normal absence of either instrumental accompaniment or trained singers, the tunes used were the shared property of a congregation. Editions of the Old Version with set tunes were available, but apparently were not in much demand. One compiler even produced a copy of the Old Version with notes set for every syllable for every psalm, but the work was never reprinted.[380] John Playford (1623-1686), the leading English music publisher of the later seventeenth century, devoted much effort towards reforming the singing of the Old Version, but with no great results.[381]

The only recorded successful inroad made by 'conventional' music-making into the offering of the Old Version appears to have been with the approval of the congregation in the huge parish church at Grantham. There an organ was installed in 1640 to play the tune of the psalms, so that everybody could hear the note and sing after the same tune: 'And the confusion which sometimes hath heretofore happened in our church, being a very large and spacious church, in singing the psalms after divers tunes, is taken away'. [382] Unfortunately, the organ did not last many years.

Each congregation can be expected to have had its own musical tradition and, within any congregation, some would have known the tunes better than others. After the Parish Clerk had read the first line, he would start to sing the first note. Experienced singers would copy the note and the others would aim to reach the same pitch. A note would last two or three seconds before the next note began to be sounded. The less musical would slide in pitch towards the new note until they were aware of being in tune with it. They might not reach the new note before the next note had been started, equally it was possible that they might overshoot the pitch. There was no way of recording this practice in musical notation. As people would slide in their own times from one note of the tune to the next, the notes functioned as assembly points where the singers met before starting out on their individual paths to the next note. At the end of each line the process was repeated with the Clerk reading the next line. The extraordinarily slow speed of this pattern can be affirmed by citing Temperley's reckoning, on the basis of extant information, that each stanza of a psalm sung in this way took about two minutes, meaning that it would take an hour to sing 30 stanzas. It is likely that fragments of psalms were used rather than whole psalms, as the Bishop of Derry complained this 'method of singing the Meetre Psalms takes up so much time, that it is impossible to praise God in whole Psalms after that manner.' [383] No record has been traced of any attempt to sing the Old Version quietly - it seems to have been a general feature that the Old Version was sung loudly, if not as loudly as possible. The Chanter of Christ Church, Dublin, was scathing in his incomprehension of the 'English Practice' of rendering the Old Version and of its 'gross mischiefs and abortions of devotion' and of people thinking that 'they then sing best when lowdest.'[384]

Cultural Context

The form of singing associated with the Old Version was part of a much broader tradition of popular music making. Song was a crucial ingredient in the world of ordinary people,[385] but their version of song was flexible and adaptable, possibly as much a subject for play as a part of ritual. It has been asserted that, because music was not written down, tunes only existed as variants. There could not be a 'correct' version of a rendering, because such a concept was irrelevant to popular practice. Instead people, or their communities, might appropriate a musical pattern so that it might become part of the life of an extended family or of a community. Music would be ornamented as pleased the singers, with slides and changes in rhythm and pitch.[386]

The popular usage of the Old Version fitted within a general pattern of popular culture.[387] The Old Version was a cultural phenomenon, a theological marker, an instrument of social cohesion, and a means of expressing political solidarity for those who had no franchise. Whilst it was significant that there was a strong tradition of people bringing their culture into Church services, it was important theologically that there was an offering of praise and prayer rooted in popular culture, in which as many people joined as possible. One cleric acknowledged the widespread affection for the Old Version, although it was rendered in:

> ... a way of singing and canting which hath neither Law of the Land nor Canon of a Synod to justify its use, nor any Approbation upon Record, either of Civil or Ecclesiastical Superiors; but the people love to have it so .... [388]

There is also evidence for the respect in which the Old Version was held by the ordinary people. It was noted at one visitation in 1670 that men uncovered their heads for their psalm-singing, but kept their hats on for the reading psalms and the lessons in the course of the office.[389] A long-serving Essex clergyman recorded disapprovingly in his diary for 1650 that '... the unreverent carriage of divers in sitting with their hatts on when the psalme is singing is strange to mee....'.[390]

It is also necessary to take account of the text of the Old Version, which was subject to variation between 1641 and 1700. Four verses may be cited in parallel to demonstrate these changes, but whether the printed copies changed in response to modifications in popular usage, or whether the printed copies were trying to engender such a change, or even whether there were differing textual traditions associated with different printers would require further investigation:

Psalm 1: first line
'The man is blest that hath not bent to wicked read his eare' (1641)
'The man is blest that hath not lent to wicked men his ear' (1700)

Psalm 1: last line
'And eke the way of wicked men shall quite be overthrown' (1641)
'Also the way of wicked men shall quite be overthrown' (1700)

Psalm 75: first verse
'Unto thee (God) will we give thanks, we will give thanks to thee
Sith thy Name is so near, declare thy wondrous works will we' (1641)
'To thee, O God, will we give thanks, we will give thanks to thee:
Since thy Name is so near, declare thy wondrous works will we'.(1700)

Psalm 150: first line
'To praise the Name of God the Lord agree with one accord' (1641)
'To praise his great and mighty Name, agree with one accord' (1700)

In using the various printings of the Sternhold & Hopkins version of the Psalms, the patterns of thought of the Psalter were popularised and made widely accessible. People were taught to both address God and to reflect about God. It is impossible to know which of the contents of the Old Version were the more widely preferred, if any, but the overall impact can be summarised from the broad character of the text.

The Role of the Old Version

The Old Version was in many ways the prayer book of the poor and of those with low levels of literacy. God was acknowledged as the protector of the poor, the protector of the good and the godly and the vindicator of the oppressed. The main character of the Old Version was that it contained both encouragements to offer praise and also patterns of praise. The recurring theme of asking God to hear prayer, was matched by the frequent declaration that God did hear prayer. Thus, in examples from a 1661 edition, God was declared to hear prayer:

... for I do call to thee, O Lord, surely thou will me aid:
Then hear my prayer, and weigh right well the words that I
have said. (17v6).

God was affirmed to hear the prayers of the poor:

All ye that fear him praise the Lord, thou Jacob honour him:
And all ye seed of Israel with reverence worship him.
For he despiseth not the poor, he turneth not awry
His countenance when they do call, but granteth to their crie.
(22v23,24).

There was an undertone of a royalist message:

A man of might I have erect, your king and guide to be:
And set him up whom I elect among the folk to me.   (89v20).

Congregations could offer assertions of commitment to praise:

But I will talk of God, I say, of Jacobs God therefore:
And will not cease to celebrate his praise for evermore. (75v9).

There was an implied linkage between 'riches' and 'wickedness':

Doubtless the just mans poor estate is better a great deal more
Then all these lewd and wicked mens rich pomp and heaped
store. (37v16);

with an opportunity for subversive comment about the social scale:

Behold the man that would not take the Lord for his defence:
But of his goods his God did make, and trust his corrupt sense.
(52v7).

God was affirmed to safeguard national standards of justice:

Then shall the world shew forth and tell, that good men have
reward:
And that a God on earth doth dwell, that justice doth regard.
(58v11).

The Old Version interpreted the psalms as teaching about Christ:

> The kings and rulers of the earth conspire and all are bent
> Against the Lord and Christ his Sonne, which he among us
>   sent. (2v2),

and discipleship was declared to be the preparation for eternity:

> My soul from death thou dost defend, and keep'st my feet
>   upright:
> That I before thee may ascend with such as live in light.
>   (56v13).

The Old Version retained the pattern of its parent in its mixture of direct speech addressed to God, meditation about God, addresses to one's fellow worshippers and reflections upon the mysteries of life. The distinctiveness of the Old Version was in finding widespread popular acceptance. One writer dismissed the significance of the rendering of the Old Version by asking: "But what did laity contribute to worship besides the caterwauling of Psalms?"[391] Another writer simply ignored the Old Version: "Divine Service was long and little room for lay participation or spontaneity".[392] Such approaches miss the value of the Old Version and the significance of its inclusion in Anglican practice. The offering of the Old Version was integral to the life of the laity in the Church of England and its place was both recognised and protected. There was popular unanimity in the use of the Old Version which was complementary to the Book of Common Prayer.

Whilst the Old Version attracted its own spectrum of dissent, ranging from the desire for abolition to the desire for an improved text and/or reformed music, its pattern of usage did not make it an alternative to the Prayer Book. Those who appeared to attend the Prayer Book offices passively, were able to share in the offering of the Old Version, so that the worship offered in Parish Churches included both local and imposed cultures. The metrical psalms of the Old Version enabled the general populace to feel that, in their use of the Old Version, they were fulfilling their obligations of praise and thanksgiving. Although it is impossible to trace the understanding of sometimes illiterate participants in the process of rendering the Old Version, there are two avenues of enquiry into the extant printed evidence for the understanding of its use; firstly, from an exchange of pamphlets that has survived relating to when the Old Version was threatened with replacement at the end of the seventeenth century and, secondly, from dispersed comments that, when taken together, show the teaching that was available about the use of metrical psalms in general and the Old Version in particular.

The Defence of the Old Version

Towards the end of the century, yet another version of the metrical psalms was prepared, but the authors prepared the ground more carefully than the previous writers who had been trying to oust the Old Version. Tate & Brady's *New Version of the Psalms* was backed by an Order in Council, by which it was 'Allowed and Permitted to be Us'd in all Churches, Chappels, and Congregations, as shall think fit to receive the same.' [393] Nicholas Brady (1659-1726) had been Bishop Wetenhall's chaplain at Cork. Nahum Tate (1652-1715) became Poet Laureate in 1692. Having already registered Wetenhall's aversion to the Old Version, it is worth noting a suggestion that he may have encouraged Brady with a desire to bring out a new version.[394]

Familiar accusations were recited against the Old Version in the interests of promoting the New Version. Thus it was claimed:

> ... that I may vindicate our Church from such as asperse her ..., and are willing to impeach her Credit, and impair her reputation by alledging that the Anciens (sic) Psalms of Sternhold and Hopkins were injoyn'd as part of her publick devotion, I must crave leave to correct this great Mistake, and do acquaint them that the Old Version never had any particular Recommendation either from the King, or Bishops, or Convocation; and that this New Translation is that which has obtain'd both the Allowance and Recommendation of Authority.[395]

The Old Version was further disparaged on grounds of language:

> ... if this New Version had been so long entertain'd in our Churches, as the Old One has been, and Sternhold and Hopkins had now offer'd their Compositions instead of it, they would certainly be rejected by all degrees of Men, with the utmost contempt.[396]

> ... I am confident that should any Minister address himself to his Congregation in such language as may be met with in the Old Version, which I am too tender to instance in, that the Auditors would not only think it time ill spent to hearken to him, but

likewise conclude that his Design was nothing else but plain Abuse.[397]

But the Old Version was not undefended; such opinions met with heavy protest:

> ... it is objected, The old Psalms are written in a plain and familiar Style. So much the better, being Sutable to Scripture-Language, which for the most part ... is delivered in a plain and familiar Style, the Spirit of God delighting to express it self in plain and intelligible Words, condescending to the meanest Capacity; and withal most agreeable to the holy Text most of the Psalms being Prayers, which are wont to be deliver'd in plain and familiar Terms, ... and more sutable to the Capacities of Parochial Congregation, where plain and unlearned Auditors are the most numerous.[398]

The defence of the Old Version had no hesitation in appealing to the realities of marketplace demand:

> By the way, let me ask the Vindicator, whether the Unlearned (who are the more numerous) may not make the same Objection against hard, and to them unintelligible, Words in our politer Modes of Speaking, that the Learned and Ingenious do against those obsolete and uncouth Expressions which are in the old Translation.[399]

The most important point, theologically, in this exchange is that the Old Version was felt to enable the mass of the population to pray in familiar phrases. The Old Version was claimed to offer an authentic pattern of address to God and a genuine experience of prayer, to disrupt this pattern of use would be to dispossess the people of their means of association in prayer.

The tension between the Old Version and the New Version was set to linger for many years to come. One final reference may be made to the contemporaneous debate, specifically to a posthumously issued pamphlet of William Beveridge, who had been such an ardent champion of the Book of Common Prayer. This pamphlet was published under the title: *A Defence of the Book of Psalms collected into English Metre, by Thomas Sternhold, John Hopkins, and others. With Critical Observations on the Late New Version Compar'd with the Old* (1710).

When he came to discuss the matter of the style of the Old Version, Beveridge protested:

> ... we may first consider, who they are that made this Objection against the Old Translation: Not they for whom it was chiefly intended, the Common People, that are the far greater Part of the Kingdom. Ye never hear them, or any of them, complain, that the Psalms which they sing in their Churches are too plain, too low, or too heavy for them. But they rather love and admire them the more for it, and are more edified by the use of them. The plainer they are, the sooner they understand them, the lower their Style is, the better it is levelled to their Capacities; and the heavier they go, the more easily they can keep pace with them.[400]

The value that was attached to the Old Version was evidently recognised at episcopal level and there were articulate people willing to defend this opportunity of prayer for the ordinary people. Whilst many of the details of the use of the Old Version were unrecorded and lost, the fact of its widespread employment is indisputable. Although there was a growing body of writing on the appreciation of Prayer Book services, these only related to the contents of the Book of Common Prayer and entirely ignored metrical psalm singing. The theological implications of the use of the Old Version, however, should not be overlooked; through the Old Version the Church of England was interlaced with popular culture. Whilst the mechanism of patronage provided a parson and whilst the incumbent could appoint an assistant to officiate at services, the people themselves often chose their Parish Clerk and, thereby, their leader for their part of Sunday worship. With the slow and measured singing of the Old Version before and after the Office, as well as before and after the sermon, it is not impossible that Prayer Book devotions became quiet intervals of reflection between episodes of psalm singing.

Accordingly, the Book of Common Prayer did not have a monopoly of the material used in public prayer. The Prayer Book was complemented by the Old Version and they were often bound together in one volume. It was not unusual for the Old Version to be bound in with the folio desk editions of the Prayer Book for use by the Parish Clerk and the parson. The scope of the understanding of the Church's prayers has to be widened accordingly and the use of the Old Version has to be integrated into the Anglican theology of prayer.

The Appraisal of the Use of the Old Version

One of the few sympathetic modern comments about the Old Version has come from neither a musician nor a church historian, but from a distinguished literary scholar:

> Those who used it in church were not looking for poetry and such poetry as they got crept into their mind unconsciously mixed with the devotion and the music. Hence we do these artless verses a kind of outrage in wrenching them from their natural context and dragging them before the bar of criticism.[401]

The lack of serious appreciation of the significance of the Old Version has inevitably distorted the overview of the Anglican theology of prayer in this era, a theology which was founded on use. Musicians tended to dislike the rendering of the Old Version intensely. The critics of the Old Version fulminated against it as a national phenomenon. One musician, writing contemptuously of the 'Old Way of Singing', referred disparagingly to the 'general outcries of most Parochial Churches in the Nation'.[402] Richard Portman, an organist of the Chapel Royal of Charles I,[403] reflected:

> ... if you please to observe at the singing of Psalmes in the Church, you shall hear such untunable voyces, and such intolerable discords, that no man or woman that hath well tuned voyces, but are exceedingly displeased with it, it being a hinderance to devotion.[404]

Portman's work was reprinted by John Playford in 1660, and Playford's own views were similarly direct in the denunciation of the 'Old Way of Singing'. Playford thought that music should be reserved for musicians and was not common property. Hence he disliked lining-out which, he acknowledged, was meant to help the illiterate, but held that:

> Such as have no knowledge to read, may have as little ability to sing, especially aged people, whom Nature hath debilitated, and such by a silent and devout attention, may give more glory to God with their hearts than their voices.[405]

The musicians, however, went unheeded and Playford had to recognise the hold that the Old Version had on the generality of the population:

... its Antiquity and Long use in our Churches, hath taken such deep Root in the Memories of the Common sort of People, that it will be of some difficulty to pluck it up and plant a better: Many have attempted it by their more refin'd Translations, but as yet none of them received into publick use....[406]

The legality of the use of the Old Version was questioned, but the usage of these psalms had the force of custom. The singing of metrical psalms was an early characteristic of the European Reformation.[407] The intention of giving the psalms such an opportunity of use in the English Church may have been implied in a sentence in the 1549 Act of Uniformity relating to the usage of the psalter:

Provided also that it shall be lawfull for all men, as well in Churches, Chappelles, Oratories, or other places, to use openlye anye Psalm, or prayer taken out of the Bible, at anye due time not letting or omitting thereby the Service, or any part thereof mencioned in the said booke.

However, by the second half of the seventeenth century, the use of the Old Version was protected by custom. Whilst no trace has been found of any appeal to the 1549 Act in this matter, episcopal protection is recorded as emerging from a dispute between an incumbent and his parishioners in the Diocese of Salisbury. Richard Watson described the singing of the Old Version as: "rude Rhimes screamed and snuffled out".[408] When Watson stopped the use of the Old Version in his congregation, the Churchwardens appealed to the Bishop who directed that their "Custom-musick should be re-induced".[409] And not even citing Cosin's opinion against the Old Version could deflect the pressure put upon Watson to comply. Whilst the Bishop of Salisbury, Dr Seth Ward, had a reputation of severity towards nonconformity, it would appear that in this controversy he supported the use of the Old Version.

Another aspect of the use of the Old Version which was disliked clerically was that of the discretion of the Parish Clerk in the choice of the psalm. When Luke Milbourne, an Anglican clergyman, published his new work: *The Psalms of David in English Metre* (1698), besides making the usual complaint against the quality of the English of the Old Version, he added:

If it be a Part of Divine Service, how comes it to pass that our Ecclesiastical Representatives have not thought Uniformity in singing of Psalms as beautiful, and as valuable, as in any other Part of the Publick Service? Why not in the Poetical, as well as in the Prose-Version? This would take the Choice of them out of the Parish-Clerk's Power, and make it a Priest's Business, whose Discretion might be farther relied on in it.[410]

If the customs of the Old Version could not be abolished, there was still the hope that the custom could be controlled but, like Milbourne's psalter, this hope was still-born. The ambition of shaping popular culture was also implied in the motivation behind the Bishop of Chichester's metrical psalter of 1651. Bishop Henry King produced psalms in the same metre as in the Old Version for each psalm so as to fit the old tunes and thereby to try and reform the custom of psalm singing by harnessing the way that the singing of the metrical psalms was practised. He felt that this way he could:

> ... prevent that disturbance which the Alteration might bring, whose difference in this Version will not be much discerned, when the Congregation, perfect in their antient Tunes, may with as much ease repeat every verse read before They sing (according to the practice) as They did the Old.[411]

However, the Old Version was not susceptible of reform in this way. Meanwhile, not all felt that aesthetic grounds were the correct basis from which to appraise the singing of psalms. Musicians had to face the wariness of those who were suspicious of only using musical quality as the touchstone of the offering of the psalms. When resort was made to the example of the early church it was found that:

> The Fathers use to reprove the abuses which were too often found in singing Psalms in the Churches, especially, that they were many times more pleased with the sweetness of the voyce then the divine matter, or when onely a few of the Church did sing, that they so sung that few understood what they sung. ... It is no perfect singing nor pleasing to God, when mens hearts do not sing unto the Lord as well as their voyces.[412]

Once one looked away from the idiosyncrasies of the Old Version and its usage and instead looked at the meaning of that usage, the Old Version took on a very different perspective. The offering of the Old Version constituted a pattern of prayer which engaged a generality of people. This usage of the psalms was appreciated across a wide spectrum of theological outlook. For example, a tract of 1644, clearly not of Anglican provenance, offered the explanation of the offering of metrical psalms that: "... singing for the most part is but more deliberate meditationall praying." [413] Another tract may be cited, again from a non-Anglican background, that distinguished two sorts of prayer: 'Metricall with musick' and 'Prosaycall' and which gave precedence to the first.[414]

The Old Version was also acknowledged as an instrument of teaching. When William Nicolson, the Bishop of Gloucester, prepared a book about the Psalms, he noted the power of this metrical material compared with attempts at didactic teaching:

> Scarce any Prophetical Prediction, or Prophetical Precept, is by the Vulgar remembered beyond the Church-door; but the tune of the Psalms, and the words too, are longer lived.[415]

Other observations recorded that:

> ... daily Experience proves that what is writ in Metre, to be sung, is more grateful to mens fancies, sooner imbib'd, makes a deeper impress, and is longer retained in memory; yea it elevates the hearts and minds to more heightened contemplations, and excelse divine rapture than Prose.[416]

> ... Psalms have a peculiar fitness for teaching and instructing, because the pleasantness of Metre said or sung, is very helpful to the Memory.[417]

A key feature of the appraisal of the use of the Old Version is to determine its significance as understood by ministers who were prepared to be immersed in its use. Two clergy have left their analyses of the spirituality articulated by the Old Version: Francis Roberts and John Lightfoot. Roberts (?1599-1675) was an assistant to the Commissioners for the ejection of scandalous ministers and schoolmasters under Parliament. He served at St Augustine's, London, and then was Rector of Wrington, Somerset, 1650-1675.[418] Lightfoot (1602-1675), the biblical and rabbinical scholar, was Rector of Ashley, Staffordshire, 1630-1642, and became a member of the Westminster Assembly in 1643. Also in 1643, he became Master of Catharine Hall, Cambridge, and Rector of Much Munden, Hertfordshire. He held both these posts to the end of his life.

Roberts knew the way that the Old Version could effectively channel the spiritual aspirations of the common people, but also recorded his reservations about these matters. He was uneasy about some aspects of the text, which he had come to regard as a paraphrase, and also about some aspects of its usage, which he thought should be bettered. Lightfoot preached about singing the psalms in a sermon to the congregation of St Mary's, Cambridge, on 24th June, 1660.[419]

Despite his unease about the Old Version, Roberts did record his understanding of the strengths that were inherent in the way that the Old Version was rendered:

> Vocal Singing of Psalmes, &c. 1. Gives more space of time and deliberate Scope for spiritual Meditation upon that which is sung. The words being as it were produced and drawn out at length, the thoughts have the longer opportunity to fix, ponder, dwell, and be detained thereupon in a more deliberate and distinct Meditation. And this use we should constantly make of Singing Psalmes: viz. thereby to enlarge our Meditation.
> 2. Excites and expresseth our spiritual affections exceedingly. (Roberts wrote of joy, love, delight, zeal, penitence).
> 3. Edifies our selves and others.
> 4. Declares our more rich furniture with the Word of God dwelling in us in all wisedom, and our more ample profession of Piety consequently.
> 5. Glorifies God more magnificently, triumphantly, and gloriously: Singing aloud, stirring up greater attention, affection, and admiration in the Auditory....
> Singing of Psalmes, &c. to God with the voice, seems to be a part of God's natural Worship.... Singing of Psalmes, &c. to God is a kind or sort of Prayer, A Prayer not in prose, but in Meetre with melody.[420]

To use the metrical psalter as a focal point for doctrine, spiritual experience, teaching and self-understanding, placed considerable emphasis upon its contents and upon its use. To put the psalms in such a central position could even have meant that the rest of scripture and worship revolved around the psalms. Hence, Roberts shared the expectation of inward sincerity in the use of these psalms:

> ... without the Conjunction of minde and heart with the audible voice, vocal Singing is but Hypocritical.[421]

Such a high estimate of the value of the psalms demanded a total absorption into their usage. There was no possibility of an objective detachment from offering the psalms; the exercise engaged the whole of one's being. In the approach represented by Roberts, the characteristics of the offering of the Old Version, which had been regarded by others as faults, became virtues; the extremely slow pace of the rendering of the Old Version became an asset. With the book of Psalms being regarded as the 'Epitome of Holy Scriptures',[422] to linger on the psalms was to encounter both revelation and truth. Accordingly, participation in the offering of the Old Version meant involvement in a process of absorbing that revelation and truth.

The use of the Old Version was found to assist meditation by elongated attention based on simple metres. By contrast, the psalters of Patrick and Abbot attempted to encourage meditation on the text by expanding and enlarging the text of the psalms in discursive verse.[423] However, popular preference remained with the more simple and familiar text.

Lightfoot presented himself as a key supporter of the singing of psalms in the deliberations of the Westminster Assembly.[424] In his Cambridge sermon of 1660, he enthused about the importance of this pattern of devotion:

> First, It is an action, that helps up and keeps the heart, in a spiritual frame, as much as any. Singing calls up the soul into such a posture, and doth, as it were, awaken it: it is a lively rousing up of the heart.
>
> Secondly; This is a work of the most meditation of any we perform in public. It keeps the heart longest upon the thing spoken. Prayer and hearing pass quick from one sentence to another; this sticks long upon it. Meditation must follow after hearing the word, and praying with the minister; for new sentences, still succeeding, give not liberty, in the instant, well to muse and consider upon what is spoken: but in this, you pray and meditate, praise and meditate, speak of the good things of God and meditate. God hath so ordered this duty, that, while we are employed in it, we feed, and chew the cud together.
>
> Thirdly; This is a service in which we profess delight in the thing we have in hand. It is a noise of joy and gladness. It speaks that we delight in God's ordinances, that we are about.
>
> Fourthly; This is a service, wherein one is cheered from another.... One takes mirth, life, and warmth from another; a

holy fervour and emulation, as the seraphims [Isa. vi] strive to outvie one another in praising God. Who is there, but, while he is joining with the congregation in this duty, feels such an impression and excitation, his own string wound up by the concert of the choir? We do, as it were, jog one another to put on all as much as we can, to join together in the praise and honour of God.[425]

Lightfoot used an interesting rhetorical device to explain the practice of psalm singing:

If I were in a vulgar or unlearned congregation, I would give rules for singing of psalms, with profit: and among divers, especially these two:
1. To mind what is sung: not only that the heart go along with the tongue in general, but to be carefully observant of what is sung. There is a variety of matter in most psalms: they pass from one thing to another. This we should carefully observe: now I pray, now I mourn for my sins, for the church of God, &c.
2. To apply to ourselves the matter we sing, as far as it may concern us: to bear a part with David, not in word and tune, but affection. This way, we must use in hearing or reading the Scripture, to bring it home to our own concernment. ... sing David's Psalms, but make them your own. Let the skill of composure be his, - the life of devotion, yours.[426]

Lightfoot indulged in a rousing conclusion:

Fail not to join with the congregation in the performance of it; stir up your hearts, while you are conversant about it. Praise only, of all the services we perform to God here, goes along with us to heaven. There is no praying, no hearing, no receiving sacraments there, - nothing but praising, lauding, and celebrating, God: and that is the work of saints and angels to all eternity. Amen. [427]

The Old Version may not have appealed to those with educated sensitivities, but within its ambit decried weaknesses became strengths and vices became virtues. It is interesting to have reviewed some of the evidence for the desire to control and even suppress the Old Version and the way that these tendencies were handled culturally and administratively. The explanations of Roberts and Lightfoot show that participation in this psalm-singing was esteemed as a corporate seal of discipleship: a participation in a divine calling.

Scrivener was another Anglican minister who touched on this dimension of congregational life and, in writing about the use of gifts to edify the Church rather than individuals, emphasised the singing of psalms to be a spiritual gift, the exercise of which required the laying aside of personal preferences in favour of corporate edification:

> For as he that sings with the Congregation ought to lay aside his private Tunes, though possibly far more excellent than that which is set for all to follow, so must the singular Devotion of a higher strain than ordinarie, complie with the meaner, to avoid scandal and confusion: as that which may better agree with the whole Bodie, than sublimer strains or Tunes. And this is the case of that plain and easie recitative way of using the Psalmes in our Church, which requires a cheerfull Spirit, without difficulty or tediousnesse of modulating the Voice, which for that reason might have been preferred before the more Artificiall and hard, of private mens Invention, had it not pleased men of designe, and unquiet Spirits, to bring it into disgrace, for no other faults but which are found to be more notorious in that they have introduced in its stead. [428]

There is in Scrivener's words the implication that people had to sacrifice individuality and work to establish an aural para-society. Accordingly, Scrivener felt that the Old Version and its singing had to be protected. Whilst the contrast was acknowledged between the popular rendering of the Old Version and other more elegant ways of singing the psalms, the Old Version did not remain unsupported:

> ... the Translation in Prose, which is sung in Cathedrals with sutable Notes and ravishing Accents, bearing some Resemblance to the Hallelujahs above; which the Vulgar may stare at, and admire, but cannot join, or bear a part in that kind of Psalmody. So that Thousands, and Ten Thousands, since the Reformation, had been deprived of the Benefit, and Pleasure, and Solace, and Comfort of singing the Praises of God in the Psalms of David, the sweet Singer of Israel, had not those charitable Authors condescended to their Capacities, by composing a plain and familiar Metre.[429]

Two books dating from the Interregnum were specifically directed to support Psalm-singing and were subsequently appealed to as carrying a degree of authority by Anglican authors.[430] Whilst it was said that:

> ... none can sing a Psalm as he ought, but he that hath grace in his heart, and is renewed in the spirit of his minde.[431]

and whilst psalm-singing was made out to be an integral and indispensable part of Christian spirituality; neither work offered the insights that Lightfoot and Roberts summarised. Whilst exuberant psalm-singing was encouraged,[432] the benefits that Roberts and Lightfoot expounded were not presented.

It had been a non-Anglican contention at the Savoy Conference that:

> Common Observation tells us, That there is more order, and less hinderance to Edification in the peoples singing, then in their reading and praying together vocally.[433]

The use of the word 'edification' in describing the effects of psalm-singing was a recurring theme. The offering of the Old Version was regarded as building-up a congregation in the matter of divine truth, in fellowship and in their encounter with God. The Old Version and the Book of Common Prayer not only co-existed but also cohabited in the same acoustic space. There were some who were enthusiasts for both but these two patterns only consistently overlapped in the person of the Parish Clerk. Just as the people often chose the man to lead them in their 'custom-musick', so also they chose the same man to represent them in the prayer book offices.

The Old Version was both a resource for use in church and was also received into people's homes and figures in the consideration of Family Prayer in the next chapter. The fact that ordinary people were able to offer praise within their own cultural idiom, when coupled with the inward sincerity which was extolled and expected, made that praise authentic and a worthy offering. In contrast with the services authorised by Parliament, the Old Version was authorised by custom and had been adopted and appropriated as a norm of popular devotion and association within the broad sweep of parish life.

9

FAMILY PRAYER

The broad phenomenon of Family Prayer across the whole spectrum of Church history, let alone in the history of the Anglican Church, has been largely overlooked.[434] Family prayer has been acknowledged to be an important historical element in Christian devotion, but it awaits investigation.[435] Accordingly, it has not proved to be possible to seek the guidance of secondary sources in the material that follows.

Church Services and Family Prayer

The instructions in the Book of Common Prayer for the daily offering of Morning and Evening Prayer included the aspiration that people would come to share in the service.[436] However, any emphasis on the value of the daily office in the life of the Church did not meet with any known general response. All the literature designed to encourage attendance at the daily services bewailed the lack of popular support for these occasions.

Writings calling for mass participation in the daily office became particularly significant during the troubled reign of James II.[437] This leads one to suspect that the call to daily public prayer in the time of James II was related to the dawning religious instability of the State. In the long term, despite all exhortation, even if people had wanted to go to Church for a week-day service, they might have had some difficulty in finding one. This was noted by a Hertfordshire Vicar, contrasting country life with towns and cities:

In Towns and Cities where People may conveniently meet, ... they ought to resort to the Temple and the House of God, to offer unto him their Morning and their Evening Sacrifice.... We are not so happy in Countrey Villages, that we should meet publickly every day in the week to worship God....[438]

Indeed, it was possible to say that, broadly, as a general rule:

> ... in most places Christian People cannot meet together at the
> Church every Day, Morning and Evening, to give to God the
> Glory that is due unto his Name.[439]

The general omission of week-day prayers in a largely rural country
underlined the implied importance of Family Prayer. However, the
tension between the idealism that encouraged people both to attend
week-day services and household family prayers may not have divided
people's loyalties as much as one might have imagined.

The theology of a continual offering to God in the Parish Churches of
the land was one thing, the practical reality was another. In the more
sober atmosphere of the 1690's, two bishops were content to encourage
their clergy to have a daily office in their Parish Churches and hoped
that they might be joined by a small congregation.[440] However, there is
also the record of a complaint from these years that parishioners were
staying at home on Sundays, reading and praying in their own families,
rather than going to Church.[441]

It was possible to set great store by the hope that people would join
in regular church attendance:

> ... the most ignorant and illiterate may, by the frequent audience
> of publick set forms of prayer ..., when these are distinctly
> pronounced ..., by the Minister of a congregation, or the Master
> of a Family, fix and remember some things and expressions, for
> their more private and single use, and at last be able to express
> their supplications to God for the private relief of their
> necessities, and in this the publick language of the Church, when
> no such thing can possibly be accomplished, by hearing the same
> matter variously phrased.[442]

In the absence of week-day services, with people staying at home on a
Sunday and using their own material, one has to enquire what resources
were available for family prayer. A clear indication of the material then
in general use survives from 1692:

> The authors of the Common-Prayer-Book did never design it for
> the use of Private Families. For otherwise 'A Form of Prayer to
> be used in Private Houses every Morning and Evening' had
> never been Printed with our Bibles after the Singing Psalms.[443]

Family Prayer from the Sternhold & Hopkins Metrical Psalter

The large number of editions of the Sternhold & Hopkins metrical psalter (the Old Version) has already been discussed, and the Old Version is extremely significant for Family Prayer. In all the comments about the Old Version no remark, other than that cited immediately above, has been noted about its concluding devotional section, suggesting that there was little point in remarking upon common practice. As Sternhold & Hopkins often came at the back of the book with which it was bound, the prayers at the end of the Old Version were immediately accessible. The importance of these prayers is not to be underestimated, bearing in mind the huge number of copies of the Old Version. The Old Version was often bound with the Book of Common Prayer or with the Authorised Version of the Bible. Consequently, the metrical psalter, with its concluding devotional section, assumed the credentials of an Anglican devotional handbook and may be viewed as effectively having been regarded as a quasi-official supplement to Scripture and to the Book of Common Prayer. Different editions of the Old Version usually contained various prayers, but the common denominator between editions in which prayers have survived is the prayers for morning and evening. These two prayers derived directly from the use of the sixteenth century congregation at Geneva. [444] These prayers were so different from the Anglican pattern and practice of the Book of Common Prayer that it may seem difficult to enlarge the boundaries of the Anglican theology of prayer to include them. However, the enormous number of printings of Sternhold & Hopkins may have meant that there were in existence more copies of these prayers for morning and evening than copies of the Prayer Book at any time in the seventeenth century. Other prayers that figured at the end of this metrical psalter included prayers to be said before and after food, 'a godly prayer to be said at all times', 'a confession of all estates and times', 'a prayer to be said before a man begin his work', 'a prayer for the whole state of Christ's church', and 'a prayer containing the duty of every true Christian'.

Both the Morning and Evening Prayers in the Old Version express a reliance on the forgiveness available through the death of Christ and carry clear implications both about the value of obedience in discipleship and the division between the saved and the rejected. The form of morning prayer includes prayer for the Church (including those in persecution) and for the mission of the Church. The reference to 'thy flock' in both Morning and Evening read as a metaphor for a family at prayer and could be suggested to have offered a household some self-understanding. There is a reciprocity between the two forms which dwells on the pattern of day and night, so that a night of dedicated rest is the prelude to a day of dutiful service. One phrase that is especially significant for this pair of prayers, which is a direct linkage to the theology of the Office of Morning Prayer that has already been outlined, is the clause that occurs in the opening sequence of both prayers: 'present ourselves ... before thy Majesty'. The assurance that prayer was offered in the presence of God was a basic attribute of the Anglican theology of prayer. Here the assurance of access to God being obtained through the atonement leads to prayer being offered in his presence.

In beginning to discuss the importance of these prayers, one can point to the certainty of a generality of distribution, but intimations of any general usage have been elusive beyond the quotation already cited. However, the fact that these devotions were available to people can be taken to imply that there was a popular awareness of these words. When one begins to consider their use there are so many variables that could be discussed and not just the question of literacy. There was a question of available time as well as of adequate domestic lighting. It was possibly more likely that these prayers would be used once a week in the leisure of a Sunday, rather than every day. In a country where the population was mostly rural, the expectations of employers, the shortness of winter daylight and the long hours demanded by the harvest, for example, all had an incidence on the lives of working people and affected the possibility of time for prayer. However, those who adopted the prayers from Sternhold & Hopkins could at least read the words at their own pace and appropriate them to their own understandings. Considering how slowly they sang their psalms, it could be that they read prayers at a similar speed. It could also be that some chose to abbreviate the prayers, so that they would be able to fulfil their duty to pray but would at the same time not have to reach beyond either their concentration span or the time available.

Theologically, there was a significant balance in these prayers between the acknowledgement of the degradation of the human condition and the assurance of the gracious presence of God. Accordingly, those who used these prayers could have been enheartened as well as ennobled by embracing the words that were provided. To have used these prayers could have reminded the poorest cottagers of their status as citizens of heaven. It is conceivable that the offering of these prayers from the metrical psalter had a far greater appeal than the prayers of the official liturgy. Another dimension has been added to the understanding of the popularity of the Old Version in the suggestion

that this work was utilised as a school textbook.[445] The possibility that
the Sternhold & Hopkins metrical psalter was therefore part of popular
training in both literacy and devotion could explain why its pages would
have been so significant in popular usage.

The Fundamental Anglican Understanding of Family Prayer

Probably the most authoritative statement of the Anglican view of
Family Prayer was offered in a sermon of 1684 by John Tillotson.[446]
Tillotson (1630-1694), who became Dean of St Paul's in 1689 and
Archbishop of Canterbury in 1691, asserted this area of concern to be 'a
great and very essential part of Religion'.[447] He preached from a clearly
paternalistic background of household organisation:

> ... it is incumbent upon us to make those, who are under our
> Charge and subject to our Authority, God's subjects, and his
> Children and Servants, which is a much more honourable and
> happy Relation, than that which they bear to us.[448]

Tillotson was able to speak about the practice of devotion as well as the
ideal of devotion. He recommended that people should proceed:

> ... by setting up the constant Worship of God in our Families. By
> daily Prayers to God every Morning and Evening; and by
> reading some portion of the Holy Scriptures at those Times,
> especially out of the Psalms of David, and the New Testament.
> And this is so necessary to keep alive and to maintain a sense of
> God and Religion in the minds of men, that where it is neglected
> I do not see how any Family can be esteemed a Family of
> Christians, or indeed to have any Religion at all.[449]

Tillotson regarded the offering of daily prayer to be as important as
daily family instruction. He encouraged people to use 'Helps',[450]
particularly 'The Whole Duty of Man'. Whilst Tillotson was able to
recommend this help for instruction, he avoided giving direction as to
what 'help' should be used for the matter of prayer. He encouraged the
saying of grace before meals and wanted masters of households to
ensure that:

> Children and servants ... be instructed in how to pray by
> themselves. ... And in order to this, they ought to take care that
> their Children and Servants be furnished with such short Forms

of Prayer and Praise, as are proper to their capacities and conditions....[451]

Tillotson did not mention the Book of Common Prayer as a source for family prayers. When Tillotson recommended daily morning and evening prayers, with the reading of scripture,[452] it is quite possible that he felt no need to specify any prayers, because those at the back of the Old Version were most probably recognised as being in general use, even if in recommending 'short' prayers he implied personal reservations as to the length of the prayers derived from Geneva. Tillotson was emphatic as to the importance of 'Family Religion':

> Families are the first Seminaries of Religion, and if care be not there taken to prepare persons, especially in their tender years, for publick teaching and instruction, it is like to have but very little effect.[453]

Family Prayer According to Richard Allestree

In *The Whole Duty of Man*, Allestree described family devotions as a 'sort of publick prayer'.[454] *The Whole Duty of Man* was first published in 1657 and achieved 38 recorded editions by 1700. It was specifically designed for regular reading in households and, despite having been issued anonymously, has been attributed to Richard Allestree.[455] Allestree (1619-1681) carefully assembled the book in the form of a manifesto for a renewed society. Allestree received recognition after the Restoration; he became Regius Professor of Divinity at Oxford in 1663 and Provost of Eton in 1665.

The 'master' of the family and all its members, including children and servants, were expected to join in devotions. The master of the family was regarded as having special responsibility to ensure that these prayers took place, "it being as much his part thus to provide for the Souls of his Children and Servants, as to provide food for their Bodies".[456] According to Allestree, there could be no excuse for the omission of prayers, not even by the "meanest householder". Allestree did not necessarily hold it to be the role of the master of a family to offer prayers. If the master was illiterate, then the duty of offering prayer was implied to devolve upon anyone who could read. For Allestree, against the trend of general practice, the Book of Common Prayer was preferred as the source of family prayers, but its exclusive use was not insisted upon. If no-one in a family could read, prayers drawn from the Prayer Book were still preferred, so that people could:

be taught without Book some form of prayer which they may use in the Family, for which purpose again some of the prayers of the Church will be very fit, as being most easie for their memories by reason of their shortness and yet containing a great deal of matter.[457]

Allestree felt that the necessity of family prayer was so vital that he would prefer to acquiesce in the use of prayers not drawn from the Anglican service book rather than omit family prayers. A family where the members did not join for prayers was labelled as "heathenish" and, just as it was the duty of the master of a family to provide prayers for the family, so it was the duty of every member of the family to join in these gatherings.

Family Prayers and Prayer Book Prayers

It was held that it was the duty of a family to pray.[458] Concern about the offering of family prayers was linked to a concern about the good state of the nation and the whole movement to promote family prayer received episcopal support. Clergy were told to encourage their people:

Put them upon worshipping God in their families, upon praying with their children and servants. If it be possible bring every family to it; press upon them the absolute necessity of it, assist and direct them that they may do it as they ought. Furnish them with books and helps, and where you cannot afford to be at that expence get the help of those that are able and willing.[459]

Patrick composed a sequence of prayers for each day for regular use morning and evening through the week. Patrick refused to consider the use of the Prayer Book in routine domestic prayer:

... the Reverence due to that book will be best preserved, by employing it only in the publick Divine Service; or in the private, where there is a Priest to officiate. However, the design of it is not to furnish the People with Prayers, for all those particular occasions, wherein devout souls would make their request to God. And the constant opinion of pious Divines, in this and other Churches ... hath been; that other Books of Prayers, which they have composed, are necessary for the flock of Christ, besides their publick Liturgy.[460]

Patrick's prayers engage in subtle theological legerdemain in that his family prayers for use at home described the devotional perception of God as being located in 'a sense of our dependance' upon God,[461] and that worshippers at home only had a 'sense of thy divine presence'.[462] There was an implication of being at one remove from the presence of God, as worshippers prayed: 'preserve in me always a religious Sense of thee' [463] and 'enable me to maintain a constant Sense of Thy Divine Presence'.[464] Patrick reserved the declaration of conviction that one was in the presence of the Divine for a private prayer to be offered in Church entitled: 'A Short Prayer before Divine Service begins'.[465] Patrick's prayers do not necessarily represent a development of Anglican theology; it is more likely that these differences arise from an agenda of heightening the public estimation of Church services.

This implicit distancing of God from the home in the prayers devised by Patrick contrasted with Bishop Lewis Bayly's long established work,[466] which included a section on the matter of family prayer. Bayly insisted that its provision was the responsibility of the master of a house, but made no mention of the use of the Book of Common Prayer. Instead, Bayly set out a specimen morning prayer some eight pages in length in a duodecimo volume[467] and another eight page specimen prayer for the evening.[468] Whilst the wide-ranging appeal of Bayly's work has been acknowledged,[469] his book can fit into Anglican teaching on prayer bearing in mind his commendation of common prayer in use in church services,[470] its royal dedication and its consistent prayers for the King and the royal family. Bayly chose words and imagery to imply the proximity of the worshipper to God, such as 'we are unworthy to appear in thy sight and presence'; 'we thine unworthy Servants ... do cast down our selves at the foot-stall of thy grace'.[471]

The anonymous *Domestick Devotions for the Use of Families and of Particular Persons, whereunto are prefixed some earnest Perswasives to Prayer and Devotion* (1683) lamented the neglect of family prayers. This tract contrasted the privileged position of public worship with its formal protection and legal incentives to attendance with the weak emphasis on family prayers. This tract denied that the Church had set any form of prayer for use in family devotions, and totally disregarded any contribution from the Old Version. The author of *Domestick Devotions* took the view that:

> ... considering the general temper of men, it would much abate their veneration of the publick service, and make them more slack and regardless in their attendance at the Church, if the

Devotions there were no other than what they have every day in their own Houses.[472]

In support of this opinion, the author referred to the *Practicall Catechisme* of Henry Hammond. However, the author of *Domestick Devotions* misrepresented Hammond, for Hammond's teaching was that family prayer was a form of public prayer and that only once the prescribed liturgy had been observed was there liberty to append prayers of personal choice.[473]

The text of *Domestick Devotions* insisted that heads of households had an overwhelming responsibility to ensure that family devotions took place, which should include both prayer and scripture reading.[474] The resulting prayers in this tract were lengthy, but comprehensive, and set for both morning and evening. However, like many other volumes of prayers in the time-span of this study, these prayers only survive in one edition. Meanwhile, one cleric was so anxious that family prayer be offered that he designed prayers that could be shortened to fit the time available as he felt strongly that any prayer was better than no prayer.[475] Another vicar was so concerned that masters lead their families in prayer, that he only specifically itemised the Lord's Prayer for use.[476]

Some clergy provided patterns of family prayer for morning and evening for their parishioners.[477] Alternative opinion could still insist on the rigid use of the Book of Common Prayer:

> Whoever has the Charge and Government of a Family should take care that God be dayly Worshipt in it by Publick Prayer....[478]

A compromise solution that commended itself to many people was published as: *The Common-Prayer-Book the Best Companion in the House and Closet as well as in the Temple: or, a Collection of Prayers out of the Liturgy of the Church of England....* (1686). From its first issue, this anthology earned the approbation of the Bishop of Ely, who recommended it to his clergy.[479] By 1700, seven further editions had been issued. This book also affirmed that it was the duty of the master of every house to provide spiritual fare for all those under his roof and gave into a master's hands the means to do so in prayers drawn from Anglican liturgy. At least one further compilation proceeded on similar lines.[480] The tract: *The Family-Prayers of those poor Christians who in Court and Country, in Cities, Towns, Cottages and Farm Houses, are in good earnest with Religion....* (1675) chose a very simple pattern drawn from the liturgy to enable a working family's duty to be discharged simply and briefly.

The Domestic Use of the Psalms

A pattern of devotion for family use that was mentioned in the literature of these years was the singing of psalms in the family. Tillotson specifically commended the use of Psalms.[481] The Rector of Ubley in Somerset wrote a whole chapter entitled 'Incitements to Singing of Psalms in Families'.[482] He felt that the psalms were a great resource to assist people:

> ... To Pray wisely and effectually, there being in the Psalms very many Prayers made to our hands, whereby we may go to the Lord, and 'take with us words' (Hosea 14.2), to express before him our necessities and desires of every kind.[483]

This author valued psalms as providing material for family use, rather than trusting to the abilities of families to construct their own material.

The use of the psalms in family prayer was already a well-established principle of guidance. Bayly had recommended the singing of a Psalm in the evening in families. Bayly advised his readers that when singing psalms they should:

> 1. Beware of singing Divine Psalmes for an ordinary recreation.... They are Gods Word, take them not in thy mouth in vain.
> 2. Remember to sing Davids Psalms with Davids spirit.
> 3. Practice St. Pauls Rule, I will sing with the spirit, but I will sing with the understanding also.
> 4. As you sing, uncover your heads, and behave your selves in comely reverence, as in the sight of God, singing to God, in Gods own words; but be sure that the matter make more mellody in your hearts, than the Musick in your ears; for the singing with a grace in our hearts, is that which the Lord is delighted withall....
> 5. thou mayest ... sing all the Psalms over in order; for all are most divine and comfortable; but if thou wilt chuse some special Psalms, as more fit for some times and purposes; and such as by the oft usage, thy people may the easier commit to memory.[484]

Bayly listed psalms for singing in particular circumstances. Whilst his comments on family prayer did not add anything to the general pattern of alternatives already established, Bayly's 'Rules' for the singing of psalms in the family give an insight into the attitudes which were encouraged in undertaking this activity.[485]

Review

Four alternative positions have been represented:

1. The normal pattern of daily devotion was shaped around the prayers drawn from the Old Version.
2. Family prayer was a form of public prayer and should exclusively use the Book of Common Prayer.
3. Family prayer was a form of public prayer and should primarily consist of the appropriate Office of the Book of Common Prayer and once that had been offered then other material could be added; but it was better to pray and not use the Prayer Book than not to pray at all.
4. Families at prayer would best avoid the use of the Book of Common Prayer and should use alternative material.

Such a diversity of teaching presented a bewildering range of advice as to how to go about household devotional duties. Meanwhile, the writings of the time indicate that there was a sense of unease at the prospect of a low level of popular response to encouragements in the practice of family prayer. For example: "there is a more general want of Family-Prayers ..." [486] To add to the confusion, the open debate about extempore prayer versus set prayer created uncertainty in the matter of family prayer as well:

And some, as experience hath shewn, finding that they could not pray in their Families ex temporare or on the sudden as they have been urged, without many vain repetitions and broken impertinent expressions, have quite left off the Duty itself.[487]

Overall, the need of printed devotions for family use was affirmed. Advice and encouragement continued to be offered in the matter of family prayer. A huge amount of material was available for popular use and there was general Anglican insistence that this sort of prayer was required. However, the heads of households were under a wide range of competing (and contradictory) pressures as to how to approach their duties. That there was the reading of the Bible and the offering of prayer and the singing of psalms in many households cannot be doubted, but it may be less problematical to consider private prayer.

10

PRIVATE PRAYER

Private Prayer Mandatory

The words of Jesus recorded in Matthew 6 v. 6 were regarded as a direct instruction requiring obedience:

> But thou, when thou prayest, enter into thy closet, and when thou hast shut the door, pray to thy Father which is in secret; and thy Father which seeth in secret shall reward thee openly.

This verse entailed a response which reveals a broad consensus of understanding across the period under scrutiny. The response of individuals can be suggested to have been, in effect, part of the understanding of the nature of a human being. As people were encouraged towards obedience to this command, it was part of the Anglican treatment of this gospel imperative that set forms of prayer were commended for use. The Church of England cannot be accused of having undervalued private prayer:

> As for Private Prayer, it cannot be imagined, that any good Christian can live a Day, nor scarce an Hour without it; so many are his Necessities, so great his Infirmities, and so violent his Temptations....[488]

It has been claimed that private devotion was 'non-controversial' in the seventeenth century,[489] but there were issues of great sensitivity associated with private prayer. The fact that forms of prayer were made available for private use was an important provision within Anglicanism. These forms were drawn so that people would not fail to follow dominical teaching. People could draw help from an abundance of material. The variety of advice and printed matter commended for use left it to individual choice as to how each person could meet their Lord's expectation of private prayer. Initially, consideration will be offered of two large-scale works that were frequently published in this period which contained prayers intended specifically for private use: *The Whole Duty of Man* and *Holy Living*.

Allestree's Teaching on Private Prayer

The author of the *Whole Duty of Man* emphasised that the day should begin and end with private prayer, both as a matter of duty to God and also as a safeguard for one's own existence. Allestree accepted that it was possible for people to find that pressure of time could preclude a proper measure of 'set and solemn Prayer', but insisted that it was still possible for people to offer short prayers whilst they worked. In the direct style that typified *The Whole Duty of Man*, Allestree added:

> And let no man that can find time to bestow upon his vanities, nay, perhaps his sins, say he wants leisure for Prayer....[490]

The early editions of *The Whole Duty of Man* contained this advice without giving examples of practice. In 1660, a supplement of prayers was appended to *The Whole Duty of Man* which subsequently became part of the text, duly amended to take account of the Restoration. This supplement, *Private Devotions for Several Occasions Ordinary and Extraordinary* (1660), contained prayers enabling readers to put these directions into practice.

The day, according to Allestree, should begin with a brief prayer on waking[491] and he advised the pursuit of some very sober reflections whilst one was getting dressed. As soon as possible, people were encouraged to 'retire to some private place', to kneel and after two short prayers to offer an extended thanksgiving. After its opening formula, this prayer promptly adopted Biblical phraseology to declare: "In thee, O Lord, I live & move and have my being".[492] These lines immediately took the petitioner into the assurance of human life being lived in the Divine presence. This thanksgiving was followed by a Confession, which opened with another statement affirming the Divine presence: "I thy sinful creature cast my self at thy feet".[493] Accordingly, the ensuing prayer for Grace presupposed the proximity of the Divine. The accompanying prayers of intercession and 'For Preservation' shared the presupposition of God being close enough to be able to be involved in the matters in which divine aid was sought. The whole sequence ended with the Lord's Prayer.

The 'Prayers for Night' did not make any significant statement of one's relationship to God, but were more concerned to enable one to deprecate evil. These prayers led to a further prayer 'For Preservation' which referred to the presence of God and his protection. The assurance of the presence of God as the context of life was not taught as a specific element in *The Whole Duty of Man*, but was an implied doctrinal presupposition in the prayers that were made available for morning and evening. More prayers were penned by Allestree for use during the day, in conjunction with the Lord's Prayer, in case people wished to experiment with the ancient Hours of Prayer. But it was stressed that this was a matter of personal choice, not a matter of obligation.

Allestree did not attempt to elide any distinction between earth and heaven in reflecting upon the proximity of the Divine,[494] but intimated that heaven and earth were adjacent. Consequently, Allestree could offer an awareness of the sovereign presence of God as being the context both within which prayer was made and also within which human life was lived. Perhaps the most revealing statement theologically of Allestree's perception of the individual's experience of prayer was in one of the prayers that he wrote for use at one's personal discretion during the day entitled: 'For devotion in Prayer' :

O Gracious Lord God, who not only permittest, but invitest us miserable and needie creatures, to present our petitions to thee; grant I beseech thee, that the frequencie of my prayer may be somewhat proportionable to those continual needs I have of thy mercie: Lord, I confess, it is the greatest honour and greatest advantage, thus to be allowed access to thee, yet so sottish and stupid is my profane heart, that it shuns or frustrates the opportunities of it. My Soul, O Lord, is possest with a spirit of infirmitie, it is bowed together, and can in no wise lift up it self to thee. O be thou pleased to cure this sad, this miserable disease, to inspirit and enliven this earthly drossie heart, that it may freely mount towards thee, that I may set a true value on this most valuable priviledge, and take delight in approaching to thee, and that my approaches may be with a reverence some way answerable to that awful Majestie I come before, with an importunitie and earnestness answerable to those pressing wants I have to be supplied, and with such a fixedness and attention of mind, as no wandring thoughts may interrupt; that I may no more incur the guilt of drawing near to thee with my lips, when my heart is far from thee, or have my prayers turn into sin, but

may so ask that I may receive, seek that I may find, knock that it
may be opened unto me: that from praying to thee here, I may be
translated to the praising thee eternally in thy glorie, through the
merits and intercession of Jesus Christ.[495]

This prayer, having affirmed God to invite the presentation of petitions
before him, also articulated the conviction of being allowed access to
God and asked that this approach may be truly valued. Allestree was
aware of the pitfalls possible in prayer, particularly when prayer was
understood as a process of recognising the Divine presence, and he
determined to protect the dignity of prayer. There was also here a sense
of continual accountability to God which can only have affected
personal conduct in society.

Jeremy Taylor's 'Holy Living'
The Rules and Exercises for Holy Living (1st ed. 1650; 18th ed. 1700),
incorporated significant material on private prayer. The suggested
devotions for daily use (Chapter I, Section III) are prefaced by guidance
on 'The Consideration and Practice of the Presence of God'. This
section is quite separate from Taylor's section on the motivation and
regulation of prayer (Chapter IV, Section VII). However, his section on
the practice of the presence of God carried particular theological
significance. The omnipresence of God was explained to be of great
consequence for devotional practice:

... we may imagine God to be as the air and the sea, and we all
inclosed in his circle, wrapt up in the lap of his infinite nature, or
as infants in the wombs of their pregnant mothers; and we can no
more be removed from the presence of God, than from our own
being.[496]

The ineluctable nature of the Divine presence carried implications for
the practice of everyday life, as well as for the practice of prayer:

He walks as in the presence of God that converses with him in
frequent prayer and frequent communion, that runs to him in all
his necessities, that asks counsel of him in all his doubtings, that
opens all his wants to him, that weeps before him for his sins,
that asks remedy and support for his weakness, that fears him as
a judge, reverences him as lord, obeys him as a father, and loves
him as a patron.[497]

To live in a continued awareness of the Divine presence meant that particular devotional attitudes developed, which Taylor saw as penetrating deeply into life:

... this exercise of considering the divine presence is,

1. An excellent help to prayer, producing in us reverence and awfulness to the divine majesty of God, and actual devotion in our offices.

2. It produces a confidence in God, ... since God is so nigh in all our sad accidents....

3. It is apt to produce joy and rejoicing in God, we being more apt to delight in the partners and witnesses of our conversation....

4. This exercise is apt also to enkindle holy desires of the enjoyment of God....[498]

Against this background of thought, Taylor constructed an office that he thought appropriate to enable prayer to be offered three times a day. He recorded two alternative forms for the morning, and noted that clergy were also obliged to offer the appointed public prayers, 'and other devout persons that have leisure to accompany them'. The noon office assisted people to continue to reflect on the difficulties of the Christian life and two alternative forms of evening prayer were provided for those 'who have not time or opportunity to say the public prayers appointed for this Office'.

The sense of the interweaving of the Divine presence with human existence meant that people could be alerted to their continual involvement with the Divine. The availability of Taylor's work meant that this pattern of understanding helped people to ensure that their devotional practice remained within the broad Anglican ethos.

The Prayer Book and Private Prayer

One author recommended private prayers at noon and expected public attendance at Morning and Evening Prayer in the parish churches of the land.[499] The impossibility of so ambitious a programme has already been considered. However, whilst the Book of Common Prayer did not contain explicit teaching on private prayer, it was nevertheless widely circulated and, by implication, widely used. By 1700, more than one hundred editions of the 1662 Prayer Book had been issued in octavo or smaller.[500]

The Prayer Book and its lectionary were commended for private use.[501] The Prayer Book was also treated as a resource that could be re-fashioned for use in private.[502] Thus, out of concern for public ignorance of the prayers of the Church, one writer hoped to familiarise people with the manner, form and method of the Prayer Book:

> ... For I am persuaded, that all the Prejudice which some People have against our Common Prayer, arise from their unacquaintedness with it.[503]

Prayer Book material could be fashioned so as to provide for prayers morning, noon and night, with Morning and Evening Prayers directly drawn from their counterparts in the Prayer Book and prayers for noon derived from the Litany.[504] Equally, the Prayer Book could be mixed with other material and marshalled into the service of a gentleman or of a soldier.[505]

The Practice of Prayer and the Presence of God

There was consensus on the priority that private prayer should have in life. Advice was given on deciding how much time should be spent on one's daily devotions:

> By affording to God one hour in twenty-four, thou mayest have the comforts and rewards of devotion. But he that thinks this is too much, either is very busy in the world, or very careless of heaven.[506]

> What number of hours do many of us squander away in poring on the News-books and those trivial Pamphlets, which swarm amongst us. Should we not do much better, if instead of those which are the most Innocent and most Diverting (how much rather, if instead of those which are good for nothing but to debauch our Minds, by stamping on them a relish of Vice, even of those Vices, which we have not, perhaps, as yet dared to practice.) If, I say, instead of these, we took some times the Writings of the Inspired Pen-Men into our hands....[507]

Although there were occasional personal examples of prayer that reached a wide public[508] and even if there was material enough available to satisfy the needs of those who wished for assistance in private prayer, there was still a question of frequency and timing.

The question as to when private prayer should be offered was generally answered from Psalm 55 v. 17:

> Evening, and morning, and at noon, will I pray, and cry aloud;
> and he shall hear my voice. (Psalm 55 v. 17).

If the fact of which material earned a market and was reprinted can be taken as a guide to popularity, then it can be affirmed that the option of seven times of prayer each day (Psalm 119 v. 164) met with little enthusiasm. Whilst certain literature[509] recommended the observance of the seven hours of prayer, the only work to recommend seven times of prayer each day and to be re-printed in this era was Cosin's *Devotions* (1st ed. 1627; 9th ed. 1693).[510]

The Countess of Morton's Daily Exercise was entrenched in a theology of living in the presence of God: On waking one blessed God; on rising one knelt and declared in prayer that one was kneeling before God. On confession of one's sins one cast oneself down before God. Before the end of the prayers allocated for the morning, one prayed:

> Possess my mind, O Lord, continually with thy Presence, and make me to have a perpetual fear and love of Thy Holy Name, teaching me to do those things that may be pleasing to Thee and profitable to my salvation, through Jesus Christ our Lord, Amen.[511]

A short litany followed for use every day, then 'Rules and Prayers for the Afternoon'. The Rules included:

> VI. And forget not (as often as you can) to be present, and to assist at the publick Offices and Divine Services of the Church, there to attend and perform the Homage and Worship of Almighty God, and to be instructed in his holy Word; for that is a Duty and a Service most highly pleasing to him.
> VII. Remember (and you will much help yourself, if you remember it) that you are continually in the presence of God, and ought to live continually in his Fear, and in Obedience to his Commandments.[512]

The repeated affirmations of the divine presence were part of the broad drift of the teaching about God implied in this genre of material. God was portrayed as involved with the lives of petitioners so that one could aspire to live in dialogue with him.

One particular position that could have caused controversy was the declaration of Patrick that private prayer only became valid if the petitioner also went and shared in public prayers. Patrick was prepared to go as far as to say that:

> ... private Worship is then acceptable unto God, when performed by a true Member of Christ's Body: that is, by one who attends upon the public Assemblies: by which he procures acceptance for his secret and private Services. Which are so far from being most acceptable, that we cannot reasonably think, they are acceptable at all: when they are set in opposition to the other; or when the other is constantly neglected.[513]

However, the validation of private prayer through attending public worship was not a view that was echoed by others but, considering the importance that was attached to Patrick as a teacher about prayer, this view should be noted.

It was recognised that some people could find themselves disadvantaged by pressure of time and that those in service could find themselves lacking the privacy to be able to pray. Reassurance was given that it was acceptable to "say as much as you can",[514] and those who employed servants were reminded that it was their duty to provide for their servants spiritual nurture so that they came to a living faith.[515] Equally, it was recognised that not everyone lived under pressure and that 'persons of leisure' were expected to read, to meditate and to pray:

> ... according to that rule, To whom much is given, from them shall much be required.[516]

This obligation of reading, meditation and prayer was part of the framework of the teaching of the Church for those who were able to follow such expectations. People were encouraged to take a daily portion of the psalms in their course, followed by readings from the Old and New Testaments.[517] The process of meditation did not have a straightforward recipe of practice and was only taught in outline:

> Now Meditation here I take not for the simple thinking of anything divine, which shall offer it self, but for an orderly and serious consideration of the particulars following.
> 1. Upon that portion of Scripture, which I have read.
> 2. Upon my own state and waies.

3. Upon the prayers (that is, confessions petitions and thanksgivings) which I am presently to offer up to God.[518]

Taylor defined meditation as:

... an attention and application of spirit to Divine things, a searching out all instruments to a holy life, a devout consideration of them, and a production of those affections which are in a direct order to the love of God and a pious conversation.[519]

However, such a definition needed some pages of explanation as to how this advice could be followed in life.[520] Teaching on private prayer did not emphasise meditation as an element to be pursued on its own. Meditation was regarded as being only part of a process, reserved for those who had the time and the capacity. The demands of the foundation verse (Matthew 6 v. 6) for private prayer were understood to be discharged by the following pattern:

1. In entring into our Closets ... and there Praying to our Father which is in secret.
2. In frequently Conversing with the Scripture and such good Books as treat about Religious Matters.
3. In private Meditation upon Spiritual things.
4. And lastly, In secret Reflexions and short Ejaculations in all places, at all times of the day, and in all transactions of Life.[521]

Jeremy Taylor emphasised individual choice in the matter of format for private prayer:

In private prayer it is permitted to every man to speak his prayers, or only to think them, which is a speaking to God: vocal or mental praying is all one to God, but in order to us they have their several advantages, the sacrifice of the heart and the calves of the lips make up a holocaust to God; but words are the arrest of the desires, and keep the spirit fixed and in less permissions to wander from fancy to fancy, and mental prayer is apt to make the greater fervour, if it wander not: our office is more determined by words, but we then actually think of God, when our spirits only speak.[522]

Taylor sensed the boundaries of human ability. His analysis reflected the difficulties of offering prayer and whilst words could give shape to formless yearnings there could be a loss of fervour in giving words to the sacrifice of the heart. Printed forms were available but in secret prayer the role of words became more debatable:

> It is not Clamour, or Noise, that our God is taken with; nor needs he it to awaken, or make him understand our meaning; for his Ear is in our Closets, and within our Hearts, to hear and observe the most secret and retir'd Prayer we can frame there.[523]

The regular routine of private devotion was considered to variously lead to solemnity and joy:

> 1. That hereby we shall be prompted to perform all Religious Duties with much greater Strictness and Accuracy.
> 2. That we shall hereby gain for our great satisfaction and comfort one of the most convincing Arguments of our own sincerity.
> 3. That we shall hereby be best inabled to perform all Acts of Publick Worship after the most Solemn manner.
> 4. That this will be a most excellent Preparation for Death, which is so uncertain.
> 5thly, and Lastly, That it will very much increase our Joy hereafter, to be openly rewarded for what we have done thus in Secret.[524]

> ... Prayer refines the Thoughts, purifies the Heart, and exalts the Soul above its natural pitch, so that he who did enter upon his Prayers with some coldness, shall often receive wonderful joy in his Mind, before he comes to the end of them. Nothing will make the Soul partake so much of the Divine Nature, and so closely unite it to God as devout Prayer.[525]

In writing of private prayer in such vibrant terms, many Anglican writers of this period mutually reinforced each other's teaching. There was no substantial controversy, even if only because secret prayer and public discussion did not go together. However, of the nature of things, these writings reached the literate. Those who had little or no cognition of the printed word could not use this material 'in secret' and had to rely on a 'trickle-down' effect that can only have been highly variable.

11

PROCESS IN ANGLICAN WORSHIP

Dimensions in Worship

A congregation gathered for public worship was observing a national legal requirement. However, as the congregation worshipped, a pattern unfolded that became the internal life of the congregation. It has been noted that the ambition of the Church was to move from uniformity to unanimity so that an external observable conformity should lead to an inner coherence, both local and national. This chapter sets out to explore the theological contours of that inner living and direction.

The use of the Book of Common Prayer subjected every congregation to the same guided process of theological perception, interpretation and reflection. This process was subtle and vulnerable. The subtlety of the process lay in that it was an open door for people to enter if they chose to participate in the service, and the process was vulnerable in that it required individual sincerity and congregational accord. The process of common prayer required no more than that words be read, but those words also had to be appropriated by congregations and, in a greater sense, to be offered to the Deity. There are questions here not only of self-understanding at an individual and at a communal level, but also the nurturing and emergence of dimensions of experience that whilst they were intangible carried significant implications for human association.

The theology of the Offices has already been surveyed, but there is still a deeper question to explore as to the process of prayer itself. The dispersed structure of teaching about prayer drawn from the Prayer Book informed the understanding and practice of prayer. The theology of the process of worship was broadly painted in terms of an interaction with and an offering to the God who was adored as being present. The quality of the character of worship came to be seen as a key factor in commending Anglican services to God:

... Gladness is the only Qualification which makes our Services acceptable unto God. 'Tis only a chearful, a free-will Offering, in which he delights; and our Worship is never so grateful unto Him, as when it is pleasing to Our selves.[526]

The mere description of worship, or the listing of the contents of worship, cannot adequately reflect the complexity of the subject. In 1642, Thorndike had asked:

What means so powerful to obtain the peace of the Church from God, to preserve it with men, as to joyn in the same uniform service of God for the purpose?[527]

The period 1641-1700 can be viewed as an extended experiment, searching for an answer and containing all the alternatives that can be the lot of a national church and its practice of prayer. Thus, in these years, the Anglican Church was disestablished, restored to a monopoly and then expected to survive in a legitimated Reformed pluralism. Anglican prayer was debated, proscribed, reinstated, revised, given unique authority as the compulsory norm of devotion and then had to compete for its credibility in a 'free market'. The functions of the forms of Anglican devotion included a form of regulation, a form of protest against the Commonwealth, a means of affirming the royal supremacy and a means of demonstrating the identity of a local community. In order to understand the nature of the Anglican experience in these years, it is necessary to consider various patterns of explanation and to consider their appropriateness to a complexity of material which is not easily susceptible to broad summary.

The Divine Presence - Mediated and Immediate
The attempt to expound the vision that unfolded within Anglicanism of its understanding of the worship that was offered had many dimensions. Sparrow could say with enthusiasm that:

... the whole Church typifies heaven, but the chancel, parted and separated from the Nave or body of the Church, so as that it cannot be seen into by those that are there, typifies the invisible heaven, or things above the heaven, not to be seen by the eye of flesh. The Nave or body resembles the lowest visible heaven or Paradise....[528]

As a Church building could be understood in such terms, talk of ministering angels was quite natural. The Prayer Book itself contained some explicit references to angels: '... as thy holy Angels alway do thee service in heaven, so by thy appointment, they may succour and defend us on earth.' (Collect for St Michael and all Angels); 'to thee all angels cry aloud' (Te Deum); 'The angel of the Lord tarrieth round about them that fear him: and delivereth them' (Ps34v7 - Day6E); 'Praise him all ye angels....' (Ps148v2 - Day30E). The presence of angels was not seen as in any way fanciful and the conviction of their presence accorded with the understanding that the liturgy affirmed the proposed world of the kingdom of heaven. The recognition of the divine was part of sharing in that proposed world.

There was nothing innovative about the contemporaneous view of angels. In the previous century, Hooker had insisted upon their presence during liturgical celebration.[529] From the obscure to the great, there was an Anglican acknowledgement of the ministry of angels:

The Angels are in Churches and Oratories, and therefore Minister unto us in several ways: they carry our Prayers to the Throne of glory. ... they are there in the right of God, and are the exhibition of the Divine presence.[530]

Behold the Angels assembled in their Quires, and the blessed Saints ready with their Hymns; behold the Church prepares her Solemn Offices, and summons all her children to bring their praises; the King of Heaven himself invites us, and graciously calls us into his own presence.[531]

If it now be enquired, how or in what manner, God is more peculiarly present in Church Assemblies, than in any other places? ... I answer briefly, by the Presence of his Heavenly Attendants, the Holy Angels. (cf. Gen. 28. 16,17) Now that the Angels are present in the Assemblies for his worship we have sufficient evidence, both in the Old Testament and in the New. (cf. Ps 68.17; I Cor. 11.10)[532]

... we are in the House of God, in the Place of his Special Residence and Presence: And ... here the Hosts of Glorious Angels attend, when the Saints meet to Worship.[533]

No hint has been found of the implication of a distant God, removed

from the congregations. The emphasis is always on the presence of God
and the privilege of access:

> This I have made my present task, to convince souls of Gods
> special Presence, in the places, and assemblies of publick
> instituted Worship of God. This truth, if once admitted with
> rational satisfaction to the mind ..., by a sound and solid
> discovery of God in his Publick Ordinances....[534]

John Stillingfleete, a Lincolnshire Rector, taught that God was present
to worshippers by his angels, by his word, by his ministers and by his
Holy Spirit. There was the implication of the view of worship as a
mediated process leading to an unmediated access to the Divine. When
another cleric preached on this area he held that the presence of God:

> ... signifieth that Communication of himself face to face in
> Glory, whereby God for ever maketh Blessed the Holy Angels
> and Saints in Heaven; which is called by Divines, the Beatifical
> Vision; and by St Jude ... 'the Presence of his Glory'... v.24.[535]

It could become unclear whether people gained access to God by
encountering him locally, or whether their prayers were the gateway to
heaven:

> Say not in thine heart, who shall go up into heaven? Prayer shall
> bring thee thither. ... Prayer will breed those ravishing, and
> glorious joys, because it brings us into a communion with the
> fountain of joy and glory. It opens heaven to us, gives us
> approach into the unaccessable glory.[536]

This blend of an immediate presence and the prospect of eternal glory
meant that those engaged in this process of worship could combine both
strands of vision. Heaven could be perceived as a parallel world:

> If therefore in our Publick Assemblies we stand up to Bless and
> Magnifie the Lord, and repeat part of the Divine Raptures
> contained in Davids Psalms fitted for that purpose. I know not
> what Service can be more Caelestial, it is for us whilst we are
> here below to joyn in Consort with that heavenly Quire of
> Angels and Saints, that continually sound forth the high Praises
> of God.[537]

Public worship was considered to attest the greatness of God[538] and the parish church was regarded as:

> ... the place where His Honour dwelleth: where he does exhibit His special Presence and hath resolv'd to have His rest and residence for ever: and where we must also take up our Habitation; and preserve the Unity of the Spirit in the bond of Peace.[539]

These encouragements implied a blurring of any distinction between earth and heaven. Such teaching also carried implications about the way that the national and local hierarchy were legitimated by participation or acknowledgement in these devotions. In a time of increasingly centralised, and therefore more remote, authority, the acknowledgement of the presence of God precluded the possibility of a power vacuum. Consequently, there was a need to explain what was happening in worship and the nature of prayer.

The Presence of Heaven

One of the distinguishing features of Anglican worship, as has already been noted, was that every phrase that was offered had a scriptural basis. This meant that scripture provided the aural and intellectual context for the scripture read in the lessons, so the whole enterprise of liturgy became a deliberate exercise in the reading and interpretation of scripture. Allusion has been made to the idea that a function of the Anglican liturgy was to affirm the proposed world of the kingdom of heaven. Just as spectators to a play were required to suspend disbelief and accept the proposed world of the drama, worshippers were required to accept that the proposed world of the kingdom of God was more credible and more real than normal existence. The eternal that was proclaimed was more important than the temporal. The affirmed kingdom was permanent; the world was transient. The affirmation of the kingdom was effected by the reading of scripture and by the phrases of a liturgy which were themselves scripture.[540]

A pattern of worship that was scripture through and through engendered its own presuppositions. The regular pattern of address to God coupled with the assertion of his proximity, the affirmation of his kingship and of his kingdom ('... For thine is the kingdom and the power and the glory ...'), meant that the liturgy had an extra dimension. Those present, by their presence, were sharing in an act of affirmation. This suggests a possible resolution of the vexed question of non-participation by those present at services that has been noted above. Those many who, it seems, only gave their voice to metrical psalms, and maybe did not utter a single sound during the offering of the liturgy, may have been doing much more than being stubborn. There may well have been an offering as worship by participating in the affirmation of the Kingdom of God.

When such esteem was felt for the presence of God, the ordinary folk who roared out their metrical psalms may well have been making their own offering in their own way. They were rendering psalms, songs of praise addressed to God, which by virtue of being addressed to him implied his presence, let alone any direct text that acknowledged his presence.

> Fall down and worship ye the Lord
> within his temple bright:
> Let all the people of the world
> be fearfull at his sight.[541]

> To praise the Lord our God devise,
> all honour to him do:
> Before his footstool worship him,
> for he is holy too.[542]

It would be totally speculative to suggest that the conviction of the presence of God meant that there was no extensive pressure to celebrate the sacrament of the presence of Christ, as was noted in the first chapter of this study. One could begin to suspect that the overriding conviction of the divine presence contributed to the way that the Anglican minimum requirement for the annual number of celebrations of the Lord's Supper often became a maximum.

The worship of the Church did not function to locate God, but to affirm his Kingdom. Praise brought worshippers closer to heaven:

> ... Praise is Faiths and reasons Triumph, a bright, unmixt, immaculate Joy, and only wants some few degrees of being all we can conceive of Heaven.[543]

> ... Praise is our most Excellent Work; a Work common to the Church Triumphant and Militant, and which lifts us up into a Communion and Fellowship with Angels.[544]

When St Paul's Cathedral was re-opened, royal authority was used to prescribe a prayer for inclusion in the Communion Service on that occasion. The references in this prayer to the function of the divine presence and the human response summarise the thought of the period, expressed in a catena of phrases gathered from scripture:

> Thou, O Lord, dwellest not in houses made with hands, Heaven and the Heaven of Heavens cannot contain Thee. But tho' thy Throne is in Heaven, earth is thy footstool. Vouchsafe therefore, we beseech Thee, thy gracious Presence in this thy House, to hear our prayers and accept our sacrifices of praise and thanksgivings....[545]

The structure of the pattern of prayer in which God is regarded as the enabler and the goal of prayer and praise, reciprocated with the perception of his presence and the affirmation of his kingdom. Accordingly, it was not surprising that liturgy was seen as an agent of reformation and as an instrument of ethical transformation.[546] Liturgy transformed and renewed participants inwardly just as it transformed the poor from the squalor of their circumstances to being citizens of heaven. Prayer also had a potential to renew participants:

> Observe the admirable power and efficacy of devout Prayer; It is able to transport the soul, to ravish the spirit, to lift up the heart into an heavenly rapture, and to fill soul and body with unspeakable glory.[547]

Liturgy was regarded as a practice, a dynamic process and a directed enterprise, in which individuals took responsibility for the quality of their involvement. As one cleric wrote:

> As much Stress as ever some are pleas'd to lay upon it, I will not be so much enquir'd after in the great Day of Accounts, How we used to Express ourselves in our Prayers: As how our Hearts stood Affected to the Service.[548]

Common Prayer came to be envisioned as the means to a renewed society. Prayer was declared to be "an instrument of Holiness".[549] Having already explored the theology of the Offices, core questions of the definitions of prayer and worship remain.

Towards the Definition of Prayer

Anglicans wrote vigorously on prayer in the seventeenth century. And it was not the exclusive role of diligent minor clergy to be passionate about prayer - there was a degree of concern that reverberated throughout the structure of the Church of England. For example, the Dean of Lichfield wrote that, in prayer:

> ... you unbosom your self, and open your heart unto him, as a man would do unto his friend in whom he most confides. ... you cannot be truly said to pray, unless the Soul so far gets loose from the entanglements of the world and the body, as not only to look up to the place from whence it came, but to make some sort of approaches towards it, and to him that dwelleth there, and who is the author of its being, and the proper Object of its love. There must be an earnest endeavour to be united to God, to become one with him, to partake of his Divine nature, or at least to bear as much of his image and likeness, with respect to holiness and purity, as we can: In the Act of Praying (if we do it as we ought) we make an oblation of our souls and bodies to the Eternal Being, and declare our dependence upon his infinite Goodness, and an entire subjection to his Infinite Power.[550]

and a future Bishop of Derry declared:

> ... Worship itself is an Act, not of our Reason but our Affections: 'Tis the workings of an exalted Love; the out-goings of an inflam'd Desire; the breathings of a pious Soul, in the extasies of his Joy and Admiration. These are the noble Springs of our Devotion, the lively Elements that compose our Worship; and these are the Tendernesses of our Nature, that lie not in the Head, but in the Heart of Man; and there lie too deep to be reached, and too fine to be wrought upon by so gross a Faculty as Reason is.[551]

It could have been possible to accept a fairly straightforward explanation of the nature of prayer:

> Prayer, as to the sorts of it, is at least threefold; Publick, or Private, Stated, or Occasional (sic), Mental, or Oral, conceived only in the Mind, or delivered by Word of Mouth. - Prayer, as to the Parts of it, consists of Three too: Confession, Supplication,

and Thanksgiving. Prayer, as to the Nature of it, is a solemn Address of a pious Person to the Throne of Grace, with an humble Confession of his Defects and Deserts, with an earnest Entreaty for Pardon and Mercy, and a free Oblation of his best Thanks, for all Benefits and Favours however thence received.[552]

However, prayer was too complex to be accommodated so simply. During the Civil War and Interregnum, Bishop Duppa[553] had written on the definition of prayer during his enforced idleness. In a chapter headed 'Of Prayer what it is', Duppa brought together three classic explanations of prayer and tried to harmonise them. He drew on Gregory Nyssen's definition of prayer "to be the conversing or discoursing of the Soul with God"; John Damascene's description of "Prayer to be an ascending of the Soul to God"; and Augustine's recognition of prayer as: "figured by that mysterious Ladder, whose foot being on the Earth, the top of it reached unto Heaven, seen by Jacob in a Vision...." [554] The pastoral encouragement in Duppa's writing was sensitive:

> The devotion of the Heart (saith St Bernard) is the Tongue of the Soul, without this it is silent and shut up; but actuated and heated with Love, it pours itself forth in Supplications and Prayers, and Discourses with God; sometimes praising Him for the Infinite Blessings received from Him, sometimes praying to Him for those we yet want. This is that conversing of the Soul with God, which Gregory Nyssen speaks of, as a Son conversing with his Father, or a Friend with a Friend into whose bosom he may pour forth with confidence all the secrets of his Soul.... But though every devout Soul mounts not to this pitch, this top of the Ladder, let none be dismaied at it. For God knows whereof you are made, he sees the Body of flesh which you bear about you, and the Plummets which it hangs upon your Soul; and therefore when you cannot rise high enough to Him, He comes down to you, for so you find in this Vision, there were descending as well as ascending Angels.[555]

Prayer was declared to be open to all under God. Prayer was also regarded as a direct approach:

> It is an immediate, hearty calling upon the true God, through Christ, according to his will, for the obtaining of any blessing to,

or diverting any judgement from our selves, or others for whom there is hope God will be entreated.[556]

Worship as Polyphony

To thee all Angels cry aloud the heavens and all the powers therein.
To thee Cherubin and Seraphin continually do cry,
Holy, Holy, Holy Lord God of Sabaoth;
Heaven and earth are full of the Majesty of thy glory.
The glorious company of the Apostles praise thee.
The goodly fellowship of the Prophets praise thee.
The noble army of Martyrs praise thee.
The holy Church throughout all the world doth acknowledge thee....
    (Te Deum - Morning Prayer)

Part of the challenge of seeking a corporate metaphor for the range of material covered in this study is that account has to be taken of family and private devotion, and the question of how they inter-related with each other, as well as with public prayer. A picture which indicates the importance of holding these potentially disparate practices in some sort of creative inter-relationship is the analogy of polyphony.

In polyphony, there can be suggested to be an inter-weaving of the worship of heaven, the public worship of the Church and the practices of family prayer and private prayer. In this model, the whole picture is bound up with the celestial worship that is offered in the presence of God. Polyphony implies many voices and the many facets of each congregation, as well as the rich variety of the national church, can be seen to be each adding their distinctive contribution to the overall totality of prayer. The suggestion of polyphony as an explanatory model reflects the lines:

> ... multiformity with mutual charity advanceth God's glory, as much as uniformity itself in matters merely indifferent; which as the pipes of an organ may be of several lengths and bigness, yet all tuned into good harmony.[557]

> In fine then, Let all the Angels cry aloud, the Heavens and all the Powers therein: Let all the Intellectual Orders above us praise God in their exalted way, and let the same String that is struck in Heaven, resound on Earth. Let us unite our Hearts and Voices, and answer Amen to their Alleluias.[558]

> If ... in our Publick Assemblies we stand up to Bless and
> Magnifie the Lord, and repeat part of the Divine Raptures
> contained in Davids Psalms fitted for that purpose. I know not
> what Service can be more Caelestial, it is for us whilst we are
> here below to joyn in Consort with that heavenly Quire of
> Angels and Saints, that continually sound forth the high Praises
> of God.[559]

There is a need for a model which can sustain the tensions between
potentially divergent habits of prayer. A vision of an integral unity has
to be available to protect the church against the possibility of splintering
into people's individual preferences. The metaphor of polyphony would
appear to meet these requirements. Polyphony allows for differences
between the voices: polyphony is probably a far better representation
than unison when considering the variety of people and places involved
in worship. With the church's quest for a uniformity that could lead to
unanimity, it may be thought that unison would be a more relevant
image than polyphony. However, this study has emphasised the
variegations within the Church of England, to which polyphony can
offer a shared rationale, whereas unison could only suppress variation.
The metaphor of polyphony confers a quality of significance and value
on each line of music. The importance of the individual line was
stressed in referring above to the analysis of prayer book services in
terms of the way that a voice offers sounds that are linear or sequential
and mono-dimensional, and yet yields the effect of a landscape with its
own contours and colours. The polyphony of many voices implies a
vision of the grandeur of the possibilities of prayer and praise that may
carry some echoes of the ultimate and eternal praise to which these
writers aspired.

The Anglican Sense of the Localised Presence of God

It is difficult to find an appropriate label that would represent the arena
of prayer from the vocabulary of this era. It would be possible to talk
about the 'interface' between God and man, or their 'adjacency', except
that such terms would imply that God and man shared a common
boundary, whereas the language of the time implied that prayer was a
space within which worship could take place - a space apart where
human beings could come before the divine presence. 'Audience
chamber' would have been a possible candidate, except that this phrase
would have avoided the realisation that the Anglican approach to prayer
celebrated the universal access to the omnipresence of God.

Accordingly, it is convenient to utilise the word 'interspace' to speak of this realm of awareness. Technically, 'interspace' means 'an interval, a time or space between, a dividing tract in space or time'. To speak of the 'interspace' between God and man would be a recognition of their proximity and their mutuality. Interspace implies shared ground, not a no-man's land. Whilst 'interspace' is an inelegant term, it was in use in the seventeenth century (OED). Its use has not been noted in this context but it does, at this stage, summarise this dimension of the experience of prayer as found by Anglican writers.

It was not desirable on pastoral grounds to leave the interspace as unmapped territory for congregations and individuals to explore. The 'interspace' was given a structure. Set prayers enabled people to be at home in the interspace. Set prayers also gave a structure of understanding that enabled lives of worship to be built. As a Bishop of Bath and Wells emphasised:

> By Prayers are meant the publick and solemn Prayers of the Apostles and Governours of the Church. Jesus had taught them to pray, and given them a Prayer of his own. And the Apostles had now received the Holy Spirit, and prayed with the Faithful: These Assemblies the first Christians departed not from. The Prayers of the Church are by no means to be neglected. ... And where these Prayers are agreeable to God's will, we can never neglect them without just imputation of Prophaneness.[560]

> ... all Christians are obliged frequently to meet together for the performance of God's Publick Worship. By Worship I mean, that immediate Worship which is offer'd up to God in his Sanctuary....[561]

It could be said that the Anglican structures of the interspace were well guarded:

> ... you may find and know ... necessary truths, by the publick doctrine of our own Church, delivered in her Liturgy and Articles of Religion.... Acquaint your selves throughly with that publick doctrine and adhere to that, and if your own Teacher teach otherwise, believe him not.[562]

Anglicans followed a shared pattern of worship. The definitions of prayer described the sense of participation in the interspace. Duppa was not troubled about the lack of harmony among the variety of definition that he found for prayer:

> The several Properties and Excellencies of Prayer, have afforded matter enough to the Ancient Fathers to mold as many several and different Descriptions of it; which like many Stars cast into a Constellation, may give altogether a full and perfect Representation of it.[563]

So, whilst there was no one 'right' explanation of prayer, there was a variety of awareness, which was held together by the Book of Common Prayer. That so much was expected to take place in prayer required the development of people's awareness of the interspace, so that there was a sense in which there was room enough for all this to take place. Such efforts required encouragement: which usually meant that people were reminded of their duty to pray:

> There is not any one act of Religion ... which is more strictly required by the Laws of God; or better recommended to us by the practice of God's Saints, especially by the most holy Example of our blessed Saviour himself, than that of Prayer.[564]

> Prayer is the primary Duty of Christians.[565]

Pelling [566] linked the duty of prayer to the sovereignty of God. Another writer described prayer as: "Devout Homage." [567] Equally, it was declared that:

> ... to pray to God is an Act of Homage, which we owe him, as he is our Maker and Father....[568]

This sense of the divine majesty gave depth to the Anglican perception of the interspace and thought was given to the appropriate way to explain the human cognition of the Divine. The duty to pray and to participate in the interspace was universal; in Anglicanism there was the sense of an overriding duty to pray, privately and together. Avis has noted the degree of interpenetration of different groups within the Church at this time.[569] By conceding that they had an overriding duty to pray, people felt that they had to learn to worship together on earth so that they could hope to live in heaven.

The Efficacy of Prayer

Part of the test of the Anglican self-understanding was the direct question as to whether prayer could be said to work. If claims were to be made for the life of the national church as its congregations gathered for worship, then there had to be the question as to whether the hearty and sincere efforts of so many people actually had any practical effect. This concern was a subject of prayer: '... grant that those things which we ask faithfully we may obtain effectually....' (Collect Trinity 23).

This pattern of advice could be typified as broadly consisting of the structure that if petitioners sincerely wanted something, then they could ask and confidently expect to receive whatever was in the will of God. A royal Chaplain offered instruction along these lines in a sermon entitled 'Of the Efficacy of Prayer' based on Matthew 7 v. 7 ('Ask and it shall be given you...') in which he made three propositions:

> I. That God's gifts and blessings, all good things, but especially the graces of his holy Spirit, ... are very well worth the Pains of asking, seeking and using our utmost Indeavours and importunities about them.
> II. That those Gifts and Graces are not likely to be obtained without such Indeavours.
> III. That most certainly we may obtain them, if with a true Piety and earnest Care we do seek and endeavour after them.[570]

The confidence that was held in the prayers that were offered by the Church was not bolstered by an appeal to evidence of answers to prayer, but by an assurance as to the nature and purposes of God and as to the reality of his involvement in human life. Accordingly, any signs of prayers not having been answered had to be understood in other ways. For example, a distinction was drawn between prayers that that were offered with fervency, that were acceptable to God, and those that were offered from a 'cold' heart. The purposes of God required that prayer be offered. Clergy were specially reminded that:

> We may observe that St Paul is frequent in Prayer, that he may be assisted in his Ministerial Employment, and he is often requesting others to pray for him, that his labours in the Gospel may prove really Advantageous and Successful. This is that which We also are concerned in, if we expect any Blessing on our Enterprizes. We must remind those who are the peculiar

Charge of our Ministry to solicite Heaven in our behalf.... If thus with the devout Supplications of others we joyn our own fervent Petitions, we shall certainly Prosper, we shall derive the Grace and Blessing of Heaven upon us in the Performances and Offices belonging to our Calling.[571]

The exhortation to fervour in prayer was a general theme in Anglican proclamation.[572] It has already been noted that writing a book entitled *Frequent and Fervent Prayer* (1687) was part of the progress of Thomas Comber to the Deanery at Durham. This was a theme that was pursued in sermons to a wide variety of audiences:

In the Public Worship of God see that you be very Reverent and Fervent: As the Apostle exhorts, Rom 12.11 Fervent in Spirit, serving the Lord. You must know the Work is great you are about; the Divine Majesty you address inconceivably Pure, Holy, and Glorious: Be afraid then of being irreverent and sottish in his presence.[573]

The Fire of Prayer must never go out, if we expect that such Mettal as a Hard Heart consists of, should ever be melted by it.[574]

... to pray always, and not to faint, imports Continuance and Perseverance in our Prayers. That we do not pray by Fits and Starts, and then intermit our Devotion; but constantly keep up the Fervour of our Minds towards God....[575]
... we should be always in a praying Temper, in such a Disposition of mind, that we always carry about us, and have within us the necessary Requisites of hearty Prayer....[576]

... careless and frigid Prayers, which make no alteration in our selves, have no effect with God. To whom we must addres our selves with such fervent and earnest Desires, as turn our Hearts towards him....[577]

It would not be inappropriate to classify some Anglican exhortation in this area of concern as being passionate. There was more here than a desire to adulate ecclesiastical structures. When Thomas Bradley preached at the Archbishop's Visitation to the Dean and Chapter at York in 1662, he spoke forcefully:

... Zeale is the wings of the soule that lifts it up, and carries it on swiftly in holy performances, the oyle of the wheeles of our obedience that makes them run chearfully; it will put us upon all our Duties with earnestnesse, fervency, devotion, affection, and that which we doe for God, or to God, it will make us doe it heartily and throughly; of all others we had need to be fervent in spirit, serving the Lord, from whose Zeal, all our People are to take Fire....[578]

Inevitably, the encouragement to fervour was balanced by the uncertainty associated with the issue of 'why God delays the giving what we ask?' [579] When this question was addressed by George Stanhope, the Vicar of Lewisham in Kent, the answers were of a piece with the overall pattern of Anglican understanding:

... these Delays enhance and add to the Blessing, when we do at last receive it. ... he may by this means improve our Virtue, and illustrate it to the World, and so both make and shew us in some good Degree fit, and worthy to receive the Blessings we pray for.[580]

Stanhope was not the only writer on this theme:

Despair not ... of an answer to your Prayers, though you have long sought God alone, and no answer hath come; though you cannot prevail your self, yet be not hopeless until you have tried others: You see 'tis not unusual with God to defer his answers, and to seem to take no notice of our own Prayers till we crave the Prayers of others....[581]

Stanhope's immovable conviction was that:

... it is impossible for Men to Pray in vain, provided they do but Pray as they ought....[582]

This last point was a long-standing tenet of Anglican teaching:

The faithfull have this comfort (saith a learned man [Hooker Eccles. polit lib. 5]) that whatsoever they rightly ask the same (no doubt) but they shall receive, so farre as may stand with the glory of God, and with their everlasting good, unto either of which two it is no vertuous mans purpose to seek or desire to obtain any thing prejudicial.[583]

The confidence in the efficacy of Anglican prayer was founded in a theology of the ultimate beneficence of God, rather than any mechanical vision of devotion:

> ... what is prayer else but the acknowledging of God the Author of all good things we hope to receive, as praise is for those good things we have already received.... Prayer at one end for blessings expected, and Praise at the other for blessings enjoyed.[584]

> ... No Prayer can be lost which is put up in Faith and Charity: If our Prayers do no good to those particular men for whom we pray, if they be not fit or worthy to receive the Mercies we pray for, yet our prayers, our peace, our blessing, shall return into our own bosoms, 10 Matt.13.
> ... praying for other men intitles us to their Prayers for us; and though we are not particularly names in their Prayers, God knows to whom they belong, and will apply them himself.[585]

However, there was another dimension to these matters in that significance became attached to parochial ministers by virtue of the processes within which they officiated. The role of ministers was not neutral:

> The readiest way to have our Prayers speed, is to mingle them with those of Christian community. Commune requests are strong by Union, and prevail with Heaven, and while the single Votes of Saints in secret are deny'd, the joint Petitions of devout Assemblies prove effectual, and return laden with most happy answers. One singular advantage they have to this purpose, is, that the Minister presents them unto God, whom He has authoriz'd to speak to His Majesty, and ordained to supplicate or intercede for the people. And he many times shall be accepted for them, when they shall not be accepted for themselves. Yea, by virtue of his Function, he shall be heard for them, when he shall not be heard for his own person.[586]

The spectrum of view of the Anglican process of worship, from proceedings receiving validation by the zeal of the officiants through to the subject of intercession being granted when it becomes a communal matter, through to the prayer being dependent upon the status of the officiants, indicates a breadth of perspective that cannot be neatly packaged but which may be held within a structure of polyphony.

Review

The overall theological strategy of the Anglican understanding of prayer had its counterpart in the perception of church buildings and in the life of congregations as they gathered throughout the land, as well as around domestic hearths and as individuals knelt in privacy. It has been stressed that theology in this era was regarded as a practical discipline. However, it may not be inappropriate to surmise that there was, in modern terms, a mystical side to Anglican experience. These apprehensions were not just expressed in terms of the conviction of the presence of angels, but also in the shared assurance that prayer and worship brought people before the throne of God. A point of access to this experience could be located in the Venite:

Let us come before his presence with thanksgiving
and shew ourselves glad in him with psalms.

O come, let us worship, and fall down
and kneel before the Lord our Maker.
For he is the Lord our God and we are the people of his pasture, and
the sheep of his hand.
(Venite - Morning Prayer)

However, the threshold of the entry into the interspace, the limen, remains elusive if the quest is for a formula that made no demands of those who aspired to gain access to the throne of grace. Just as ministers in their role were not neutral, neither was the posited interspace which may be viewed as having been an arena in which divine sovereignty and patterns of discipleship explored each other. If the notion of the interspace as common territory between God and the people in their awareness of the divine is a plausible conceptual construct, then it could be suggested that this 'space' was, in part, inhabited by the aural community. Further, it may be useful, for the sake of building an understanding of the practice of prayer in this era, to consider that it was from this 'space' that the polyphony of earthly prayer and praise arose, from individuals, from households, from congregations in their common assurance that their devotions were offered in the presence of God. In this 'space' the prayers of earth mingled with the praises of heaven. Whilst these perceptions may have been unspoken, it may be hypothesised that the putative significance of this 'space' was such that it generated its own patterns of authority and its own political implications. Thus the Crown had to strive to harness these dimensions of life, knowing what had happened when a de-regulation of these structures in favour of local preferences and processes had undermined the fabric of the State.

12

CONCLUDING REVIEW

Hundreds of original printed sources have been examined in the course of this exploration. The broad classifications that have been utilised in gathering data into chapters have reflected the primary concerns and patterns of usage that have been detected. The size of the range of primary material means that any further material that may be identified can be expected to conform to this pattern.

This study has sought to delineate the structure of the devotional life that was focused in and through the Church of England. This structure was deliberately inclusive, although people could and did opt for the alternatives of recusancy, nonconformity and non-attendance. The forgotten character of the theological integrity of Anglican worship in these years has been explored, as well as its broad-based appeal.

Objection could be raised that, because so many documents have been represented in this study, the self-understanding of Anglicanism in those days has been left behind. It could be asserted that this study has constructed a fictional synthesis of Anglican writing and that no one person in those years would have read the output that has been surveyed in these pages. Indeed, this extended exploration of seventeenth century Anglican material may have produced a harmonisation of views that is quite illusory.

However, if prayer was offered by the faithful, then the faithful were to some extent labelled by the prayer that they offered. This was especially true when the people clustered in their parish churches to offer the liturgy of the Church. The offering of its set services was the Anglican Church's act of self-definition. In an era of practical theology this mattered far more than any theoretical attempts to define the Church. Consequently, this study has not pursued a unitive theology but has sought to capture a spectrum of opinion and practice - a spectrum that illuminated a quest for consensus. A unitive approach, for example, could have treated the practice of prayer as an exercise in channelling allegiance and suggested that the throne of the earthly kingdom of England participated in the role of the throne of heaven. Whilst this would have had the attraction of putting a political gloss on personal sincerity as people voluntarily offered their devotions in their cottages and their closets, this would overlook the strict theological divide between a king on earth and the King in eternity.

This investigation has been an estimate of an area of Anglican practice and popular association in a particular period. If it is possible to talk about an Anglican identity, rather than about the histories of individual dioceses, parishes and particular persons, then there has to be both summary and summation. The reality of local life and variety may imply that there were as many 'Anglicanisms' in the seventeenth century as there were parishes and as many different patterns of prayer as there were people who offered devotion. So the question has to be raised as to whether it can be claimed that this study can purport to represent satisfactorily the range of the belief and practice in Anglicanism during this period within such a variety of historical and local contexts. However, it has been found that such concerns are met by the coinherence within Anglicanism that has been evinced.

The word 'Anglican' in this study has been shown to refer to a nexus of processes and many layers of association. The differentiations within Anglicanism arose from its hierarchy and its geographical spread. Parish boundaries were probably more significant than retrospective theological labels and the distinctive ethos of any parish church was probably more dependent upon its customs than upon any particular theological nuance associated with successive clergy in local pastoral charge. Whilst people prayed as equals, in the process they subscribed to, and reaffirmed their place within, a socially differentiated nation.

The complexity of national life in the period 1641-1700 challenged the Anglican Church to reflect upon its practice and to develop its self-understanding. It has also been possible to look into the conceptual substrata of prayer and worship. Prayer and worship carried their own sense of place and this was recognised in the appreciation of the parish church. As a result of the need to limit this study, attention has been given neither to the rubrics of Anglican ritual, nor to the devotions associated with the Holy Communion. An unexpected implication emerged to support this latter decision; entrance to the Divine presence was found to be associated with the offering of standard texts rather than with the consecration of sacramental elements.

This study has focussed on a generality of practice and behaviour as reflected in printed documents. The variety of local practice and preference was underpinned by common texts as the basis for common prayer and shared experience. Although the result may be viewed as reflecting a theologically undifferentiated Anglicanism, it has been possible to gain some insight into the common factors across the Church of England.

Reflection

Whilst Common Prayer may have been originally, to some extent, an implement born of political necessity, it nevertheless eventually received a theological rationale. If the Book of Common Prayer had been an instrument of statecraft under the Tudors and James I, and then an instrument of ideological tyranny under Laud, after 1645 the Prayer Book became a symbol of royal allegiance and of yearning for political stability. The Prayer Book had been deposed and its theological justification then became a political necessity.

The theological vindication of Anglican practice was undertaken in direct dialogue with the text of the Bible and the early Fathers. A pattern called 'transgenerational consensus' [587] may be suggested to have been sought in these years to establish the authority of Anglican liturgy, using a literary bridge between the seventeenth and the early centuries. Furthermore, one can feel that Kermode's suggestion of a midrashic process, appropriating an ancient book to contemporary usage is a useful contribution to understanding. Midrash has been explained as a creative process of combining and recombining verses from the Bible so as to allow perceived implicit meanings to become explicit, as well as allowing new meaning to unfold.[588] The assurance that developed of the legitimacy of the Book of Common Prayer, due to its biblical and patristic phraseology, gave it the status of an authorised midrash.[589] Prayer book piety was given distinctive shape by an intermingling of precept and prayer, of praise and lection, of familiar response and direct address to the divine. Voices orchestrated by the Prayer Book were heard in aural communities in which God heard and in which God himself was heard.

The Anglican experience of prayer that has been outlined in this investigation has been shown to be an interplay between the conviction of the sovereignty of God, the certainty that he heard prayer and the assurance of his presence and his present voice. The fact that these convictions were exteriorised, articulated and shared, was not the simple product of an agreed set of conventions. People regarded the activity of worship as being a joint action that was jointly understood and as being part of a national programme of worship and cohesion. Just as it is difficult to pinpoint the limen of the entry into the Divine presence, so it is also awkward to locate the offering of worship, whether oral or aural, whether participatory or non-participatory. This study has suggested that worship was taking place in the mutuality of the spoken and the heard. The dimensions of the aural community, therefore, have to be extended to recognise that God was also a participant in this community - that he was hearing prayer and praise and that his voice was heard in the enunciation of his word in scripture. The elusive limen to the posited congregational experience consequently shifts from being an identifiable sequence of words within the process of worship to an act of faith. The shared convictions of congregational life rested upon the use of the phrases of scripture in communal address to God. The faith that was implied was that all that was offered was within the will of God and that he would honour such obedience with his blessing.

The Fruits of Anglican Worship - A Flawed Harvest

The earnest and repeated exhortations to prayer reflected the importance that was attached to prayer and worship in the era under consideration. The public prayers of the church broadly followed a prescribed pattern, though there was variation in the details of services throughout the land. However, it has already been noted that this uniformity was hoped to bear the fruit of unanimity. By the close of the century, this dream had already been surrendered with the advent of legitimised toleration, but a greater discord was apparent in the life of the church even before the Toleration Act of 1689.

The accession of William and Mary produced a new factor which precluded unanimity. The Non-Jurors did not accept William and Mary and they labelled set prayers in the liturgy for the new King and Queen as 'immoral prayers'. It has also been noted that Archbishop Sancroft declared that those who attended services where the new prayers were being used would be in need of absolution at the end of the service as well as at the beginning.[590] Plainly, once uniformity was rejected, there could no longer be unanimity. The majority of those who rejected this uniformity were simply of scrupulous conscience, but they were led by Anglican clergy. Once there was a rejection of uniformity, there could be neither unity nor unanimity.

A further ground of anxiety was that ambitions for a renewed society were not bearing fruit. There had been such a groundswell of optimism attached to the Restoration, but this faded. One tract had recited the ideal that:

The publique prayers require Unanimity, so we read of the first Christians They were altogether with one accord in one place. The multitude of them that believed were of one heart and one soul.... St Cyprian commenting on those words of our Blessed Saviour 'I say unto you that if two of you shall agree on earth, touching any thing that ye shall ask....' Notes judiciously from thence, that very much is ascribed not to the multitude but to the unanimity of those that pray. [Cypr. *de unitate 10.11*] [591],

whilst an Essex clergyman recorded his despair at the difficulties of building communal harmony, let alone unanimity towards God:

To think to get Peace with God by our Supplications, when we have unpeaceable Hearts towards others; to have Forgiveness from God, while we forgive not our Brethren; to have God's Love, while we love not one another; is a vain Delusion. To pray together at Church, and quarrel at home; to sit in one Seat here, and to fight one with another abroad; to say Amen to the Prayer for Peace, and yet to study Strife; is monstrous Hypocrisie. To praise God in singing Psalms here, and yet to curse and revile one another abroad, is horrible Impiety. [592]

Crucially, the Anglican programme, with its ambitions for mass education in spirituality, cannot be claimed to have eroded popular ignorance. Part of the educational drive of the Anglican Church had been the tendency to rely on printed materials, or 'Helps' as some clergy termed them. Whilst print made knowledge and understanding accessible, print also made that knowledge easy to avoid. [593] It also has to be recognised that, for many people, life was short and the population was growing, so the Church was overwhelmed by the educational needs with which it was confronted. As the population grew, so the possibility of success in any national programme that placed major reliance upon the parish system receded. Sunday services had been expected to tutor the nation in prayer, but the proportion of the population that attended services is as undiscoverable as the answer to the question as to what fraction of the population could be physically accommodated in the nation's churches.

The Integrity of Anglicanism
The conviction of the seventeenth century writings that have been used in this study affirmed that, in worship, one could encounter a reality

beyond one's ordinary experience in life. The usages of Anglican worship, both in their response to the requirements of the Prayer Book and in the popular instinct for metrical psalmody, set out a structure in the realm of spiritual experience that offered a sense of location in the interspace of prayer. This sense of structure was sustained in being by regular participation in the liturgy.

The text of the liturgy was held in aural communities in which people entered the divine presence. The theology of the worship of the Church of England was a process of response to God's revelation that was observed nationally on a localised basis. This suggestion is not a euphemism that avoids saying that the Church of England was everywhere and nowhere. The Church as national institution was both centralised and diffused; but in each situated congregation a theology of the whole was articulated. This conspectus raises theological questions as to the relationship between the individual congregations and the whole and what models may be appropriate to affirm the reality of a 'whole', when the only evidence of a 'whole' is of usage amongst varied and dispersed congregations. Clearly, this is a question for Anglican ecclesiology and a separate enquiry. However, it is important that this question is raised in this context because the commitment of congregations and individuals to their worship gave popular approbation to a system that was imposed centrally. There has to have been a difference between, on the one hand, the voluntary offering of prayer to the divine and, on the other hand, the requirements of the national focus of allegiance in the sovereign and the disciplinary focus in the Bishop and his staff. This dichotomy was part of the reason why prayers offered privately and in family households merited such emphasis in the teaching of the Church, because these devotions arose out of individual fiat rather than a centrally driven compulsion. The separate loci of congregational, family and private prayer had different parts in the polyphony of the offering of the human to the divine.

The suggested model of polyphony preserves the vision of the multi-voiced nature of the worship offered to Almighty God against any over-simplification. The tensions implied in polyphony were as real as the layers of accord. For example, it has been noted that it was taught that all people enjoyed an equality before God, yet the set forms of prayer reinforced patterns of social differentiation. There were tensions between the way that the observance of set forms of prayer affirmed the nation and sovereign and subverted the significance of the individual, but there were also tensions in the way that the local congregational appropriation of the set forms subverted the ideal of national uniformity.

Prayer implied belief. The liturgy implied the recognition of the divine presence. Common prayer implied a shared apprehension of the divine. The discovery of glory is reflected in this antique literature and it was acknowledged that it was possible for people to cross into an experience of God in prayer that might now be labelled as 'mystical'. It is a matter of some ambiguity as to whether common prayer harnessed individual devotion to a national enterprise or whether common prayer enriched and facilitated personal sincerity. However, these differing strands subsisted in the rendering of the polyphony of the life of the Church of England and the life of heaven. Even when the ambition that uniformity of prayer would lead to unanimity of heart and mind had been shattered by toleration and the Non-Jurors, still the multi-voiced polyphony of prayer and praise remains a viable explanatory and descriptive metaphor.

To conclude this study in a way that demonstrates empathy with Anglican theology of the period 1641-1700, the final notes have to be of praise. It is fitting to take leave of this research with a majestic paragraph on the polyphony of praise written by a revered Anglican bishop to conclude his long work on prayer:

The Saints in Heaven have no other prayer but thanksgiving; they cry, Amen, Blessing & Glory, and Wisdome, & Honour, & Power, be to God, Rev. vii 12. All their song is Amen, Halleluiah, Rev. xix 4. Therefore, if we will come where they are, we must sound out the praises of God, as they do; If we will be like the heavenly Angels, we must speak with the tongue of Angels; If we say Amen to his praise and honour, he will ratifie his word towards us, so that his promise to us shall be Yea, and Amen.[594]

NOTES,
BIBLIOGRAPHIES
and
INDEX

[1] I Green *Print and Protestantism in Early Modern England* (2000) p.565

[2] J Spurr 'Anglican Apologetic and the Restoration Church' (Oxford University Ph.D. thesis, 1985) pp.210-242

[3] A Hunt 'The Lord's Supper in Early Modern England' *Past and Present* Issue 161 1998 pp.39-83

[4] DA Spaeth 'Parsons and Parishioners: Lay-Clerical Conflict and Popular Piety in Wiltshire Villages, 1660-1740' (Brown University Ph.D. thesis, 1985) pp.48-72 offers some analysis of popular failure to participate in the Holy Communion

[5] Cf. C Haigh 'Communion and Community: Exclusion from Communion in Post-Reformation England' *Journal of Ecclesiastical History* Vol. 51 No 4 Oct. 2000, pp.721-740

[6] J Gardiner *Advice to the Clergy of the Diocese of Lincoln* 2nd ed.. (1697) pp.12-13 (James Gardiner (1635-1705) 1661 Prebendary at Lincoln; 1669 DD; 1671 Sub-dean at Lincoln; 1695 Bishop of Lincoln)

[7] Ed. G Ornsby *The Remains of Denis Granville DD, Dean and Archdeacon of Durham, &c.* Durham, Surtees Society, Volume 47, 1865, p.59 - Letter of 9th December 1680

[8] The *Oxford English Dictionary* cites two sources from 1661

[9] I Green *The Christian's ABC: Catechisms and Catechizing in England c.1530-1740* (1996) pp. 30, 479-485

[10] J Maltby ' "By this Book": Parishioners, the Prayer Book and the Established Church' in ed. K Fincham *The Early Stuart Church 1603-1642* (1993) p.115

[11] DH Davies *Worship and Theology in England 1690-1850* (1961) p52

[12] FR Arnott 'Anglicanism in the Seventeenth Century' in ed. PE More & FL Cross *Anglicanism* (1935) p. lxvi f

[13] L Potter *Secret Rites and Secret Writing - Royalist Literature 1641-1660* (1989) p.138-9

[14] N Temperley *The Music of the English Parish Church* (1983) p86

[15] J Morrill *Reactions to the English Civil War 1642-1649* (1982) p.20

[16] Cf. M Thornton *English Spirituality* (1963) pp.230-256, 261-270

[17] RD Townsend 'The Caroline Divines' in ed. GS Wakefield *A Dictionary of Christian Spirituality* (1983) p.73f

[18] P Christianson 'Reformers and the Church of England under Elizabeth I and the Early Stuarts' *Journal of Ecclesiastical History* Vol. 31 (1980) p.465

[19] J Geree *The Character of an Old English Puritan* (1646) cited in BR White 'The Twilight Years of Puritanism in the years before and after 1688' in eds. OP Grell and JI Israel and N Tyacke *From Persecution to Toleration* (1991) p.308; and also in MR Watts *The Dissenters: From the Reformation to the French Revolution* (1992) p.15

[20] RW Williams 'The Puritan Concept and Practice of Prayer' (London University Ph.D. thesis, 1983)

[21] E.g. ed. G Rowell *The English Religious Tradition and the Genius of Anglicanism* (1993); the sequence of chapters jumps from Lancelot Andrewes to John & Charles Wesley

[22] WH Hutton 'Divines of the Church of England 1660-1700' in eds. AW Ward & AR Waller *The Cambridge History of English Literature* Vol.8 (1912) p.308

[23] AW Brink 'A Study of the Literature of Inward Experience, 1600-1700' (London University Ph.D. thesis, 1963) p.404

[24] WG Simon *The Restoration Episcopate* (1965) pp.31, 32

[25] RB Knox 'Bishops in the Pulpit in the Seventeenth Century: Continuity amid Change' in ed. RB Knox *Reformation Conformity and Dissent* (1977) pp.93, 94

[26] FL Kelly *Prayer in Sixteenth Century England* (1966)

[27] HC White *English Devotional Literature (Prose) 1600-1640* (1931)

[28] CJ Somerville *Popular Religion in Restoration England* (1977) p.9

[29] DH Davies *Worship and Theology in England from Andrewes to Baxter, 1603-1690* (1975)

[30] R Hutton *The Restoration: A Political and Religious History of England and Wales 1658-1667* (1985) p.177, 178

[31] A Argent 'Aspects of the Ecclesiastical History of the Parishes of the City of London 1640-49 (with special reference to the Parish Clergy)' (London University Ph.D. thesis, 1983); DM Barratt 'The Condition of the Parish Clergy between the Reformation and 1660, with special reference to the Dioceses of Oxford, Worcester, and Gloucester' (Oxford University Ph.D. thesis, 1949); F Bussby 'A History and Source Book on Training for the Ministry in the Church of England 1511-1717' (Durham M.Litt. thesis, 1952); GI Ignjatijevic 'The Parish Clergy in the Diocese of Canterbury and Archdeaconry of Bedford in the Reign of Charles I and under the Commonwealth' (Sheffield University Ph.D. thesis, 1986); JH Pruett *The Parish Clergy under the Later Stuarts: The Leicestershire Experience* (1978)

[32] Cf. B Reay *Popular Culture in Seventeenth Century England* (1985) p.5

[33] Cf. E Duffy 'The Godly and the Multitude in Stuart England' *Seventeenth Century* Vol. I, 1986, p.34

[34] E.g.: C W Dugmore *Eucharistic Doctrine in England from Hooker to Waterland* (1942); K Stevenson *Covenant of Grace Renewed: A Vision of the Eucharist in the Seventeenth Century* (1994); D Cressy *Birth Marriage & Death - Ritual, Religion and the Life-Cycle in Tudor and Stuart England* (1997); R Houlbrooke *Death, Religion, and the Family in England, 1480-1750* (1998); B D Spinks *Sacraments, Ceremonies and the Stuart Divines* (2002)

[35] Cf. A Johns *The Nature of the Book: Print and Knowledge in the Making* (1998) pp.230-248

[36] GV Bennett 'Conflict in the Church' in ed. G Holmes *Britain after the Glorious Revolution 1689-1714* (1969) p.163

[37] D Wing *Short Title Catalogue ... 1641-1700* (1972, etc.)

[38] S Letsome *The Preacher's Assistant, ... A Series of the Texts of all the Sermons and Discourses Preached upon, and published Since the Restoration, to the Present Time* (1753)

[39] MSG McLeod, KI James, and DJ Shaw *The Cathedral Libraries Catalogue. Books printed before 1701 in the libraries of the Anglican cathedrals of England and Wales. Vol. 1 Books printed in the British Isles and British America and English books printed elsewhere* (London, British Library, 1984)

[40] 17 Car. I cap.11

[41] Ed. SR Gardiner *The Constitutional Documents of the Puritan Revolution 1625-1660* (1899) pp.197-199

[42] Ed. SR Gardiner *The Constitutional Documents of the Puritan Revolution 1625-1660* (1899) p.232

[43] J Maltby 'Approaches to the Study of Religious Conformity in late Elizabethan

and early Stuart England: with special reference to Cheshire and the Diocese of Lincoln' (Cambridge University Ph.D. thesis, 1991) pp.99ff

[44] Cf. J Morrill 'The attack on the Church of England in the Long Parliament, 1640-1642' in ed. D Beales and G Best *History, Society and the Churches* (1985) pp.105-124

[45] SR Gardiner *The Constitutional Documents of the Puritan Revolution 1625-1660* (1899) pp. 247-248

[46] E.g. I Green *The Re-Establishment of the Church of England 1660-1663* (1978) p.5; JRH Moorman *A History of the Church in England* (1967) p.258; CJ Stranks *Anglican Devotion* (1961) p.149

[47] Ordinance of 23rd August 1645: 'for the more effectuall putting in execution the Directory for Publique Worship....' p.2

[48] *Two Letters of Great Concernment* (1645) p.8

[49] *Proclamation concerning the Book of Common-Prayer and the Directory for Publike Worship* p.2

[50] Ibid. p.2

[51] Ibid. p.2

[52] E Husband *A Collection of all the publicke orders, ordinances and declarations of both Houses of Parliament....* 1646 pp.715, 755

[53] LS York 'In Dens and Caves: The Survival of Anglicanism during the Rule of the Saints 1640-1660' (Auburn University, Alabama, Ph.D. thesis, 1999) p.118

[54] Cf. S Roberts 'Local Government Reform in England and Wales during the Interregnum' in ed. I Roots *Into Another Mould: Aspects of the Interregnum* (1981) p.26

[55] AM Coleby *Central Government and the Localities: Hampshire 1649-1689* (1987) p.63

[56] Cf. E Trotter *Seventeenth Century Life in the Country Parish with special reference to Local Government* (1968) Preface p.vii

[57] Cf. ed. J Brewer and J Styles *'An Ungovernable People': The English and their Law in the Seventeenth and Eighteenth Centuries* (1983) passim.

[58] *The Kingdomes Weekly Intelligencer* No.231 19th-26th October 1647 p.704

[59] 'Act repealing several clauses in Statutes imposing penalties for not coming to Church' in ed. SR Gardiner *The Constitutional Documents of the Puritan Revolution 1625-1660* (1899) pp. 391-394

[60] J Morrill 'The Church in England 1642-9' in ed. J Morrill *Reactions to the English Civil War 1642 - 1649* (1982) pp.107-8

[61] J Morrill 'The Church in England 1642-9' in ed. J Morrill *Reactions to the English Civil War 1642 - 1649* (1982) p.108

[62] The Directory 1645 edition, p.21

[63] Cf. RS Bosher *The Making of the Restoration Settlement* (1957) p16-18

[64] GB Tatham *Puritans in Power* (1913) pp.226, 227

[65] *Kingdomes Weekly Intelligencer* No. 230 12th-19th October 1647

[66] *Perfect Weekly Account* 3rd-10th May 1647

[67] J Morrill 'The Church in England 1642-9' in ed. J Morrill *Reactions to the English Civil War 1642 - 1649* (1982) p.104

[68] Loc.cit.

[69] A Argent 'Aspects of the Ecclesiastical History of the Parishes of the City of London 1640-49 (with special reference to the Parish Clergy)' (London

University Ph.D. thesis, 1983) pp.220, 228

[70] Cf. C Durston 'Puritan Rule and the Failure of Cultural Revolution 1645-1660' in eds. C Durston and J Eales *The Culture of English Puritanism 1560-1700* (1996) pp.226-232

[71] Bodleian pressmark CP 1645 f1

[72] DN Griffiths *The Bibliography of the Book of Common Prayer 1549-1999* (2002) p.106 - 1645/1

[73] Bodleian pressmark CP 1647 f1

[74] Bodleian pressmark Bib. Eng. 1650 f1

[75] E.g. TH Darlow and HF Moule *Historical Catalogue of the Printed Editions of Holy Scripture in the Library of the British and Foreign Bible Society* (1963), Vol. I lists 29 bibles bearing dates in the years 1645-1659. Of these, six are bound with copies of the Book of Common Prayer, variously dated 1639, 1641, and 1642

[76] DN Griffiths *Bibliography of the Book of Common Prayer....* (2002) 1641/2, 1641/3

[77] RS Bosher *The Making of the Restoration Settlement* (1957) p.5; A Argent 'Aspects of the Ecclesiastical History of the Parishes of the City of London 1640-49 (with special reference to the Parish Clergy)' (London University Ph.D. thesis, 1983) p.205

[78] Deduced from G Clark *The Later Stuarts 1660-1714* (1965) p.23 n.1

[79] Ed. GH Sabine *The Works of Gerrard Winstanley* (1941) p.504 cited in PH Hardacre *The Royalists during the Puritan Revolution* (1956) p.88

[80] JH Pruett *The Parish Clergy under the Later Stuarts: The Leicestershire Experience* (1978)

[81] JH Pruett *The Parish Clergy under the Later Stuarts: The Leicestershire Experience* (1978) pp.10-28

[82] I.W. *Certain Reasons why the Booke of Common-Prayer Being Corrected should continue* (1641); *The Protestation of the Two and Twenty Divines for the Setling of the Church: and the Particulars by them excepted against in the Liturgie: Not that the Book of Common Prayer of the Church of England should be utterly abolished, but purged of all Innovations and Absurdities* (1643).

[83] J Davies *The Caroline Captivity of the Church: Charles I and the Remoulding of Anglicanism 1625-1641* (1992) p.295

[84] *The Use of Daily Publick Prayers* 1641, pp.1,2

[85] D Whitby *The Vindication of the Forme of Common Prayers Used in the Church of England....* (Oxford, 1644) p.24

[86] H Hammond *The View of the New Directory* (Oxford, 1645) and the anonymous *Dirge for the Directory* (Oxford, 1645)

[87] Cf. JB Hibbitts 'Henry Hammond (1605-1660) and English New Testament Exposition' (Oxford University Ph.D. thesis, 1954) p.431

[88] Cf. JW Packer *The Transformation of Anglicanism 1643-1660, with special reference to Henry Hammond* (1969) passim.

[89] H Hammond *Ευσχημονως και Κατα Ταξιν: or, The Grounds of Uniformity From I Cor. 14.40* (1657) p.10

[90] H Hammond *Ευσχημονως και Κατα Ταξιν: or, The Grounds of Uniformity From I Cor. 14.40* (1657) p.20

[91] H Jeanes *Uniformity in Humane Doctrinall Ceremonies ... or, A Reply unto Dr Hammonds ... Grounds of Uniformity* (Oxford, 1660) pp.19,78

[92] *A Dirge for the Directory* (Oxford, 1645) p.5

[93] J Taylor *An Apology for Authorized and Set Forms of Liturgie* (1649) p.67

[94] J Taylor *An Apology for Authorized and Set Forms of Liturgie* (1649) p.74

[95] Loc. cit

[96] J Doughty *Velitationes Polemicae* (1652) p.155

[97] J Allington *A brief Apologie for the Sequestred Clergie....* (1649); L Gatford [?-1665; 1631 Vicar of St Clements, Cambridge; 1637 Rector of Dennington, Suffolk; 1644 Chaplain to Pendennis Castle, Cornwall; 1647 minister on Jersey and Chaplain to Sir Edward Hyde; 1654-1660 itinerant ministry; 1660 DD; 1661 Vicar of Plymouth; 1663 curate of Great Yarmouth] *A Petition For the Vindication of the Publique use of the Book of Common-Prayer* (1655)

[98] A Sparrow *A Rationale upon the Book of Common Prayer....* (1655) Preface, np. [Anthony Sparrow, ejected 1644, & 1648, Archdeacon of Sudbury & DD 1660, Bishop of Exeter 1667, Bishop of Norwich 1676, Died 1685]

[99] J Gauden - 1605-1662; 1640 Vicar of Chippenham; 1641 DD and Dean Of Bocking; 1660 Chaplain to the King & Bishop of Exeter; 1662 Bishop of Worcester

[100] Cf. ed. PA Knachel *Eikon Basilike* (1966) pp.xxviii-xxxii

[101] L Potter *Secret Rites and Secret Writing - Royalist Literature 1641-1660* (1989) p.170

[102] Cf. SN Zwicker *Lines of Authority: Politics and English Literary Culture 1649-1689* (1993) p.37; K Sharpe 'The King's Writ: Royal Authors and Royal Authority in Early Modern England' in ed. K Sharpe and P Lake *Culture and Politics in Early Stuart England* (1994) p.136; R Targoff *Common Prayer: the Language of Public Devotion in Early Modern England* (2001) p.12f; A Lacey *The Cult of King Charles the Martyr* (2003) p.12

[103] Cf. references listed in C Wordsworth *Who Wrote Εικων Βασιλικη?* 1824 pp.104-110

[104] E.g. *A Forme of Prayer Used at Newport in the Isle of Wight; by His Majesties Directions, upon the 15 of September, 1648; Prince Charles, his Letany, and Prayers, For the King of Great Britane in his sad Condition ....* (1648); *A Forme of Prayer, used in the King's Chappel, upon Tuesdayes In these Times of Trouble & Distresse* (1649)

[105] The development of the royal cult is surveyed in A Lacey *The Cult of King Charles the Martyr* (2003)

[106] J Morrill 'The Church in England 1642-9' in ed. J Morrill *Reactions to the English Civil War 1642 - 1649* (1982) p.90

[107] Cf. JE Skoglund 'Free Prayer' *Studia Liturgica* Vol. 10, 1974, No.3/4, pp.151-166

[108] P Bales *Oratio Dominica: or, the Lords Prayer, pleading for Better Entertainment in the Church of England. A Sermon Preached at Saint Mary Woolnoth, London, Jan 11. 1643* 1643, p.12 cf. John Grant [Rector of St Bartholomew's Exchange] *Gods Deliverance of Man by Prayer. And Mans Thankfulnesse to God in Prayses* 1642 p.17

[109] Eds. FP Verney and MM Verney *Memoirs of the Verney Family during the*

Seventeenth Century (1907) Vol. I, pp.355f.

[110] L Potter *Secret Rites and Secret Writing - Royalist Literature 1641-1660* (1989) p. 168f.

[111] A Hunt 'The Art of Hearing: English Preachers and their audiences 1590-1640' (Cambridge University Ph.D. thesis, 1998); cf. R Bozell 'English Preachers of the Seventeenth Century on the Art of Preaching' (Cornell University Ph.D. thesis, 1938)

[112] J Black 'Some Structural Features of Sumerian Narrative Poetry' in eds. ME Vogelzang and HLJ Vanstiphout *Mesopotamian Epic Literature: Oral or Aural?* (1992) pp. 71, 72, 75, 76

[113] 1841 edition, p.162

[114] In a population of roughly 5 million people, childhood was regarded as running from ages 7-14 cf. SR Smith 'Religion and the Conception of Youth in Seventeenth Century England' *History of Childhood Quarterly* Vol. 2, Part 4, 1974/75, p.495

[115] K Dillow 'The Social and Ecclesiastical Significance of Church Seating Arrangements and Pew Disputes 1500-1740' (Oxford University Ph.D. thesis, 1990) pp.142-150

[116] Cf. T Lacqueur 'The Cultural Origins of Popular Literacy in England 1500-1850' *Oxford Review of Education* Vol. 2 No 3, 1976, pp.255-275

[117] D Jenkins *A Scourge for the Directorie and the Revolting Synod....* 1647 p.1 (this work had previously been issued anonymously as *A Dirge for the Directory* (Oxford, 1645))

[118] JA Russo 'Oral Theory: its Development in Homeric Studies and Applicability to Other Literatures' in eds. ME Vogelzang and HLJ Vanstiphout *Mesopotamian Epic Literature: Oral or Aural?* (1992) pp. 13,14

[119] H Thorndike *Of Religious Assemblies, and the Publick Service of God....* (1642) pp.214-215).

[120] J Hall *The Devout Soul....* (1644) pp.4-5

[121] J Hall *The Devout Soul....* (1644) p.7

[122] J Hall *The Devout Soul....* (1644) p.10

[123] M Casaubon *A Treatise Concerning Enthusiasme* (1655) p.274

[124] M Casaubon *A Treatise Concerning Enthusiasme* (1655) p.275

[125] M Casaubon *A Treatise Concerning Enthusiasme* (1655) pp.275-276

[126] M Casaubon *A Treatise Concerning Enthusiasme* (1655) p.276

[127] M Casaubon *A Treatise Concerning Enthusiasme* (1655) p.277

[128] M Casaubon *A Treatise Concerning Enthusiasme* (1655) p.278

[129] H More *Enthusiasmus Triumphatus* (1656) p.2

[130] H More *An explanation of the Grand Mystery of Godliness* (1660) p.538

[131] H More *An explanation of the Grand Mystery of Godliness* (1660) p.539

[132] J Taylor *A Discourse concerning Prayer Ex tempore....* (1646) p.13

[133] J Taylor *A Discourse concerning Prayer Ex tempore....* (1646) p.33

[134] J Taylor *An Apology for Authorized and Set Forms....* (1649) p.21

[135] J Taylor *An Apology for Authorized and Set Forms....* (1649) p.31-32

[136] J Doughty *Velitationes Polemicae* (1652) p.155f

[137] J Doughty *Velitationes Polemicae* (1652) p.159

[138] J Doughty *Velitationes Polemicae* (1652) p.161

[139] P Heylyn *Ecclesia Vindicata....* (1657) p.101

[140] H Thorndike *An Epilogue to the Tragedy of the Church of England* (1659) Book III pp.277-278

[141] H Leslie *A Discourse of Praying with the Spirit and with the Understanding* (1660) p.1

[142] H Leslie *A Discourse of Praying with the Spirit and with the Understanding* (1660) p.28

[143] H More *An Explanation of the Grand Mystery of Godliness* (1660) p.539

[144] Richard Sherlock - 1612-1689; Oxford MA 1633; BD 1646; Chaplain to the Earl of Derby 1658; Rector of Winwick, Lancs, 1662-1689

[145] R Sherlock *Principles of Holy Christian Religion....* (1659) Preface

[146] Cf. CC Weston *English Constitutional Theory and the House of Lords, 1556-1832* (1965) pp.88, 89

[147] See: GJ Cuming *A History of Anglican Liturgy* (1969)

[148] As noted by IM Green *The Re-Establishment of the Church of England 1660-1663* (1978) pp. 145,146

[149] R Hutton *The Restoration: A Political and Religious History of England and Wales 1658-1667* (1985)

[150] E.g. C Durston 'By the book or with the spirit: the debate over liturgical prayer during the English Revolution' *Historical Research* Vol. 79, No 203 (February 2006) pp. 50-73: a selective survey which inclines to this view.

[151] Cf. FG Healey *Rooted in Faith: Three Centuries of Nonconformity 1662-1962* (1961)

[152] J Gauden *Ecclesiae Anglicanae Suspiria* (1659) p.105

[153] G Clark *The Later Stuarts 1660-1714* (1965) p.27; EAO Whiteman 'The Episcopate of Dr Seth Ward, Bishop of Exeter (1662 to 1667) and Salisbury (1667 to 1688/9) with special reference to the ecclesiastical problems of his time' (Oxford University Ph.D. thesis 1951) pp. 362-442

[154] A Browning *Thomas Osborne, Earl of Danby and Duke of Leeds 1632-1712* (1951) Vol. I p.198

[155] Cf. ed. A Browning *English Historical Documents 1660-1714* (1953) pp. 413f, 425

[156] A Everitt 'Nonconformity in Country Parishes' in ed. J Thirsk *Land, Church, and People: Essays presented to Professor H.P.R. Finberg Supplement to The Agricultural History Review* Vol. 18 1970 p.185; cf. ed. A Whiteman *The Compton Census of 1676* (1986) p. lxxix

[157] *The Book of Homilies* (1822) Right Use of the Church, First Chapter, p.154

[158] *The Book of Homilies* (1822) Of Common Prayer and Sacraments, p.329

[159] Declaration of Charles II of 25th October 1660 *Concerning Ecclesiasticall Affaires* p.14-15

[160] 'A Copy of His Majesties Commission' cited at the beginning of *An Accompt of all the Proceedings....* (1661)

[161] Cf. William Annand *Fides Catholica* (1661) p.517

[162] Cf. FE Ball 'A Liturgical Colloquy: An examination of the records of the Savoy Conference, 1661' (Oxford University B.Litt. thesis, 1958)

[163] FE Ball 'A Liturgical Colloquy: An examination of the records of the Savoy Conference, 1661' (Oxford University B.Litt. thesis, 1958) p.180

[164] *An Accompt of all the Proceedings of the Commissioners of both Persuasions appointed by his Sacred Majesty....* (1661) p.35

NOTES181

[165] GJ Cuming 'The Prayer Book in Convocation, November 1661' *Journal of Ecclesiastical History* Vol. 8 No.2 London 1957 p.182

[166] 'Letter from the Bishops of the Northern Province to the Prolocutor and Proctors of the Convocation of the Province of York' in *The Records of the Northern Convocation* Surtees Society Vol. 113 (1907) p.316

[167] Cf. 'But such alterations as were tendered to us ... as seemed to us in any degree requisite or expedient, we have willingly, and of our own accord assented unto....' - Preface to 1662 Prayer Book

[168] 'If any man ... shall take the pains to compare the present Book with the former; we doubt not but the reason of the change may easily appear.' Preface to the 1662 Prayer Book

[169] WJ Grisbrooke 'The 1662 Book of Common Prayer: its history and character' *Studia Liturgica* Vol. 1 No.3 1962, p.164

[170] H Thorndike *Just Weights and Measures* (1662) p.111

[171] E.g. V Powell's pamphlet *Common-Prayer-Book no Divine Service, or XXVII Reasons against forming and imposing any Humane Liturgies....* (1661) was answered by John Barbon's Λειτουργια Θειοτερα Εργια: *or Liturgie a most Divine Service....* (Oxford, 1662)

[172] Cf. A Hoffman *Bocking Deanery - The story of an Essex Peculiar* (1976) pp. 53-66).

[173] J Gauden *Considerations touching the Liturgy* (1661) pp. 9,10

[174] J Gauden *Considerations touching the Liturgy* (1661) p. 11

[175] J Gauden *Considerations touching the Liturgy* (1661) p.11

[176] J Gauden *Considerations touching the Liturgy* (1661) p.12

[177] GR Cragg *The Church and the Age of Reason 1648-1789 - Pelican History of the Church Vol. IV* (1962) p.52

[178] DL Edwards *Christian England Vol. 2* (1983) p.428

[179] J Butt 'The Facilities for Antiquarian Study in the Seventeenth Century' *Essays and Studies by Members of the English Association* Vol. 24, 1939 pp.64-79

[180] CE Whiting 'The Study of the Classics in England during the Restoration Period' *Durham University Journal* Vol. 26, 1928-1930 pp.255-269, 339-348

[181] Cf. K Thomas *The Perception of the Past in Early Modern England* (1983) p.1f

[182] Cf. JGA Pocock *The Ancient Constitution and the Feudal Law: A study of English Historical Thought in the Seventeenth Century* (1974) pp.17-47

[183] JGA Pocock *The Ancient Constitution and the Feudal Law: A study of English Historical Thought in the Seventeenth Century* (1974) p.31

[184] R Lingard *A Sermon preached before the King at Whitehall July 26, 1668. In Defence of the Liturgy of our Church* (1668) p.12 (Richard Lingard ?1598-?1670; Professor of Divinity at Dublin, 1661; Dublin DD 1664)

[185] 'Smectymnuus' *An Answer to a Booke entituled, an Humble Remonstrance* (1641)

[186] J Hall *Defence of the Humble Remonstrance....* (1641) p.13ff

[187] 'Smectymnuus' *A Vindication of the Answer to the Humble Remonstrance* (1641) p.15ff

[188] J Hall *A Short Answer to the Tedious Vindication* (1641) pp.23ff

[189] Cf. E Duffy 'Primitive Christianity Revived; Religious Renewal in Augustan England' in ed. D Baker *Renaissance and Renewal in Christian History: Studies in Church History 14* (1977) pp.287-300; especially pp.287-291

[190] PG Stanwood *Jeremy Taylor: Holy Living and Holy Dying* (1989) Vol. I, p.xlvi

[191] GV Bennett 'Patristic Tradition in Anglican Thought, 1660-1900' *Oecumenica* 1972, p.68

[192] JT Addison 'Early Anglican Thought 1559-1667' *Historical Magazine of the Protestant Episcopal Church* September 1953, Vol. 22, No. 3, p. 282

[193] Cf. RL Simpson *The Interpretation of Prayer in the Early Church* (1965); PF Bradshaw *Daily Prayer in the Early Church* (1981); GW Woolfenden *Daily Liturgical Prayer: Origins and Theology* (2004)

[194] HO Old *The Patristic Roots of Reformed Worship* (1975) p.339

[195] J Gauden *Considerations Touching the Liturgy* (1661) p.8

[196] M Casaubon *The Vindication of the Lords Prayer* (1660) Postscript to the Epistle to the Reader

[197] M Casaubon *The Vindication of the Lords Prayer* (1660) Postscript to the Epistle to the Reader

[198] J Owen *Discourse concerning Liturgies and their Imposition* (1661) p.21

[199] J Owen *Discourse concerning Liturgies and their Imposition* (1661) p.23

[200] J Owen *Discourse concerning Liturgies and their Imposition* (1661) p.63f

[201] A Sparrow *Rationale upon the Book of Common Prayer* Preface

[202] Cf. J Lloyd *A Treatise of the Episcopacy, Liturgies, and Ecclesiastical ceremonies of Primitive Times* (1661) p.37; Anon. *A True Notion of the Worship of God: Or a Vindication of the Service of the Church of England* (1673) pp.25ff.; J Arderne *A Sermon Preached at the Visitation of ... John Lord Bishop of Chester....* (1677) pp.13,14 (James Arderne 1636-1691; Curate of St Botolph's Aldersgate 1666-1682; Oxford DD 1673; Chaplain to Charles II; Dean of Chester 1682); J Shaw (Rector of Whalton, Northumberland) *No Reformation of the Established Reformation* 1685, pp.85ff

[203] W Cave *Primitive Christianity* (First edition 1673; Fifth edition 1698) (William Cave 1637-1713; Vicar of Islington 1662-1691; DD 1681; Chaplain to Charles II; Canon of Windsor 1684)

[204] E Pelling *The Good Old Way, or a Discourse offer'd to all True-hearted Protestants Concerning the Ancient Way of the Church, and the Conformity of the Church of England Thereunto....* (1680) p.49
[1674-1678 Vicar of St Helens, London; 1678-1691 Vicar of St Martin's Ludgate; 1683-1691 Prebendary of Westminster; 1691-1718 Rector of Petworth, Sussex; Chaplain-in-ordinary to William & Mary]

[205] E Pelling *The Good Old Way....* (1680) p.73

[206] CJ Stranks *Anglican Devotion* (1961) p.156

[207] DH Davies *Worship and Theology in England 1603-1690....* (1975) p.117

[208] D Clarkson *Discourse Concerning Liturgies* (1689) p.151

[209] D Clarkson *Discourse Concerning Liturgies* (1689) pp.62-64

[210] T Comber *Companion to the Temple* (1688) Part III, pp.36ff

[211] D Clarkson *Discourse Concerning Liturgies* (1689) pp.181ff

[212] T Comber *Scholastical History of the Primitive and General Use of Liturgies in the Christian Church together with an Answer to Mr Dav. Clarkson's late Discourse Concerning Liturgies* (1690)

[213] Cave's introductory letter when this work was included in the posthumously issued *Companion to the Temple....* Volume 2 (1702) with the section specifically addressed to Clarkson omitted

[214] T Comber *Scholastical History* (1690) p.206

[215] SB *An Examination of Dr Comber's Scholastical History of the Primitive and General Use of Liturgies in the Christian Church* 1690

[216] SB *An Examination....* (1690) Preface

[217] T Comber *The Examiner Examined: Being a Vindication of the History of Liturgies* (1691)

[218] T Comber *The Examiner Examined....* (1691) p.4

[219] SB *A Second Examination....* (1691)

[220] SB *A Second Examination....* (1691) p.65

[221] Ed. CE Whiting *The Autobiographies and Letters of Thomas Comber* Surtees Society Volumes 156, 157 (1946, 1947) Volume 2, pp. 188, 189

[222] W Owtram *Twenty Sermons Preached upon Several Occasions* (1697) p.134 (William Owtram, 1626-1679; Rector of St Margaret's, Westminster, 1664-79; Archdeacon of Leicester 1669; Prebendary of Westminster 1670)

[223] T Comber *Companion to the Temple....* Vol. I (1688) Preface

[224] A Carr *A Peaceable Moderator: or some plain Considerations to give Satisfaction to such as stand Disaffected to our Book of Common Prayer* (1665) p.36

[225] A Carr *A Peaceable Moderator....* (1665) p.36-37

[226] G Bright *A Treatise of Prayer* (1678) Preface

[227] Loc. cit.

[228] J Taylor *An Apology for Authorized and Set Forms* (1649) p.74, re-issued in Jeremy Taylor *Συμβολον θεολογικον: or a Collection of Polemicall Discourses....* (1674) p.29

[229] Cf. E Davies 'The Enforcement of Religious Uniformity in England 1668-1700 with Special Reference to the Dioceses of Chichester and Worcester' (Oxford University Ph.D. thesis, 1982); H Consett *The Practice of the Spiritual or Ecclesiastical Courts* (1700) pp.379f.

[230] Ed. A Macfarlane *The Diary of Ralph Josselin 1616-1683* (1991) p.602, entry for 5th September, 1677

[231] S Hinde [Vicar of St Mary's, Dover] *Englands Prospective-Glasse: A Sermon at a Metropolitical Visitation Held at The Cathedral Church of Christ in Canterbury on the 29th of April 1663* (1663) p.20

[232] J Goodman *A Sermon Preached at Bishops-Stortford August 29. 1677 before ... Henry, Lord Bishop of London, &c., At his Lordships Primary Visitation* (1677) p.29
(John Goodman (?-1690) Vicar of Watford 1651-74; Cambridge DD 1673; Vicar of Much Hadham, Herts, 1674-90; Archdeacon of Middlesex 1986-90)

[233] J Norris *A Sermon Preach'd in the Abby Church of Bath, Before ... Thomas, Lord Bishop of Bath and Wells. At his Visitation held there July 30. 1689* (1690) p.187 (John Norris (1657-1711) had specialised in the study of Platonism at Oxford and had been ordained about 1685. In 1689 he became Vicar of Newton St Loe, Somerset).

[234] T Duncumb *The Great Efficacy and Necessity of Good Example Especially in the Clergy: Recommended in a Visitation Sermon Preached at Guildford* (1671) p.23
(Thomas Duncumb Rector of Shere, Surrey 1658-1714; Oxford DD 1671)

[235] A Carr *A Peaceable Moderator....* (1665) p.36

[236] E Kemp *Reasons for the Sole Use of the Churches Prayers in Publick* (1668) p.9 (Edward Kemp ?-1671. Ejected as a Fellow from Cambridge 1644; reinstated 1660. Rector of Little Eversden, Cambs, 1667-1671)

[237] W Goulde *Domus mea, Domus Orationis. A Sermon Preached in the Cathedral of St. Peter in Exon on Palm-Sunday An. Dom. 1672* (1672) p.18f.

[238] S Patrick *A Discourse Concerning Prayer* (1686) 1848 ed. p.117 (Symon Patrick 1626-1707; 1679 Dean of Peterborough; 1689 Bishop of Chichester; 1691-1707 Bishop of Ely)

[239] H Davis *De Jure Uniformitatis Ecclesiasticae: Or Three Books, of the Rights Belonging to an Uniformity in Churches* (1667) p.164; (Chaplain to the Duke of Buckingham)

[240] H Davis *De Jure Uniformitatis Ecclesiasticae....* (1667) p.164f

[241] *Publick Devotion and the Common service of the Church of England, Justify'd and Recommended....* (1675) p.20

[242] H.C. *Brief Directions for our more Devout Behaviour in Time of Divine Service .... (1693) p.21*

[243] T Pittis *Discourse of Prayer* (1683) p.100

[244] J Kettlewell *A Discourse Explaining the Nature of Edification Both of Particular Persons in Private Grace, and of the Church in Unity and Peace. And shewiug (sic) That we must not break Unity and Publick Peace, for supposed Means of better Edifying in Private Virtues. In a Visitation Sermon at Coventry, May 7. 1684.* (1684) Preface
Cf. G Raymond *A Sermon Preached at the Primary Visitation of ... John Lord Bishop of Norwich June, 20th. 1692* (1692) p.3

[245] R Sherlock (Rector of Winwick, Lancashire) *A Sermon Preached at a Visitation, held at Warrington in Lancashire May 11. 1669* (1669) p.8
Cf. *The Irregularitie of a Private Prayer in a Publick Congregation* (1674)

[246] J Allington (Vicar of Leamington-Hastang) *The Reform'd Samaritan: or, the Worship of God by measures of spirit and truth* (1678) p.7

[247] Cf. JR Jones *Country and Court: England 1658-1714* (1980) pp. 145-147; VD Sutch *Gilbert Sheldon: Architect of Anglican Survival 1640-1675* (1973) esp. pp. 61-90

[248] *A Resolution of two Cases of Conscience* (1683) p.36

[249] F Fullwood *The Necessity of Keeping our Parish Churches An Assize Sermon at Exeter* (1672) p.27

[250] S Patrick *A Discourse Concerning Prayer* (1848) p.121

[251] S Patrick *A Discourse Concerning Prayer* (1848) p.124

[252] S Patrick *A Discourse Concerning Prayer* (1848) p.125

[253] J Mapletoft *A Perswasive to the Consciencious frequenting the daily Publick Prayers of the Church of England* (1687) p.20 (Mapletoft (1631-1721) became Vicar of St Laurence Jewry in 1688)

[254] J Mapletoft *A Perswasive to the Consciencious frequenting the daily Publick Prayers of the Church of England* (1687) p.21,22

[255] J Cave *A Sermon preached in a Country-Audience on the late Day of Fasting and Prayer: January 30* (1679) p.22; cf. W Stainforth *An Assize Sermon, Preached August 3, 1685 in the Cathedral Church of St Peter in York* (York, 1685) pp.28,29; W Sherlock *A Sermon Preached at the Temple Church, May 29, 1692* (1692) pp.24f; V Allsop *Duty and Interest United in Prayer and*

Praise for Kings, and all that are in Authority (1695)

[256] *A form of prayer, to be used upon the fifteenth of January in all churches and chappels within the cities of London and Westminster; the suburbs of each, and the burrough of Southwark. ... for the averting those sicknesses, that dearth and scarcity, which justly may be feared from the unseasonableness of the weather.* (1662)

[257] *A form of common prayer, together with an order of fasting, for the averting of Gods heavy visitation upon many places of this realm. The fast to be observ'd within the cities of London and Westminster, and places adjacent, on Wednesday the twelfth of this instant July; and both there, and in all parts of this realm, on the first Wednesday of every moneth; and the prayers to be read on Wednesday in every week, during this visitation.* (Oxford 1665)

[258] *A form of common prayer. To be used on Wednesday the tenth day of October next; ... being appointed by His Majesty, a day of fasting and humiliation, in consideration of the late dreadful fire, which wasted the greater part of the city of London.* (1666)

[259] *A form of prayer with fasting, to be us'd yearly upon the 30th of January, being the day of the martydom of the blessed King Charles the First: to implore the mercy of God, that neither the guilt of that sacred and innocent bloud, nor those other sins, by which God was provoked to deliver up both us, and our King into the hands of cruel and unreasonable men, may at any time hereafter be visited upon us, or our posterity.* (1685)

[260] *A form of prayer, with thanksgiving to Almighty God for having put an end to the great rebellion by the restitution of the King and royal family. And the restauration of the government after many years interruption: which unspeakable mercies were wonderfully completed upon the 29th of May, in the year, 1660. And in memory thereof, that day in every year is by Act of Parliament appointed to be for ever kept holy.* (1685)

[261] *A form, or order of thanksgiving and prayer, to be used in London, and ten miles round it, on Sunday the 15th. of this instant January ... in behalf of the King, the Queen, and the royal family, upon occasion of the Queen's being with child.* (1688)

[262] *A form of prayer with thanksgiving for the safe delivery of the Queen, and happy birth of the young Prince. To be used on Sunday next, being the seventeenth day of this instant June...* (1688)

[263] This prayer was used many times - for example in *A form of prayer to be used on Wednesday the tenth of May next, throughout the whole kingdom; being the fast-day appointed by Their Majesties proclamation; and on the second Wednesday of every month following, till further order. To be observed in a most solemn and devout manner, for supplicating Almighty God for the pardon of our sins, and for imploring his blessing and protection in the preservation of Their Majesties sacred persons, and the prosperity of their arms both at land and sea.* (1693)

[264] *A form of prayer to be used yearly on the second of September, for the dreadful fire of London* (1696)

[265] M D'Assigny *The Divine Art of Prayer* (1691) p.99
(Marius D'Assigny 1643-1717; BD Cambridge 1668 per literas regias; Vicar of Penrith, 1667-68; Vicar of Cutcombe, Somerset, 1672-1699)

[266] R West *The Profitableness of Piety ... An Assize Sermon Preached at Dorchester* (1671) p.11
(Richard West (?1615-1690) Rector of Shillingston, Dorset 1649-1690; Oxford DD 1660; Rector of Durweston, Dorset 1664-1690)

[267] J Templer *A Treatise relating to the Worship of God* (1694) p.177
(John Templer (?-1697) Rector of Balsham, Cambs 1654-1693; Cambridge DD 1666)

[268] DN Griffiths *Bibliography of the Book of Common Prayer....* (2002) p.106f

[269] Cf. ed. WK Clay *Liturgies and Occasional Forms of Prayer set forth in the Reign of Queen Elizabeth* (1847) p. xiii

[270] G Meriton *A Guide for Constables, Churchwardens, Overseers of the Poor, Surveyors of the Highways ... A Treatise briefly shewing the extent and latitude of the several offices, with the powers of the officers herein, both by common law and statute....* (1669) p.152

[271] Cf. ed. E Arber *A Transcript of the Register of the Company of Stationers 1554-1640* Vol. 4 (1877) pp.21, 22

[272] The Articles of Visitation for the Dioceses of Worcester and Durham had required two Prayer Books, one for the minister and one for the clerk, even in 1662

[273] Ed. A Macfarlane *The Diary of Ralph Josselin 1616-1683* (1991) p.491; entry for 16th August 1662

[274] IM Green *The Re-Establishment of the Church of England 1660-1663* (1978) p.144ff

[275] W Beveridge *Works* Vol. VI (1842) p.373

[276] Cf. O Blackall *A Sermon Preached at Brentwood in Essex, October the 7th, 1693. At the Visitation of ... Henry, Lord Bishop of London.* (1699) 2nd ed. p.29

[277] W Beveridge *Works* Vol. VI (1842) p.373; cf. Robert Whitehall *A Sermon concerning Edification in Faith and Discipline, preached before the University of Oxford. Sept. 1. 1689* (Oxford, 1694) p.24

[278] J Scott *Certain Cases of Conscience Resolved ...* Part I (1683) pp.45, 46

[279] M Hole *A Sermon Preached at the Triennial Visitation of ... Richard L. Bishop of Bath and Wells. Held at Bridgewater, on the 19th Day of August, 1695* (1696) p.11

[280] J Kettlewell *The Religious Loyalist: Or a Good Christian Taught How to be a Faithful Servant both to God and the King in a Visitation-Sermon. Preached at Coles-Hill in Warwickshire, Aug. 28, 1685 At the Triennial Visitation of my Lords Grace of Canterbury, During the Suspension of the Bp. of Litchfield and Coventry.* (1686) p.23

[281] T Lodington *The Honour of the Clergy Vindicated from the Contempt of the Laity in a Sermon preached at the Arch-Deacon of Lincoln his Visitation, holden at Grantham, Oct 15. 1672.* (1673) pp.62f

[282] E Gibson *Codex Juris Ecclesiastici Anglicani* (Oxford, 1761) Vol. 2, p.962

[283] J Godolphin *Repertorium Canonicum* (1680) p.192

[284] P Joyce *Visions of the People - Industrial England and the Question of Class 1848-1914* (1991) p.150; cf. A Fox *Oral and Literate Culture in England 1500-1700* (2000) pp.259-281

[285] T Puller *The Moderation of the Church of England* (1679) p.167
(Timothy Puller (?1638-1693) 1673 DD; 1679 Rector of St Mary-le-Bow,

London)

[286] T Seymour *Advice to the Readers of Common Prayer* (1683) p.61

[287] *Rules for our more Devout Behaviour in the time of Divine Service in the Church of England* (1687) p.32,33

[288] T Seymour *Advice to the Readers of Common Prayer* (1683) pp.58,59

[289] L Atterbury *Ten Sermons preach'd before Her Royal Highness The Princess Ann of Denmark At the Chappel at St James.* (1699) p.114 (Lewis Atterbury, 1656-1731, ordained 1679; Rector of Sywell, Northamptonshire, 1684; Preacher at Highgate Chapel 1695; Chaplain to Princess Anne)

[290] Charles II *Proclamation for the Observation of the Lords Day* (1663)

[291] *Act of Uniformity 1559*, 1Eliz. I cap 2

[292] *Publick Devotion and the Common Service of the Church of England justified, and recommended....* (1675) Preface

[293] R Sherlock *A Sermon Preached at a Visitation, held at Warrington in Lancashire May 11. 1669* (1669) p.8

[294] *A Form of Common Prayer Together with an Order of Fasting For the Averting of Gods heavy Visitation Upon many places of this Realm* (1665) Exhortation - np.

[295] R Hollingsworth *A Modest Plea for the Church of England* (1676) p.74

[296] W Sherlock *A Practical Discourse of Religious Assemblies* (1682) p.284 (William Sherlock (?1641-1707) 1669 Rector of St George, Botolph Lane; 1680 DD; 1681 Prebendary of St Paul's; 1685 Master of the Temple; 1691 Dean of St Paul's.)

[297] M D'Assigny *The Divine Art of Prayer* (1691) p.31 cf. T Tenison *A Sermon concerning the Wandering of the Mind in God's Service. Preached before the Queen at Whitehall....* (1691) [on the text 'That you may attend upon the Lord without distraction' I Cor. vii. 35];George Tullie *A Discourse of the Government of the Thoughts* 3rd ed. (1694) pp.92ff

[298] M D'Assigny *The Divine Art of Prayer* (1691) pp.91f

[299] T Manningham *Praise and Adoration* (1682) p.18

[300] J Shaw *Parish Law* (1733) p.42; cf. John Godolphin *Repertorium Canonicum* (1680) p.192

[301] Cf. J Spurr *The Restoration Church of England, 1646-1689* (1991) p.355f

[302] A Carr *A Peaceable Moderator....* (1665) p.36

[303] *Articles to be Enquired of By the Ministers, Church-Wardens and Side-men of every Parish within the Arch-Deaconry of Colchester....* (1662) p.8

[304] *Articles of Visitation and Enquiry ... of Every Parish with the Diocess of Lincoln. In the Metropolitical Visitation of ... William ... Lord Archbishop of Canterbury* (1686) p.12

[305] A Carr *A Peaceable Moderator* (1665) pp.36f

[306] B.P. *The Parish-Clerk's Vade Mecum....* (1694) Preface

[307] T Seymour *Advice to the Readers of the Common Prayer* (1683) p.57

[308] Cf. J Spurr *The Restoration Church of England, 1646-1689* (1991) p.351

[309] *An Answer to the Dissenters Objections against the Common Prayers* (1684) pp.17,19

[310] Cited in JT Cliffe *The Puritan Gentry Besieged 1650-1700* (1993) pp.92-94

[311] R Sherlock *A Sermon Preached at a Visitation, held at Warrington in Lancashire May 11. 1669* (1669) p.8

[312] J Gardiner *Advice to the Clergy of the Diocese of Lincoln*.... (1697) p.11

[313] Ed. G Ornsby *The Remains of Denis Granville*.... Surtees Society Vol. 47 (1865) p.102

[314] Ed. G Ornsby *The Remains of Denis Granville*.... (1865) pp.102, 103

[315] *Copy of the Alterations in the Book of Common Prayer prepared by the Royal Commissioners for the Revision of the Liturgy in 1689* (1854) p.92f.

[316] *Copy of the Alterations*.... (1854) p.106

[317] T Seymour *Advice to the Readers of the Common Prayer* (1683)

[318] E Stillingfleet *The Bishop of Worcester's Charge to the Clergy of his Diocese* (1691) p.23 (Edward Stillingfleet (1635-1699) 1665-1689 Rector of St Andrew's Holborn; 1678 Dean of St Paul's; 1689 Bishop of Worcester)

[319] G Burnet *A Discourse of the Pastoral Care* (1692) p.91f (Gilbert Burnet (1643-1715) 1690 Bishop of Salisbury)

[320] T Sprat *A Discourse made by the Ld Bishop of Rochester to the Clergy of his Diocese* (1696) p.8 (Thomas Sprat (1635-1713) 1669 Canon of Westminster; 1679 Lecturer St Margaret's, Westminster; 1681 Canon of Windsor; 1683 Dean of Westminster; 1684 Bishop of Rochester)

[321] T Sprat *A Discourse made by the Ld Bishop of Rochester*.... (1696) p.10

[322] T Sprat *A Discourse made by the Ld Bishop of Rochester*.... (1696) p.13

[323] T Sprat *A Discourse made by the Ld Bishop of Rochester*.... (1696) p.19

[324] Cf. DM Buley 'Eloquence as the essence of common prayer: Cranmer's liturgical language' (Drew University Ph.D. thesis 2004)

[325] J Gardiner *Advice to the Clergy of the Diocese of Lincoln*.... (1697) p.12

[326] J Clark *A Sermon Preached in the Parish Church of Grantham, July 12. 1697*.... (1698) pp. 9, 10

[327] See AP Fox 'Aspects of Oral Culture and its Development in Early Modern England' (Cambridge University Ph.D. thesis, 1992) pp.51-125

[328] ED Holley 'The English Bible and English Primary Education in the Tudor and Stuart Periods' (Florida State University Ph.D. thesis 1998) p.128

[329] Ed. B Reay *Popular Culture in Seventeenth-Century England* (1985) p.7

[330] Cf. J Watson *The Literary Qualities of the Prayer Book* (1949) pp. 38-41

[331] E.g. CS Lewis *English Literature in the Sixteenth Century* (1954) pp. 215-221; GC Richards 'Coverdale and the Cursus' *Church Quarterly Review* Vol. 110, April 1930, pp.34-39

[332] Cf. PF Baum *The Other Harmony of Prose ... an essay in English prose rhythm* (1952) p.98; DW Harding *Words into rhythm: English speech rhythm in verse and prose* (1976) p.121ff

[333] R Bridges *Milton's Prosody* (1901) p.91

[334] T Puller *The Moderation of the Church of England* (1679) p.168

[335] T Tenison *A Sermon concerning the Wandring of the Mind in God's Service*.... (1691) p.26

[336] G Burnet *Four Discourses delivered to the Clergy of the Diocese of Sarum* (1694) p.312

[337] Cf. HC Porter *Reformation and Reaction in Tudor Cambridge* (1958) pp. 323-325

[338] S Patrick 'The Bishop of Ely's Letter to his Clergy, before his Primary Visitation, 1692' in *Four Discourses sent to the Clergy of the Diocese of Ely on Four*

Several Visitations (1704) p.3,4

[339] B Laney *A Sermon Preached before His Majesty at Whitehal, April 5. 1663* (1663) p.25
(Benjamin Laney (1591-1675) Former Chaplain to Charles I,1660 Bishop of Peterborough; 1663 Bishop of Lincoln; 1667 Bishop of Ely)

[340] O.U. *Parish-Churches No Conventicles, From the Minister's reading in the Desk when there is no Communion* 1683 pp.7, 8

[341] P Browne *The Sovereign's Authority And the Subjects Duty Plainly represented in a Sermon Preached at the Visitation April the 12th, 1681* (1682) p. 30

[342] J Jeffery *A Sermon Preached in the Cathedral Church of Norwich: At the Primary Visitation of ... John, Lord Bishop of Norwich. May 18. 1692.* (1692) p.15 (John Jeffery (1647-1720) Appointed vicar of St Peter Mancroft Norwich, 1678, Archdeacon of Norwich 1694, DD 1696)

[343] H Hammond *A Paraphrase and Annotations upon the Books of Psalms* (1659) Preface

[344] E Pelling *The Good Old Way*.... (1680) p.76

[345] T Comber *The Companion to the Temple*.... Vol. I (1688) Part I p.84
cf. H.C. *Brief Directions for our more Devout Behaviour in Time of Divine Service*.... (1693) p.76; Thomas Elborow *The Reasonableness of our Christian Service*.... (1677) pp. 33f; *The Faith and Practice of a Church of England-Man* (1688) pp. 85f

[346] H.C. *Brief Directions for our more Devout Behaviour*.... (1693) p.20

[347] T Elborow *The Reasonableness of our Christian Service*.... (1677) p.35

[348] T Comber *The Companion to the Temple*.... Vol. I (1688) p.86

[349] *An Answer to the Dissenters Objections against the Common Prayers* (1684) p.17
cf. RE McFarland 'The Response to Grace: Seventeenth Century Sermons and the Idea of Thanksgiving' *Church History* Vol. 44, No. 2, pp. 199-203

[350] H.C. *Brief Directions for our more Devout Behaviour*.... (1693) p.21

[351] T Comber *A Companion to the Temple*.... Vol. I (1688) p.84

[352] H.C. *Brief Directions for our more Devout Behaviour*.... (1693) pp20,21; Thomas Elborow *The Reasonableness of our Christian Service*.... (1677) p.39; *Faith and Practice of a Church of England-Man* (1688) p.85

[353] S Patrick *The Book of Psalms Paraphras'd* (1680)

[354] The wider dimensions of this phenomenon are explored in DS Greenwood 'The Seventeenth-Century English Poetical Biblical Paraphrase' (Cambridge University Ph.D. thesis 1985)

[355] H.C. *Brief Directions for our more Devout Behaviour*.... (1693) p.9

[356] S Patrick *The Devout Christian Instructed How to Pray and Give Thanks to God* (1730) 16th ed., pp. 156, 160

[357] *The Hours of Daily Prayer in and about the City of London,* 1692

[358] B Laney *A Sermon Preached before His Majesty*.... (1663) p.14,15
[Laney's sermon of 1663 came to be entitled 'Of Prayer to God' and remained significant for many years. It was reprinted and was quoted in a publication of 1688 (*A Letter of Advice to all the Members of the Church of England to come to the Divine Service Morning and Evening Every Day* (1688) p.9) and received acknowledgement in a marginal note in another sermon given by a Royal Chaplain in the next decade, (T Manningham *A Sermon concerning Publick*

Worship (1692) p.23) (Thomas Manningham - Bishop of Chichester 1709-1722).]

[359] D Grenville *The Compleat Conformist* (1684) p.19

[360] H Hamlin *Psalm Culture and Early Modern English Literature* (2004)

[361] *The Whole Booke of Psalmes collected into English Meeter by Thomas Sternhold, John Hopkins, and others: conferred with the Hebrew, with apt notes to sing them withall. Set forth and allowed to be sung in all Churches, of all the people together, before and after Morning and Evening Prayer; as also before & after Sermons: and moreover in private houses, for their godly solace and comfort, laying apart all ungodly songs and ballads, which tend only to the nourishing of vice, and corrupting of youth.* (A 1661 version of the title.)

[362] I Green *Print and Protestantism in Early Modern England* (2000) p.509

[363] N Temperley *The Music of the English Parish Church* (1983) p.122

[364] E.g. according to eds. TH Darlow and HF Moule *Historical Catalogue of the Printed Editions of the Holy Scripture in the Library of the British and Foreign Bible Society* (1963) Vol. I, out of 106 Bibles in this collection dated 1641-1700, only four volumes did not include an edition of this metrical psalter

[365] The provenance of 'Sternhold & Hopkins' has been traced in: R Zim *English Metrical Psalms - Poetry as Praise and Prayer 1535-1601* (1987); RA Leaver *'Goostly psalmes and spirituall songes': English and Dutch Metrical Psalms.... 1535-1566* (1991)

[366] Cf. T Young *The Metrical Psalms and Paraphrases* (1909)

[367] N Temperley *The Music of the English Parish Church* (1983) p.97

[368] J Harley *Music in Purcell's London* (1968) p.96

[369] See DS Greenwood 'The Seventeenth-Century English Poetical Biblical Paraphrase' (Cambridge University Ph.D. thesis 1985); P von Rohr-Sauer *English Metrical Psalms from 1600 to 1660* (1938)

[370] E.g. LL Martz *The Poetry of Meditation: A Study in English Religious Literature of the Seventeenth Century* (1954)

[371] B Keach *The Breach Repaired in God's Worship: Or, Singing of Psalms, Hymns, and Spiritual Songs, proved to be an Holy Ordinance....* (1691) Epistle Dedicatory p.vii

[372] E.g. lists of suitable psalms in: T.M. *The Whole Book of Psalms, as they are now sung in the Churches* (1688); B.P. *The Parish-Clerk's Vade Mecum* (1694)

[373] Included in B.P. *The Parish-Clerk's Vade Mecum* (1694)

[374] R Gough *The History of Myddle* (1981) p.45

[375] *Directory for the Publique Worship of God* (1645) pp.83,84

[376] See HO Old *The Patristic Roots of Reformed Worship* (1975) p.257

[377] RA Leaver *'Goostly psalmes and spirituall songes'....* (1991) p.214

[378] Elizabeth I *Injunctions* (1559) Paragraph 49

[379] Ed. W Jacobson *Fragmentary Illustrations of the History of the Book of Common Prayer....* (1874) pp. 55, 56

[380] T.M. *The Whole Book of Psalms....* (1688)

[381] see N Temperley 'John Playford and the Metrical Psalms' *Journal of the American Musicological Society* Vol. 25 1972, pp.331-378

[382] Petition to Parliament of the Corporation of Grantham cited in M Pointer *The Glory of Grantham* (1978) p.30

[383] W King *A Discourse concerning the Inventions of Men in the Worship of God*

(1694) p.21

[384] E Wetenhall *Of Gifts and Offices in the Publick Worship of God* (Dublin, 1679) p.414,426; (Edward Wetenhall (1636-1713) Minor Canon, Exeter 1667-74; Chanter of Christ Church, Dublin; Bishop of Cork & Ross 1679-1699; Bishop of Kilmore & Ardagh 1699-1713)

[385] Cf. AP Fox 'Aspects of Oral Culture and its Development in Early Modern England' (Cambridge University Ph.D. thesis 1992) pp.14f

[386] Cf. P Burke *Popular Culture in Early Modern Europe* (1978) p.124f

[387] Cf. R Finnegan *Oral Poetry: Its Nature, Significance and Social Context* (1972) considers the importance of parallelism pp.98-102, 127-130, and offers examples of oral poetry sung or spoken very slowly p.123

[388] W Gould, Minister of Kenne in Devon *Conformity According to Canon Justified* .... (1674) (Visitation Sermon preached at Exeter Cathedral on I Cor. 14.40 'Let all things be done Decently and in Order') p.42f.

[389] W.B. *Corporal Worship, Discuss'd and Defended: in a Sermon Preached at the Visitation April 21 1670 in Saviours-Church Southwark* (1670) p.15

[390] Ed. A Macfarlane *The Diary of Ralph Josselin 1616-1683* (1971) p.208, entry for 23rd June 1650

[391] J Spurr *The Restoration Church of England, 1646-1689* (1991) p.355

[392] DA Spaeth 'Common Prayer? Popular Observance of the Anglican Liturgy in Restoration Wiltshire' in ed. SJ Wright *Parish, Church and People: Local Studies in Lay Religion 1350-1750* (1988) p.142

[393] Order of 3rd December, 1696, cited in *A Breif (sic) and Full Account of Mr Tate's and Mr Brady's New Version of the Psalms* (1698) pp.6,7

[394] Cf. FR Bolton *The Caroline Tradition of the Church of Ireland* (1958)p.149

[395] *A Breif and Full Account....* (1698) p.2,3

[396] *A Breif and Full Account....* (1698) p.12

[397] *A Breif and Full Account....* (1698) p.37

[398] *Remarks Upon a Late Pamphlet Entituled, A Brief and Full Account of Mr Tate's and Mr Brady's New Version of the Psalms* (1699) p.21

[399] *Remarks Upon a Late Pamphlet....* (1699) p.22

[400] W Beveridge *A Defence of the Book of Psalms collected into English Metre, by Thomas Sternhold, John Hopkins, and others. With Critical Observations on the Late New Version Compar'd with the Old* (1710) p.41

[401] C S Lewis *English Literature in the Sixteenth Century* (1954) p.247

[402] T Mace *Musicks Monument* (1676) p.3

[403] Cf. W Shaw *The Succession of Organists of the Chapel Royal....* (1991) p.330f

[404] R Portman *The Soules Life* (1645) p.132

[405] J Playford *Whole Book of Psalms* (1677) Preface

[406] J Playford *Psalms and Hymns in Solemn Musick* (1671) Preface

[407] Cf. C Garside 'The Origins of Calvin's Theology of Music : 1536-1543' *Transactions of the American Philosophical Society* Vol. 69 Part 4 1979

[408] R Watson *The Right Reverend Doctor John Cosin, Late Lord Bishop of Durham, His Opinion ... What slender Authority, if any, the English Psalms, in Rhime and Metre, have ever had for the publick use they have obtained in our Churches: Freely rendered in two Letters, with Annotations....* (1684) p.57

[409] R Watson *The Right Reverend Doctor John Cosin, Late Lord Bishop of Durham, His Opinion....* (1684) p.92

[410] L Milbourne *The Psalms of David in English Metre* (1698) (Preface) (Luke Milbourne (?1650-1720) Rector of Osmandiston, Norfolk, 1677-1720; Lecturer of St Leonard, Shoreditch 1688-1720; Rector of St Ethelburga, London, 1704-1720)

[411] H King *Psalmes of David* (1651) Preface

[412] J Lloyd *A Treatise of the Episcopacy, Liturgies, and Ecclesiastical Ceremonies of the Primitive Times* (1661) p.39

[413] N.H. *Gospel Musick. Or, the Singing of Davids Psalms, &c In the publick Congregation, or private Families asserted....* (1644) p.24

[414] W Fenner *The Spiritual Mans Directory* (1656) p.29

[415] W Nicolson *Davids Harp Strung and Tuned* (1662) Preface

[416] T.M. *The Whole Book of Psalms* (1688) Preface

[417] W Marshal *The Gospel Mystery of Sanctification* (1692) p.304

[418] J Holland *The Psalmists of Britain....* (1843) Vol. II, pp.60,63

[419] F Roberts *Clavis Bibliorum* (1665); John Lightfoot 'Sermon Preached at St Mary's, Cambridge June 24, 1660' in *Works* Vol. VII (1822)

[420] F Roberts *Clavis Bibliorum* (1665) pp.171, 172

[421] F Roberts *Clavis Bibliorum* (1665) p.171

[422] F Roberts *Clavis Bibliorum* (1665) p.142

[423] G Abbot *The Whole Book of Psalms Paraphrased....* (1650); S Patrick *The Book of Psalms Paraphras'd* (1680)

[424] See J Lightfoot 'Journal of the Assembly of Divines' in *Works* Vol. XIII, (1824) pp. 325, 344

[425] Lightfoot *Works* Vol. VII, (1822) pp. 36ff

[426] Lightfoot *Works* Vol. VII, (1822) p. 43

[427] Lightfoot *Works* Vol. VII, (1822) p. 44

[428] M Scrivener *The Method and Means to a true Spiritual Life* (1688) pp.357,358; (Matthew Scrivener (?-1688) Vicar of Haslingfield, Cambs, 1666-1688)

[429] *Remarks Upon a Late Pamphlet Entituled, A Brief and Full Account....* (1699) p.20

[430] T Ford *Singing of Psalms the Duty of Christians....* (1659); J Cotton *Singing of Psalmes a Gospel-Ordinance* (1650)

[431] T Ford *Singing of Psalms the Duty of Christians....* (1659) p.60

[432] Cf. J Cotton *Singing of Psalmes a Gospel-Ordinance* (1650) p.39,40

[433] *An Accompt of all the Proceedings of the Commissioners of both Persuasions....* (1661) p.31

[434] Cf. B Fischer 'The Common Prayer of Congregation and Family in the Ancient Church' *Studia Liturgica* Vol. 10 No. 3/4 1974 p.118

[435] DK Tripp *Daily Prayer in the Reformed Tradition: An Initial Survey* (1996) pp.32-36

[436] And the Curate that ministereth in every Parish-Church or Chapel, being at home, and not being otherwise reasonably hindered, shall say the same in the Parish-Church or Chapel where he ministereth, and shall cause a Bell to be tolled thereunto a convenient time before he begin, that the people may come to hear God's Word, and to pray with him. (*Book of Common Prayer*)

[437] Cf. S Patrick *Discourse concerning Prayer, Especially of Frequenting the Daily Public Prayers* (1686); J Mapletoft *A Perswasive to the Consciencious frequenting the daily Publick Prayers of the Church of England* (1687); T

Comber *A Discourse Concerning the Daily Frequenting the Common Prayer* (1687); *A Letter of Advice to all the Members of the Church of England To Come to the Divine Service Morning and Evening Every Day* (1688)

[438] N Smith, (Vicar of Braughing, Herts) *A Sabbath of Rest*.... (1675) pp.9f

[439] S Patrick *Devout Christian instructed how to Pray*.... (1730) Preface

[440] E Stillingfleet *The Bishop of Worcester's Charge to the Clergy of his Diocese* (1691) pp. 23f; Nicolas Stratford *The Bishop of Chester's Charge* (1692) p.19

[441] J Inett, The Chanter of Lincoln Cathedral *A Guide to the Devout Christian* 2nd ed. (1691) Part II, Preface

[442] T Pittis *Discourse of Prayer* (1683) p.106

[443] D Jones *A Sermon of the Absolute Necessity of Family-Duties* (1692) p.29

[444] *The form of prayers and ministration of the Sacraments, &c. used in the Englishe Congregation at Geneua: and approued, by the famous and godly learned man, Iohn Caluyn* (1556) pp, 156-160, pp. 162-165; cf. WD Maxwell *John Knox's Genevan Service Book 1556* (London. Oliver & Boyd, 1931) pp. 65, 76.

[445] I Green *Print and Protestantism in Early Modern England* (2000) p.510

[446] 'Concerning Family Religion. A Sermon Preached at St Lawrence Jury, July the 13th. 1684' in J Tillotson *Six Sermons* (1694) pp.49ff.

[447] J Tillotson *Six Sermons* (1694) p.50

[448] J Tillotson *Six Sermons* (1694) p.50

[449] J Tillotson *Six Sermons* (1694) pp.53,54

[450] J Tillotson *Six Sermons* (1694) p.55

[451] J Tillotson *Six Sermons* (1694) pp.65,66

[452] J Tillotson *Six Sermons* (1694) pp.53, 54

[453] J Tillotson *Six Sermons* (1694) pp.83, 84

[454] R Allestree *The Works of the Learned and Pious Author of the Whole Duty of Man* (1684) p.44

[455] Cf. P. Elmen 'Richard Allestree and the Whole Duty of Man' *The Library (Transactions of the Bibliographical Society)* 5th Series Vol. VI No. 1, 1951, p.19-27

[456] R Allestree *Works*.... (1684) p.44

[457] R Allestree *Works*.... (1684) p.44

[458] Cf. R Morse *The Clergyman's Office* (Visitation Sermon) (1699) p.14; L Addison *The Christians Daily Sacrifice*.... (1698) pp.89,90; T Pollard *The Necessity and Advantages of Family Prayer* (Dublin, 1696) p.5; G Barker *Sermons upon Several Texts of Scripture* (York, 1697) p.83

[459] R Kidder *The Charge of Richard, Lord Bishop of Bath and Wells, to the Clergy of his Diocese*.... (1692) pp.14,15 [Richard Kidder, ? - 1703; ejected 1662; Anglican rector 1664-1691; Canon of Norwich 1681; Dean of Peterborough 1689; Bishop of Bath & Wells 1691-1703]

[460] S Patrick *The Devout Christian instructed how to Pray and give thanks to God: or, a book of devotions for Families: and for particular persons in most of the concerns of humane life* (1st ed. 1673; 11th ed. 1700.) Preface

[461] S Patrick *The Devout Christian instructed how to Pray*.... (1730) p.1

[462] S Patrick *The Devout Christian instructed how to Pray*.... (1730) p.33

[463] S Patrick *The Devout Christian instructed how to Pray*.... (A short prayer at home, after we are come from Church, before Dinner) (1730) p.158

[464] S Patrick *The Devout Christian instructed how to Pray*.... (A Thanksgiving for any publick or private Mercies) (1730) p.464

[465] S Patrick *The Devout Christian instructed how to Pray*.... (1730) p.146

[466] L Bayly *The Practise of Piety Directing the Christian How to Walk that he may Please God* (31st ed. 1642; 42nd ed. 1695)

[467] L Bayly *The Practise of Piety*.... (1661) pp.294ff

[468] L Bayly *The Practise of Piety*.... (1661) pp.315ff

[469] See CJ Stranks *Anglican Devotion* London, SCM Press, 1961, pp.41-63

[470] L Bayly *The Practise of Piety*.... (1661) p.399

[471] L Bayly *The Practise of Piety*.... (1661) pp.294-5, 315

[472] *Domestick Devotions for the Use of Families and of Particular Persons, whereunto are prefixed some earnest Perswasives to Prayer and Devotion* (1683) Preface, np

[473] H Hammond *A Practicall Catechisme* (Oxford, 1645) pp.259, 267 (Benjamin Jenks, the Rector of Harley in Shropshire, and Chaplain to the Earl of Bradford, similarly misrepresented Hammond's position - cf. Jenks' Preface to: *Prayers and Offices of Devotion, for Families*.... (1697))

[474] *Domestick Devotions*.... (1683) p.59

[475] J Meriton, [Rector of St Michael Cornhill & Lecturer of St Martins-in-the-Fields] *Forms of Prayer for every Day of the Week; Morning and Evening. Composed for the use of Private Families* (1682) Preface

[476] W Bell (Vicar of St Sepulchres) *Joshua's Resolution to Serve God with his Family* (1672) [A Sermon on Joshua 24.15]

[477] E.g. J.A. *Secret and Family Prayers*.... (Cambridge, 1677) 'Fitted for the Use and Benefit of the Inhabitants of Cartmel in Lancashire'; W Assheton, (Rector of Beckenham) *A Method of Daily Devotion* (1697); B Jenks, (Rector of Harley in Shropshire) *Prayers and Offices of Devotion* (1697)

[478] W Payne, (Rector of St Mary White-Chappel, Chaplain in Ordinary) *Family Religion* (Sermon on Joshua 24v15) (1691) p.20

[479] F Turner *A Letter to the Clergy of the Diocese of Ely* (Cambridge, 1686) p.15

[480] *An Earnest Exhortation from a Minister to his Parishioners to Discharge the Duty of Morning and Evening Prayer in their Families* (Worcester, 1700)

[481] J Tillotson *Six Sermons* (1694) p.54

[482] W Thomas (Rector of Ubley in Somerset) *A Preservative of Piety* (1662) Part 2, Chapter 4

[483] W Thomas *A Preservative of Piety* (1662) p.201

[484] L Bayly *The Practise of Piety*.... (1661) pp.312ff

[485] Further consideration of the careful reflection of this time on this issue can be found in J Wells (Minister of St. Olave, Jewry) 'How may we make melody in our hearts with singing of Psalms? [A sermon on Ephes. v. 19.]' in ed. S Annesley *A Supplement to the Morning-Exercise at Cripplegate* (1676) pp. 174-190

[486] J.A. *Secret and Family Prayers* (Cambridge 1677) Preface

[487] J.A. loc. cit.

[488] R Morse *The Clergyman's Office ... A Sermon preached at the Triennial Visitation of ... Edward Lord Bishop of Gloucester*.... (1699) p.13 (Robert Morse (?1661-1703) Rector of Willersley, Gloucestershire 1691; Rector of Tredington, Worcestershire 1701)

[489] C. Garrett 'The Rhetoric of Supplication: Prayer Theory in Seventeenth Century England' *Renaissance Quarterly* Vol. 46 No. 2 1993, p.329

[490] R Allestree *Works*.... (1684) p.45

[491] R Allestree *Private Devotions for Several Occasions Ordinary and Extraordinary* (1660), p.2

[492] R Allestree *Private Devotions*.... (1660) p.4

[493] R Allestree *Private Devotions*.... (1660) p.6

[494] R Allestree *Private Devotions*.... (1660) cf. the 'Brief Paraphrase on the Lord's Prayer' pp. 32-35

[495] R Allestree *Private Devotions*.... (1660) pp.21-22

[496] J Taylor *The Rules and Exercises for Holy Living*.... (1817) p.22

[497] J Taylor *The Rules and Exercises for Holy Living*.... (1817) p.28f

[498] J Taylor *The Rules and Exercises for Holy Living*.... (1817) p.29f

[499] T Comber *Frequent and Fervent Prayer* (1687) p.16

[500] DN Griffiths *Bibliography of the Book of Common Prayer*.... (2002) pp.115-133

[501] *A Brief Exhortation with the means to promote Piety*.... (1669) p.19

[502] E.g. *Prayers in the Closet* (Oxford, 1689; London, 1692)

[503] *Forms of Private Devotion for Every Day in the Week in a Method agreeable to the Liturgy*.... (1691) Preface

[504] *The Church of England-Man's Private Devotions* (1691)

[505] *Private Devotion and a Brief Explication of the Ten Commandments* (Oxford, 1689); *Forms of Prayer Collected for the Private Use of a Soldier* (1687)

[506] J Taylor *The Rules and Exercises for Holy Living*.... (1817) p.46

[507] T Lynford, Royal Chaplain, *A Sermon Concerning the Worship of God in Private* (1691) p.10f

[508] E.g. L Andrewes *A Manual of Private Devotions* 1st ed. 1648; 5th ed. 1692; A Douglas *The Countess of Morton's Daily Exercise* 1st ed. 1666; 17th ed. 1696

[509] *Of the Daily Practice of Piety* (1660); W Laud *A Summarie of Devotions* (1667)

[510] Much of the contents from *Of the Daily Practice of Piety* was re-issued, but under a different title (*Preparations to a Holy Life* (1684)) and without the material about the seven hours.

[511] A Douglas *The Countess of Morton's Daily Exercise* np

[512] A Douglas *The Countess of Morton's Daily Exercise* np

[513] S Patrick *A Discourse concerning Prayer* (1848) p.137

[514] T Ken *Directions for Prayer, for the Diocess of Bath and Wells* (nd, ?1686) p.11

[515] R Allestree 'The Gentleman's Calling' in *Works* (1684) p.436f

[516] E Wetenhall *Enter into thy Closet* (1666) p.36

[517] E Wetenhall *Enter into thy Closet* (1666) p.43f

[518] E Wetenhall *Enter into thy Closet* (1666) p.47f

[519] J Taylor *The Great Exemplar* (1st ed. 1649, 7th ed. 1684) (1849) p.148

[520] J Taylor *The Great Exemplar* (1849) pp.148-166

[521] T Lynford *A Sermon Concerning the Worship of God in Private* (1691) p.2

[522] J Taylor *The Great Exemplar* (1849) pp. 537f

[523] N Resbury *Of Closet-Prayer* (1693) pp.19f
(Nathanael Resbury (?1643-1711) Vicar of Wandsworth, Surrey 1674-1687; Rector of Broughton Gifford, Wiltshire 1687; Rector of St Paul, Shadwell 1689; Chaplain to William & Mary from 1691; Oxford DD 1692)

[524] T Lynford *A Sermon Concerning the Worship of God in Private* (1691) p.17f

[525] J Moore *Of Religious Melancholy* (1692) p.33
(John Moore: Prebendary of Ely 1679-1691; Cambridge DD 1681; Rector of St Andrew's Holborn 1689-1691; Bishop of Norwich 1691-1707; Bishop of Ely 1707-1714)

[526] C Hickman *A Sermon Preached at St Bride's Church on St Caecilias's Day Nov 22, 1695* (1696) p.8
(Charles Hickman (1648-1713) Oxford DD 1685; Chaplain to William & Mary; Rector of Burnham, Buckinghamshire & Lecturer of St James Westminster 1698-1702; Bishop of Derry 1703)

[527] H Thorndike *Of Religious Assemblies....* (1642) p.426

[528] A Sparrow *Rationale upon the Book of Common Prayer* (1664) p.375

[529] R Hooker *Of the Laws of Ecclesiastical Polity* V xxiii.1; I iv.1,2; I xv.2; I vi.1; I viii.4

[530] T Wemys [Vicar of Whittingham, Northumberland] *Beth-Hak-Kodesh or the Separation and Consecration of Places for God's publick Service and Worship and the Reverence due unto them vindicated* (1674) pp.137,138

[531] *A New-years-Gift Composed of Prayers and Meditations with Devotions for Several Occasions* (3rd Edition, 1683) Part III 1685, pp.191f

[532] N Stratford [Bishop of Chester 1689 - 1707] *Of the Reverence due to God in his Publick Worship. A Sermon Preach'd before the King and Queen, at Whitehall, March 25, 1694* (1694) p.13

[533] T Dorrington [Rector of Hopton Castle, Shropshire] *Family Devotions for Sunday Evenings throughout the Year, Being Practical Discourses with Suitable Prayers* Vol. 4 (1695) p145

[534] J Stillingfleete [Rector of Beckingham, Lincolnshire; Late Fellow of St Johns Cambridge] *Shecinah: Or a Demonstration of the Divine Presence in the Places of Religious Worship* (1663) Preface to Reader
cf. W Beveridge *The Great Necessity and Advantage of Publick Prayer and Frequent Communion* (9th Edition, 1750) p.11; S Patrick *A Discourse Concerning Prayer* (1848) pp.45,46; J Kelsey [Rector of Newton-Tony, Wiltshire] *A Sermon Preached at the Consecration of a Chappel in the House of John Collins, Esq. of Chute in Wiltshire* (1674) p.26

[535] H Felton [Rector of Melford, Suffolk, Royal Chaplain] *The Eternal Joys of God's Presence - A Sermon preached at the Temple-Church upon All-Saints Day* (1699) p.14

[536] R Brownrig [Appointed Bishop of Exeter 1642] *Twenty Five Sermons* Vol.2 (1664) p.56

[537] *A True Notion of the Worship of God, Or a Vindication of the Service of the Church of England* (1673) pp.38f

[538] *A True Notion of the Worship of God....* (1673) p.62; cf. T Manningham [Rector of St Andrews Holborn, Chaplain-in-ordinary] *A Sermon concerning Publick Worship, Preached before the Queen on Wednesday the 23^d of March, 169½* (1692) pp.7,8,19,20; G Burghope [Rector of Little Gaddesden, Hertfordshire, & Chaplain to the Earl of Bridgwater] *An Essay to Revive the Necessity of the Ancient Charity and Piety* (1695) p.79,80

[539] T Thurlin [Rector of Gaywood, Fellow of St John's Cambridge] *The Necessity of Obedience to Spiritual Governours, Asserted in a Sermon at an Episcopal Visitation in Kings-Lyn, Norfolk, on the Tenth day of May, 1686.* (Cambridge,

1686) pp. 13,14

[540] Cf. S Biderman *Scripture and Knowledge - An Essay on Religious Epistemology* (1995) pp.102-103

[541] Sternhold & Hopkins (1661) Ps. 96v9

[542] Sternhold & Hopkins (1661) Ps. 96v5

[543] T Manningham *Praise and Adoration. Or, A Sermon on Trinity-Sunday before the University of Oxford* (1682) p.6

[544] F Atterbury [Appointed Royal Chaplain 1694, DD 1701, Bishop of Rochester, 1713-1723] *A Sermon before the Queen at White-Hall May 29. 1692* (1692) pp. 17, 24

[545] *A Prayer to be Used at the Opening - the Cathedral Church of St Paul December 2 1697 Being the Thanksgiving Day* (1697); this particular extract draws on: 2 Chr. 6 v. 18; Is. 66 v. 1; 2 Chr. 20 v. 9; I Pet. 2 v. 5; Heb. 13 v. 15.

[546] Cf. R Targoff 'The Performance of Prayer: Sincerity and Theatricality in Early Modern England' *Representations* Issue 60, 1997 p.60

[547] R Brownrig *Twenty Five Sermons* Vol. II (1664) p.56

[548] *The Liberty of Prayer Asserted, and Garded from Licentiousness* (by a Minister of the Church of England) (1695) p.54

[549] R Lucas [Vicar of St Stephens, Coleman Street] *Practical Christianity, or an account of the Holiness which the Gospel enjoins....* (1693) Part 4, p.296

[550] L Addison [? - 1703; Royal Chaplain 1670; Oxford DD 1675; Prebendary of Salisbury 1678; Dean of Lichfield 1683; Archdeacon of Coventry 1684] *The Christians Daily Sacrifice, Duly Offered. Or, A Practical Discourse Teaching the Right Performance of Prayer* (1698) pp.2, 4

[551] C Hickman *A Sermon Preached at St Bride's Church, on St. Caecilia's Day, Nov 22. 1695. Being the Anniversary Feast of the Lovers of Musick* (1696) p.15

[552] W Gostwyke [Rector of Purley 1684-1719] *Pray for the Peace of Jerusalem: A Sermon Preach'd at St Mary's, in Reading, at the Visitation of the Reverend Mr William Richards, Arch-Deacon of Berks. April the 12th 1692* (1692) p.2

[553] Bryan Duppa (1589-1662) Dean of Christ Church, Oxford 1629-1638; Bishop of Chichester 1638-1641; Bishop of Salisbury 1641; Bishop of Winchester 1660-1662

[554] B Duppa *Holy Rules and Helps to Devotion, Both in Prayer and Practice; written in the time of his Sequestration* (1679) pp. 2,3,4,6

[555] B Duppa *Holy Rules and Helps to Devotion* (1679) pp.24-26

[556] W Annand *Fides Catholica* (1661) p.473

[557] T Fuller 'The Appeal of Injured Innocence' cited in FJ Trott 'Prelude to Restoration: Laudians, Conformists and the struggle for 'Anglicanism' in the 1650's ' (London University Ph.D. thesis, 1992) pp.188f

[558] T Naish [Sub-Dean, Salisbury Cathedral] *Sermon Preach'd at the Cathedral Church of Sarum Novemb. 22. 1700 Before a Society of Lovers of Musick* (1701) p.24

[559] *A True Notion of the Worship of God: OR a Vindication of the Service of the Church of England* (1673) pp. 38, 39

[560] R Kidder *Twelve Sermons* (1697) p.235

[561] L Atterbury [? -1731; Rector of Sywell, Northants 1685-1707; one of the Preachers to Princess Ann of Denmark] *Ten Sermons preach'd before Her Royal Highness The Princess Ann of Denmark At the Chappel at St James*

(1699) p. 106f

[562] A Sparrow *The Bishop of Exons Caution to his Diocese Against False Doctrines Delivered in a Sermon at Truro in Cornwall at his Primary Visitation* (1669) p.14

[563] B Duppa *Holy Rules and Helps to Devotion* (1679) pp.2,3

[564] E Pelling *A Practical Discourse upon Prayer* (2nd ed. 1694) p.1

[565] J Moore *Of the Wisdom and Goodness of Providence - Two Sermons preached before the Queen at Whitehall on August 17, 24 MDCXC* (1690) p.7

[566] E Pelling *A Practical Discourse upon Prayer* (1694) p.12

[567] E Bagshaw [Chaplain to the Earl of Anglesey, Student of Christ Church] *A Brief Treatise about the Spiritual Nature of God and of his Worship* (1662) p12

[568] W Sherlock *A Discourse concerning the Knowledge of Jesus Christ and our Union and Communion with Him* (1674) p.193

[569] P Avis *Anglicanism and the Christian Church* (1989) p.86

[570] A Littleton [Rector of Chelsey, Middlesex, Royal Chaplain] *Sixty One Sermons* (1680) Part II, p.50
cf. T Horton *One Hundred Select Sermons* (1679) p.446; cf. J Conant *Sermons preach'd on Several Occasions* Vol. 3 (1698) p.506: 'fervent Prayers do much prevail with God. ... Because these fervent breathings of the heart in Prayer are from the Spirit of God.'

[571] J Edwards *Sermons on Special Occasions and Subjects* (1698) - A Sermon Preach'd before the Clergy at the Archdeacon of Ely's Visitation - p. 106.
cf. E Reynolds [Bishop of Norwich] *The Pastoral Office Opened in a Visitation-Sermon preached at Ipswich October 10.1662* (1663) p.39

[572] Cf. C Garbett 'The Rhetoric of Supplication: Prayer Theory in Seventeenth Century England' *Renaissance Quarterly* Vol. 46 No.2 Summer 1993 pp.338-345

[573] E Hough [Minister of Penistone, near Barnsley, Yorkshire] *A Country Minister's Serious Advice to his Parishioners: Containing many Profitable Directions, Tending both to Inform their Understanding and Reform their Lives* (1700) p.10

[574] R Neville [Rector of Ansty] *The Nature & Causes of Hardness of Heart, Together with the Remedies against it. Discovered in a Sermon, Preached first before the Honourable Society of Lincolns-Inn, and afterwards before the University in Great St Maries Church in Cambridge* (1683) p.20

[575] J Sharp [?1645-1714; Dean of Norwich 1681-1689; Royal Chaplain 1686-1691; Dean Of Canterbury 1689-1691; Archbishop of York 1691-1714] *A Perswasive to Prayer - A Sermon preach'd before the King at St James's March 13 1698* (1700) p.9

[576] J Sharp *Fifteen Sermons* (1700) p.489

[577] S Patrick *The Work of the Ministry Represented to the Clergy of the Diocess of Ely* (1698) p.20 in *Four Discourse sent to the Clergy of the Diocese of Ely on Four Several Visitations* (1704)

[578] T Bradley *A Sermon Ad Clerum At the Visitation of the Deane and Chapter there, holden the 19th day of November, Anno Dom. 1662 By ... Acceptus ... Arch-Bishop of York....* (York, 1663) p.18

[579] G Stanhope [Royal Chaplain; Vicar of Lewisham, Kent] *A Sermon concerning*

*God's Deferring to answer Mens Prayers: Preached before the King and
Queen at Whitehall November the 11th 1694* (1695) p.7

[580] G Stanhope *A Sermon concerning God's Deferring to answer Mens Prayers....*
(1695) pp.7, 14

[581] J Conant *Sermons Preach'd on Several Occasions* Vol. 3 (1698) p.487

[582] G Stanhope *A Sermon concerning God's Deferring to answer Mens Prayers....*
(1695) p.28

[583] W Gearing *Clavis Coeli: or a Treatise setting forth the Nature, the Parts, and
Kinds of Prayer....* (1663) p. 91

cf. T Bradley [Rector of Ackworth, Prebendary of York] *Elijah's Epitaph, and
the Motto of all Mortalls in the Other Reason in the Text, persuading him into a
willingness to Dye, in these words, I am no better than my Fathers, I Kin. 19.4*
(York 1670) p.40

[584] A Littleton *Sixty One Sermons* (1680) Part 2, p.55

[585] W Sherlock *A Sermon Preached at the Temple Church, May 29. 1692* (1692) pp.
11-13

[586] E Warren [Rector of Worlington, Suffolk] *A Defence of Liturgies* (1687) p.10

[587] F Kermode *Forms of Attention* (1985) p.77

[588] Cf. D Boyarin *Intertextuality and the Reading of Midrash* (1990) p.128

[589] Cf. Hl Bailey *The Liturgy Compared with the Bible* (1853) in which a Biblical
root is traced for every phrase of the Prayer Book.

[590] J Findon 'The Non Jurors and the Church of England 1689-1716' (Oxford
University Ph.D. thesis, 1978) p.153

[591] *Publick Devotion and the Common Service of the Church of England, Justify'd
and Recommended, to all honest and well meaning (however prejudic'd)
DISSENTERS* (sic) (nd - BL cat records 1680) pp.20, 21

[592] C Gibbes [Rector of Stanford-Rivers, Essex, Prebendary of Westminster] *XXXI
Sermons Preached to the Parishioners of Stanford-Rivers in Essex* (1677)
p.271f

[593] Cf. B Philpotts *Edda and Saga* (1931) p.162 cited in R Finnegan 'Literacy versus
Non-Literacy: The Great Divide' in ed. R Horton and R Finnegan *Modes of
Thought* (1973) p. 124

[594] L Andrewes *Nineteen Sermons Concerning Prayer* (Cambridge, 1641) p.450

Bibliography - Primary Sources

(All items purport to have been published in London, unless stated otherwise.)

A, J. *Secret and Family Prayers*.... (Cambridge, 1677)

Abbot, George. *The Whole Book of Psalms Paraphrased, or, made easier for any to understand*.... (1650)

Accompt of all the Proceedings of the Commissioners of both Persuasions, appointed by His Sacred Majesty, according to letters patents, for the review of the Book of Common Prayer, &c. (1661)

Addison, Lancelot. *The Christians Daily Sacrifice, Duly Offered. Or, A Practical Discourse Teaching the Right Performance of Prayer* (1698)

Allestree, Richard. *Private Devotions for Several Occasions Ordinary and Extraordinary* (1660)

Allestree, Richard. *The Works of the Learned and Pious Author of the Whole Duty of Man* (1684)

Allington, John. *The Reform'd Samaritan: or, the Worship of God by measures of spirit and truth* (1678)

Allington, John. *A brief Apologie for the Sequestred Clergie...In a letter from a sequestred divine to Mr Stephen Marshall* (1649)

Allsop, Vincent. *Duty and Interest United in Prayer and Praise for Kings, and all that are in Authority* (1695)

An Anti-Brekekekex-Coax-Coax. Or a Throat-Hapse for the Frogges and Toades that lately Crept abroad, Croaking against the Common-Prayer-book and Episcopacy (1660)

Anatomie of the Common Prayer-Book... (1661)

Anatomy of the Service Book (1642)

Andrewes, Lancelot. *Nineteen Sermons Concerning Prayer* (Cambridge 1641)

Andrewes, Lancelot. *A Manual of Private Devotions* (1648)

Annand, William. *Fides Catholica* (1661)

Answer to the Dissenters Objections against the Common Prayers (1684)

Arderne, James. *A Sermon Preached at the Visitation of ... John Lord Bishop of Chester, at Chester* (1677)

Articles of Visitation and Enquiry ... of Every Parish with the Diocess of Lincoln. In the Metropolitical Visitation of ... William ... Archbishop of Canterbury (1686)

Articles to be Enquired of By the Ministers, Church-Wardens and Side-men of every Parish within the Arch-Deaconry of Colchester.... (1662)

Assheton, William. *A Method of Daily Devotion* (1697)

Atterbury, Francis. *A Sermon before the Queen at White-Hall May 29. 1692* (1692)

Atterbury, Lewis. *Ten Sermons preach'd before Her Royal Highness The Princess Ann of Denmark At the Chappel at St James* (1699)

Ayliffe, John. *Parergon Juris Canonici Anglicani* (1726)

B, S. *An Examination of Dr Comber's Scholastical History of the Primitive and General Use of Liturgies in the Christian Church* (1690)

B, S. *A Second Examination*.... (1691)

B, W. *Corporal Worship, Discuss'd and Defended: in a Sermon Preached at the Visitation April 21 1670 in Saviours-Church Southwark* (1670)

Bagshaw, Edward. *A Brief Treatise about the Spiritual Nature of God and of his Worship* (1662)

Bales, Peter. *Oratio Dominica: or, the Lords Prayer, pleading for Better Entertainment in the Church of England. A Sermon Preached at Saint Mary Woolnoth, London, Jan 11. 1643* (1643)

Barbon, John. *Λειτουργια Θειοτερα Εργια: or Liturgie a most Divine Service: in answer to a late Pamphlet stiled, Common-Prayer-Book no Divine Service....* (Oxford, 1662)

Barker, George. *Sermons upon Several Texts of Scripture* (York, 1697)

Bayly, Lewis. *The Practise of Piety Directing the Christian How to Walk that he may Please God* (1661)

Bell, William. *Joshua's Resolution to Serve God with his Family* (1672)

Beveridge, William. *A Defence of the Book of Psalms collected into English Metre, by Thomas Sternhold, John Hopkins, and others. With Critical Observations on the Late New Version Compar'd with the Old* (1710)

Beveridge, William. *The Great Necessity and Advantage of Publick Prayer and Frequent Communion* (1750)

Beveridge, William. *Works* Vol. VI (Oxford, Parker Society, 1842)

Beveridge, William. *The Excellency and Usefulness of the Common Prayer* (1681)

Blackall, Ofspring. *A Sermon Preached at Brentwood in Essex, October the 7th, 1693. At the Visitation of... Henry, Lord Bishop of London* (2nd ed. 1699)

Book of Common-Prayer and Administration of the Sacraments and other Rites & Ceremonies of the Church , According to the Use of The Church of England.... (1662)

Book of Homilies (1822)

Bradley, Thomas *A Sermon Ad Clerum At the Visitation of the Deane and Chapter there, holden the 19th day of November, Anno Dom. 1662 By ... Acceptus ... Arch-Bishop of York....* (York, 1663)

Bradley, Thomas. *Elijah's Epitaph, and the Motto of all Mortalls in the Other Reason in the Text, persuading him into a willingness to Dye, in these words, I am no better than my Fathers, I Kin. 19.4* (York 1670)

Breif (sic) and Full Account of Mr Tate's and Mr Brady's New Version of the Psalms (1698)

Brief Exhortation with the means to promote Piety.... (1669)

Bright, George. *A Treatise of Prayer* (1678)

Browne, Philip. *The Sovereign's Authority And the Subjects Duty Plainly represented in a Sermon Preached at the Visitation April the 12th, 1681* (1682)

Brownrig, Ralph *Twenty Five Sermons* Vol.2 (1664)

Burghope, George. *An Essay to Revive the Necessity of the Ancient Charity and Piety* (1695)

Burnet, Gilbert. *A Discourse of the Pastoral Care* (1692)

Burnet, Gilbert. *Four Discourses delivered to the Clergy of the Diocese of Sarum* (1694)

C, H. *Brief Directions for our more Devout Behaviour in Time of Divine Service. With a short rationale on the Common-Prayer* (1693)

Carr, Alan. *A Peaceable Moderator: or some plain Considerations to give Satisfaction to such as stand Disaffected to our Book of Common Prayer* (1665)

Casaubon, Méric. *The Vindication of the Lords Prayer* (1660)

Casaubon, Méric. *A Treatise Concerning Enthusiasme, As It is an Effect of Nature: but is mistaken by many for either Divine Inspiration, or Diabolical Possession* (1655)

Cave, John. *A Sermon preached in a Country-Audience on the late Day of Fasting and Prayer: January 30* (1679)

Cave, William. *Primitive Christianity* (1673)

Charles I. *Proclamation concerning the Book of Common-Prayer and the Directory for Publike Worship* (1645)

Charles I. *Εικων Βασιλικη* (1649)

Charles II. *Proclamation for the Observation of the Lords Day* (1663)

Charles II. *Declaration of 25th October 1660 Concerning Ecclesiasticall Affaires* (1660)

Church of England-Man's Private Devotions (1691)

Clark, Joshua. *A Sermon Preached in the Parish Church of Grantham, July 12. 1697....* (1698)

Clarkson, David. *Discourse Concerning Liturgies* (1689)

Comber, Thomas. *A Discourse Concerning the Daily Frequenting the Common Prayer* (1687)

Comber, Thomas. *Scholastical History of the Primitive and General Use of Liturgies in the Christian Church together with an Answer to Mr Dav. Clarkson's late Discourse Concerning Liturgies* (1690)

Comber, Thomas. *A Companion to the Temple: or, a Help to Devotion in the Use of the Common Prayer....* (1684; 3rd ed. 1688, Vol. 2 1702)

Comber, Thomas. *The Examiner Briefly Examined....* (1691)

Comber, Thomas. *The Examiner Examined: Being a Vindication of the History of Liturgies* (1691)

Comber, Thomas. The Autobiographies and Letters of Thomas Comber, ed. by CE Whiting (Durham, Surtees Society (Volumes 156, 157) 1946, 1947)

Common Prayer-Book Unmasked, Wherein is declared the Unlawfulnesse and Sinfulnesse of it.... (1660)

Common-Prayer-Book the Best Companion in the House and Closet as well as in the Temple: or, a Collection of Prayers out of the Liturgy of the Church of England.... (1686)

Conant, John. *Sermons preach'd on Several Occasions* Vol. 3 (1698)

Confutation of M. Lewes Hewes his dialogue: Or, an Answer to a Dialogue or Conference betweene a Country Gentleman and a Minister of Gods Word, about the Booke of Common Prayer. Set forth for the Satisfying of those who clamour against the said Booke, and maliciously revile them that are serious in the use thereof (1641)

Consett, Henry. *The Practise of the Spiritual or Ecclesiastical Courts* (1700)

Copy of the Alterations in the Book of Common Prayer prepared by the Royal Commissioners for the Revision of the Liturgy in 1689 (1854)

Cosin, John. *Devotions* (1693)

Cotton, John. *Singing of Psalmes a Gospel-Ordinance* (1650)

D'Assigny, Marius. *The Divine Art of Prayer* (1691)

Davis, Hugh. *De Jure Uniformitatis Ecclesiasticae: Or Three Books, of the Rights Belonging to an Uniformity in Churches* (1667)

Directory for the Publique Worship of God (1645)

Dirge for the Directory (Oxford, 1645)

Domestick Devotions for the Use of Families and of Particular Persons, whereunto are prefixed some earnest Perswasives to Prayer and Devotion (1683)

Dorrington, Theophilus. *Family Devotions for Sunday Evenings throughout the Year, Being Practical Discourses with Suitable Prayers* (1693-1695)

Doughty, John. *Velitationes Polemicae* (1652)

Douglas, Anne. *The Countess of Morton's Daily Exercise* (1666)

Duncumb, Thomas. *The Great Efficacy and Necessity of Good Example Especially in the Clergy: Recommended in a Visitation Sermon Preached at Guildford* (1671)

Duppa, Bryan. *Holy Rules and Helps to Devotion, Both in Prayer and Practice; written in the time of his Sequestration* (1679)

Earnest Exhortation from a Minister to his Parishioners to Discharge the Duty of Morning and Evening Prayer in their Families (Worcester, 1700)

Edward Pelling *A Practical Discourse upon Prayer* 2nd ed. (1694)

Edwards, John. *Sermons on Special Occasions and Subjects* (1698)

Elborow, Thomas. *An Exposition of the Book of Common Prayer* (1663)

Elborow, Thomas. *The Reasonableness of our Christian Service....* (1677)

Elizabeth I. *Injunctions* (1559)

England, Parliament. *Act for Preventing the Frequent Abuses in Printing Seditious, Treasonable and Unlicensed Books and Pamphlets, and for Regulating of Printing and Printing-presses* (1662)

England, Parliament. *Act for the Uniformity of Common Prayer, and Service in the Church, and Administration of the Sacraments* (1559)

England, Parliament. *Act for the Uniformity of Publick Prayers, and Administration of Sacraments, and other Rites and Ceremonies: And for establishing the Form of Making, Ordaining, and Consecrating Bishops, Priests, and Deacons in the Church of England* (1662)

England, Parliament. *Ordinance of 23rd August 1645*: 'for the more effectuall putting in execution the Directory for Publique Worship'

England, Parliament. *Resolves of the Commons assembled in Parliament, Concerning such Ministers as shall Preach or Pray against the present Government established by Parliament* (1649)

Faith and Practice of a Church of England-Man (1688)

Family-Prayers of those poor Christians who in Court and Country, in Cities, Towns, Cottages and Farm Houses, are in good earnest with Religion.... (1675)

Felton, Henry. *The Eternal Joys of God's Presence - A Sermon preached at the Temple-Church upon All-Saints Day* (1699)

Fenner, William. *The Spiritual Mans Directory* (1656)

LIX Exceptions against the Book of Common Prayer (1644)

First Search after One Grand Cause of the wrath of God yet against his people, in the use of the so much Idolized Liturgie, or Common Prayer (1644)

Ford, Thomas. *Singing of Psalms the Duty of Christians....* (1659)

Form of Common Prayer, to be Used upon the Thirtieth of January, Being the
Anniversary Day, Appointed by Act of Parliament For Fasting and
Humiliation, To implore the Mercy of God, That neither the Guilt of that
Sacred and Innocent Blood, nor those other sins by which God was provoked
to deliver up both us and our KING, into the hands of Cruel and Unreasonable
men, may at any time hereafter be visited upon us or our Posterity (1661)

Form of common prayer, together with an order of fasting, for the averting of Gods
heavy visitation upon many places of this realm. The fast to be observ'd within
the cities of London and Westminster, and places adjacent, on Wednesday the
twelfth of this instant July; and both there, and in all parts of this realm, on the
first Wednesday of every moneth; and the prayers to be read on Wednesday in
every week, during this visitation (Oxford 1665)

Form of common prayer. To be used on Wednesday the tenth day of October next;
... being appointed by His Majesty, a day of fasting and humiliation, in
consideration of the late dreadful fire, which wasted the greater part of the city
of London (1666)

A Form of Common Prayer Together with an Order of Fasting For the Averting of
Gods heavy Visitation Upon many places of this Realm (1665)

Form of prayer and thanksgiving to Almighty God, for having made His Highness
the Prince of Orange the glorious instrument of the great deliverance of this
kingdom from popery and arbitrary power ... for use on 31st January 1689
(1689)

Form of prayer to be used on Wednesday the tenth of May next, throughout the
whole kingdom; being the fast-day appointed by Their Majesties proclamation;
and on the second Wednesday of every month following, till further order. To
be observed in a most solemn and devout manner, for supplicating Almighty
God for the pardon of our sins, and for imploring his blessing and protection
in the preservation of Their Majesties sacred persons, and the prosperity of
their arms both at land and sea (1693)

Form of prayer to be used yearly on the second of September, for the dreadful fire
of London (1696)

Form of prayer with fasting, to be us'd yearly upon the 30th of January, being the
day of the martydom of the blessed King Charles the First: to implore the
mercy of God, that neither the guilt of that sacred and innocent bloud, nor
those other sins, by which God was provoked to deliver up both us, and our
King into the hands of cruel and unreasonable men, may at any time hereafter
be visited upon us, or our posterity (1685)

Form of prayer with thanksgiving for the safe delivery of the Queen, and happy
birth of the young Prince. To be used on Sunday next, being the seventeenth
day of this instant June.... (1688)

Form of prayer, to be used upon the fifteenth of January in all churches and
chappels within the cities of London and Westminster; the suburbs of each, and
the burrough of Southwark. ... for the averting those sicknesses, that dearth
and scarcity, which justly may be feared from the unseasonableness of the
weather (1662)

*Form of prayer, with thanksgiving to Almighty God for having put an end to the
    great rebellion by the restitution of the King and royal family. And the
    restauration of the government after many years interruption: which
    unspeakable mercies were wonderfully completed upon the 29ᵗʰ of May, in the
    year, 1660. And in memory thereof, that day in every year is by Act of
    Parliament appointed to be for ever kept holy* (1685)
*Form of prayers and ministration of the Sacraments, &c. used in the Englishe
    Congregation at Geneua: and approued, by the famous and godly learned
    man, Iohn Caluyn* (Geneva, 1556)
*Form, or order of thanksgiving and prayer, to be used in London, and ten miles
    round it, on Sunday the 15ᵗʰ. of this instant January ... in behalf of the King,
    the Queen, and the royal family, upon occasion of the Queen's being with child*
    (1688)
*Forme of Prayer Used at Newport in the Isle of Wight; by His Majesties Directions,
    upon the 15 of September, 1648* (1648)
*Forme of Prayer, used in the King's Chappel, upon Tuesdayes In these Times of
    Trouble & Distresse* (1649)
Forms of Prayer Collected for the Private Use of a Soldier (1687)
*Forms of Private Devotion for Every Day in the Week in a Method agreeable to the
    Liturgy....* (1691)
Fullwood, Francis. *The Necessity of Keeping our Parish Churches An Assize
    Sermon at Exeter* (1672)
Gardiner, James. *Advice to the Clergy of the Diocese of Lincoln* 2nd ed. (1697)
Gardiner, SR, ed. *The Constitutional Documents of the Puritan Revolution 1625-
    1660* (Oxford, Clarendon Press, 1899)
Gatford, Lionel. *A Petition For the Vindication of the Publique use of the Book of
    Common-Prayer* (1655)
Gauden, John. *Ecclesiae Anglicanae Suspiria* (1659)
Gauden, John. *Considerations touching the Liturgy of the Church of England*
    (1661)
Gearing, William. *Clavis Coeli: or a Treatise setting forth the Nature, the Parts,
    and Kinds of Prayer....* (1663)
Geree, John. *The Character of an Old English Puritan* (1646)
Gibbes, Charles *XXXI Sermons Preached to the Parishioners of Stanford-Rivers in
    Essex* (1677)
Gibson, Edmund. *Codex Juris Ecclesiastici Anglicani* Vol. 2 (Oxford, 1761)
Godolphin, John. *Repertorium Canonicum* (1680)
Goodman, John. *A Sermon Preached at Bishops-Stortford August 29. 1677 before
    ... Henry, Lord Bishop of London, &c., At his Lordships Primary Visitation*
    (1677)
Gostwyke, William. *Pray for the Peace of Jerusalem: A Sermon Preach'd at St
    Mary's, in Reading, at the Visitation of the Reverend Mr William Richards,
    Arch-Deacon of Berks. April the 12th 1692* (1692)
Gough, Richard. *The History of Myddle* (Harmondsworth, Penguin 1981)
Gould, William. *Conformity According to Canon Justified....* (1674)
Goulde, William. *Domus mea, Domus Orationis. A Sermon Preached in the
    Cathedral of St. Peter in Exon on Palm-Sunday An. Dom. 1672* (1672)

Grand Debate between the most Reverend the Bishops, and the Presbyterian Divines, appointed by His Sacred Majesty, as Commissioners for the Review and Alteration of the Book Of Common Prayer, &c.... (1661)

Grant, John. *Gods Deliverance of Man by Prayer. And Mans Thankfulnesse to God in Prayses* (1642)

Granville, Denis. *The Remains of Denis Granville DD, Dean and Archdeacon of Durham, &c.* ed. George Ornsby, Durham, Surtees Society, Volume 47 (1865)

Grenville, Denis. *The Compleat Conformist* (1684)

H, N. *Gospel Musick. Or, the Singing of Davids Psalms, &c In the publick Congregation, or private Families asserted....* (1644)

Hall, Joseph. *Humble Remonstrance to the High Court of Parliament* (1640)

Hall, Joseph. *Defence of the Humble Remonstrance....* (1641)

Hall, Joseph. *The Devout Soul, or, Rules of Heavenly Devotion* (1644)

Hall, Jospeh. *A Short Answer to the Tedious Vindication* (1641)

Hammond, Henry. *Ευσχημονως και Κατα Ταξιν or, The Grounds of Uniformity From I Cor. 14.40* (1657)

Hammond, Henry. *A Paraphrase and Annotations upon the Books of Psalms* (1659)

Hammond, Henry. *A Practicall Catechisme* (Oxford, 1645)

Hammond, Henry. *The View of the New Directory and a Vindication of the Ancient Liturgy of the Church of England* (Oxford, 1645)

Heylyn, Peter. *Ecclesia Vindicata: Or, the Church of England Justified....* (1657)

Hickman, Charles. *A Sermon Preached at St Bride's Church, on St. Caecilia's Day, Nov 22. 1695. Being the Anniversary Feast of the Lovers of Musick* (1696)

Hinde, Samuel. *Englands Prospective-Glasse: A Sermon at a Metropolitical Visitation Held at The Cathedral Church of Christ in Canterbury on the 29th of April 1663* (1663)

Hole, Matthew. *A Sermon Preached at the Triennial Visitation of ... Richard L. Bishop of Bath and Wells. Held at Bridgewater, on the 19th Day of August, 1695* (1696)

Hollingsworth, Richard. *A Modest Plea for the Church of England* (1676)

Hooker, Richard. *Works* ed. by J. Keble 3 Vols. (Oxford, 1845)

Horton, Thomas. *One Hundred Select Sermons* (1679)

Hough, Edward. *A Country Minister's Serious Advice to his Parishioners: Containing many Profitable Directions, Tending both to Inform their Understanding and Reform their Lives* (1700)

Hours of Daily Prayer in and about the City of London (1692)

Husband, Edward. *A Collection of all the publicke orders, ordinances and declarations of both Houses of Parliament....* (1646)

Inett, John. *A Guide to the Devout Christian* 2nd ed. (1691)

Irregularitie of a Private Prayer in a Publick Congregation (1674)

Jeanes, Henry. *Uniformity in Humane Doctrinall Ceremonies ... or, A Reply unto Dr Hammonds ... Grounds of Uniformity* (Oxford, 1660)

Jeffery, John. *A Sermon Preached in the Cathedral Church of Norwich: At the Primary Visitation of ... John, Lord Bishop of Norwich. May 18. 1692* (1692)

Jenkins, David. *A Scourge for the Directorie and the Revolting Synod....* (1647)

Jenks, Benjamin. *Prayers and Offices of Devotion, for Families....* (1697)

Jones, David. *A Sermon of the Absolute Necessity of Family-Duties* (1692)

Josselin, Ralph. *The Diary of Ralph Josselin 1616-1683* ed. Alan Macfarlane (Oxford, British Academy/Oxford University Press: Records of Social and Economic History, New Series III, 1991)

Keach, Benjamin. *The Breach Repaired in God's Worship: Or, Singing of Psalms, Hymns, and Spiritual Songs, proved to be an Holy Ordinance....* (1691)

Kelsey, Joseph. *A Sermon Preached at the Consecration of a Chappel in the House of John Collins, Esq. of Chute in Wiltshire* (1674)

Kemp, Edward. *Reasons for the Sole Use of the Churches Prayers in Publick* (Cambridge, 1668)

Ken, Thomas. *Directions for Prayer, for the Diocess of Bath and Wells* (nd, ?1686)

Kettlewell, John. *A Discourse Explaining the Nature of Edification Both of Particular Persons in Private Grace, and of the Church in Unity and Peace. And shewiug (sic) That we must not break Unity and Publick Peace, for supposed Means of better Edifying in Private Virtues. In a Visitation Sermon at Coventry, May 7. 1684* (1684)

Kettlewell, John. *The Religious Loyalist: Or a Good Christian Taught How to be a Faithful Servant both to God and the King in a Visitation-Sermon. Preached at Coles-Hill in Warwickshire, Aug. 28, 1685 At the Triennial Visitation of my Lords Grace of Canterbury, During the Suspension of the Bp. of Litchfield and Coventry* (1686)

Kidder, Richard. *The Charge of Richard, Lord Bishop of Bath and Wells, to the Clergy of his Diocese....* (1692)

Kidder, Richard. *Twelve Sermons* (1697)

King, Henry. *Psalmes of David* (1651)

King, William. *A Discourse concerning the Inventions of Men in the Worship of God* (1694)

Kingdomes Weekly Intelligencer No. 230 12th-19th October 1647

Kingdomes Weekly Intelligencer No. 231 19th-26th October 1647

Laney, Benjamin. *A Sermon Preached before His Majesty at Whitehal, April 5. 1663* (1663)

Laud, William. *A Summarie of Devotions* (1667)

Leslie, Henry. *A Discourse of Praying with the Spirit and with the Understanding* (1660)

Letter of Advice to all the Members of the Church of England to come to the Divine Service Morning and Evening Every Day (1688)

Liberty of Prayer Asserted, and Garded from Licentiousness (1695)

Lightfoot, John. *Works* Vol. VII (1822); Vol. XIII (1824)

Lingard, Richard. *A Sermon preached before the King at Whitehall July 26, 1668. In Defence of the Liturgy of our Church* (1668)

Littleton, Adam. *Sixty One Sermons* (1680)

Lloyd, John. *A Treatise of the Episcopacy, Liturgies, and Ecclesiastical ceremonies of Primitive Times* (1661)

Lodington, Thomas. *The Honour of the Clergy Vindicated from the Contempt of the Laity in a Sermon preached at the Arch-Deacon of Lincoln his Visitation, holden at Grantham, Oct 15. 1672* (1673)

Lucas, Richard. *Practical Christianity, or an account of the Holiness which the Gospel enjoins....* (1693)

Lynford, Thomas. *A Sermon Concerning the Worship of God in Private* (1691)

M, T. *The Whole Book of Psalms, as they are now sung in the Churches* (1688)

Mace, Thomas. *Musicks Monument* (1676)

Manningham, Thomas. *A Sermon concerning Publick Worship, Preached before the Queen on Wednesday the 23ᵈ of March, 169½* (1692)

Manningham, Thomas. *Praise and Adoration. Or, A Sermon on Trinity-Sunday before the University of Oxford* (1682)

Mapletoft, John. *A Perswasive to the Consciencious frequenting the daily Publick Prayers of the Church of England* (1687)

Marshal, Walter. *The Gospel Mystery of Sanctification* (1692)

Meriton, George. *A Guide for Constables, Churchwardens, Overseers of the Poor, Surveyors of the Highways ... A Treatise briefly shewing the extent and latitude of the several offices, with the powers of the officers herein, both by common law and statute. ...* (1669)

Meriton, John. *Forms of Prayer for every Day of the Week; Morning and Evening. Composed for the use of Private Families* (1682)

Milbourne, Luke. *The Psalms of David in English Metre* (1698)

Moore, John. *Of Religious Melancholy* (1692)

Moore, John. *Of the Wisdom and Goodness of Providence - Two Sermons preached before the Queen at Whitehall on August 17, 24 MDCXC* (1690)

More, Henry. *An explanation of the grand mystery of Godliness* (1660)

More, Henry. *Enthusiasmus Triumphatus* (1656)

Morse, Robert. *The Clergyman's Office and the Clergyman's Due; A Sermon preached at the Triennial Visitation of ... Edward Lord Bishop of Gloucester....* (1699)

Naish, Thomas. *Sermon Preach'd at the Cathedral Church of Sarum Novemb. 22. 1700 Before a Society of Lovers of Musick* (1701)

Neville, Robert. *The Nature & Causes of Hardness of Heart, Together with the Remedies against it. Discovered in a Sermon, Preached first before the Honourable Society of Lincolns-Inn, and afterwards before the University in Great St Maries Church in Cambridge* (1683)

New-years-Gift Composed of Prayers and Meditations with Devotions for Several Occasions (3rd Edition 1683: Part III 1685)

Nicolson, William. *Davids Harp Strung and Tuned* (1662)

Norris, John. *A Sermon Preach'd in the Abby Church of Bath, Before ... Thomas, Lord Bishop of Bath and Wells. At his Visitation held there July 30. 1689* (1690)

Of the Daily Practice of Piety (1660)

Old Non-Conformist Touching the Book of Common Prayer, and Ceremonies (1660)

Owen, John. *A Discourse concerning Liturgies and their Imposition* (1661)

Owtram, William. *Twenty Sermons Preached upon Several Occasions* (1697)

P, B. *The Parish-Clerk's Vade Mecum: or an Alphabetical Concordance of the most material words and sentences in the book of Singing Psalms, used in the Parish Churches; pointing out also Psalms suited to all the great festivals of the Church of England and most other special occasions* (1694)

Patrick, Symon. *Discourse concerning Prayer, Especially of Frequenting the Daily Public Prayers* (1686)

Patrick, Symon. *The Book of Psalms Paraphras'd* (1680)

Patrick, Symon. *Four Discourse sent to the Clergy of the Diocese of Ely on Four Several Visitations* (1704)

Patrick, Symon. *The Devout Christian instructed how to Pray and give thanks to God: or, a book of devotions for Families: and for particular persons in most of the concerns of humane life* (1673)

Payne, William. *Family Religion* (1691)

Pelling, Edward. *The Good Old Way, or a Discourse offer'd to all True-hearted Protestants Concerning the Ancient Way of the Church, and the Conformity of the Church of England Thereunto: as to its government, manner of worship, rites and ceremonies* (1680)

Perfect Weekly Account 3rd-10th May 1647

Petition for Peace: with the Reformation of the Liturgy, as it was presented to the Rt. Rev. the Bishops by the Divines appointed by his Majesties Commission to treat with them about the alteration of it (1661).

Pittis, Thomas. *Discourse of Prayer* (1683)

Playford, John. *Psalms and Hymns in Solemn Musick* (1671)

Playford, John. *Whole Book of Psalms* (1677)

Pollard, Thomas. *The Necessity and Advantages of Family Prayer* (Dublin, 1696)

Portman, Richard. *The Soules Life* (1645)

Powell, Vavasor. *Common-Prayer-Book no Divine Service, or XXVII Reasons against forming and imposing any Humane Liturgies....* (1661)

Prayer to be Used at the Opening - the Cathedral Church of St Paul December 2 1697 Being the Thanksgiving Day (1697)

Prayers in the Closet (Oxford, 1689; London, 1692)

Preparations to a Holy Life (1684)

Prideaux, John. *The Doctrine of Prayer* (1841)

Prince Charles, his Letany, and Prayers, For the King of Great Britane in his sad Condition.... (1648)

Private Devotion and a Brief Explication of the Ten Commandments (Oxford, 1689)

Protestation of the Two and Twenty Divines for the Setling of the Church: and the Particulars by them excepted against in the Liturgie: Not that the Book of Common Prayer of the Church of England should be utterly abolished, but purged of all Innovations and Absurdities (1643)

Publick Devotion and the Common Service of the Church of England, Justify'd and Recommended, to all honest and well meaning (however prejudic'd) DISSENTERS (sic) (nd - BL catalogue records 1680)

Puller, Timothy. *The Moderation of the Church of England* (1679)

Pulpit-Conceptions, Popular-Deceptions: or The Grand Debate resumed, in the point of Prayer: Wherein it appears that those free Prayers so earnestly contented for have no advantage above the Prescribed Liturgie in publick Administration.... (1662)

Raymond, George. *A Sermon Preached at the Primary Visitation of ... John Lord Bishop of Norwich June, 20th. 1692* (1692)

Records of the Northern Convocation (Durham, Surtees Society, Vol. 113, 1907)

Remarks Upon a Late Pamphlet Entituled, A Brief and Full Account of Mr Tate's and Mr Brady's New Version of the Psalms (1699)

Resbury, Nathanael. *Of Closet-Prayer* (1693)

Resolution of two Cases of Conscience (1683)

Reynolds, Edward. *The Pastoral Office Opened in a Visitation-Sermon preached at Ipswich October 10.1662* (1663)

Roberts, Francis. *Clavis Bibliorum* (1665)

Rules for our more Devout Behaviour in the time of Divine Service in the Church of England (1687)

Scott, John. *Certain Cases of Conscience Resolved....* Part I (1683)

Scrivener, Matthew. *The Method and Means to a true Spiritual Life* (1688)

Seymour, Thomas. *Advice to the Readers of Common Prayer* (1683)

Sharp, John. *Fifteen Sermons* (1700)

Sharp, John. *A Perswasive to Prayer - A Sermon preach'd before the King at St James's March 13 1698* (1700)

Shaw, John. *No Reformation of the Established Reformation* (1685)

Shaw, Joseph. *Parish Law* (1733)

Sherlock, Richard. *Principles of Holy Christian Religion....* (1659)

Sherlock, Richard. *A Sermon Preached at a Visitation, held at Warrington in Lancashire May 11. 1669* (1669)

Sherlock, William *A Practical Discourse of Religious Assemblies* (1682)

Sherlock, William *A Sermon Preached at the Temple Church, May 29. 1692* (1692)

Sherlock, William. *A Discourse concerning the Knowledge of Jesus Christ and our Union and Communion with Him* (1674)

'Smectymnuus'. *An Answer to a Booke entituled, an Humble Remonstrance* (1641)

'Smectymnuus'. *A Vindication of the Answer to the Humble Remonstrance* (1641)

Smith, Nicholas. *A Sabbath of Rest....* (1675)

Sparrow, Anthony. *A Rationale upon the Book of Common Prayer....* (1655)

Sparrow, Anthony. *The Bishop of Exons Caution to his Diocese Against False Doctrines Delivered in a Sermon at Truro ... at his Primary Visitation* (1669)

Sprat, Thomas. *A Discourse made by the Ld Bishop of Rochester to the Clergy of his Diocese* (1696)

Stainforth, William. *An Assize Sermon, Preached August 3, 1685 in the Cathedral Church of St Peter in York* (York, 1685)

Stanhope, George. *A Sermon concerning God's Deferring to answer Mens Prayers: Preached before the King and Queen at Whitehall November the 11th 1694* (1695)

Stillingfleet, Edward. *The Bishop of Worcester's Charge to the Clergy of his Diocese* (1691)

Stillingfleete, John. *Shecinah: Or a Demonstration of the Divine Presence in the Places of Religious Worship* (1663)

Stratford, Nicholas. *Of the Reverence due to God in his Publick Worship. A Sermon Preach'd before the King and Queen, at White-hall, March 25, 1694* (1694)

Stratford, Nicholas. *The Bishop of Chester's Charge* (1692)

Supply of Prayer for the Ships of this Kingdom that want Ministers to pray with them; agreeable to the Directory established by Parliament (Published by Authority). (1645)

Tate, Nahum and Brady, Nicholas. *A New Version of the Psalms of David* (1696)

Taylor, Jeremy *The Rules and Exercises for Holy Living in which are described the Means and Instruments of obtaining Every Virtue and the Remedies against every vice and Considerations serving to the resisting all temptations together with Prayers containing the Whole Duty of a Christian and the parts of Devotion fitted for all Occasions and furnished for all Necessities* (1817)

Taylor, Jeremy. *A Discourse concerning Prayer Ex tempore....* (1646)

Taylor, Jeremy. *An Apology for Authorized and Set Forms of Liturgie* (1649)

Taylor, Jeremy. *An Apology for Authorized and Set Forms of Liturgie* (1649)

Taylor, Jeremy. *The Great Exemplar* (1849)

Taylor, Jeremy. Συμβολον Θεολογικον: *or a Collection of Polemicall Discourses, wherein the Church of England, in its Worst as well as more Flourishing Condition, is defended in many material Points, against the Attempts of the Papists on one hand, and the Fanaticks on the other* (1674)

Templer, John. *A Treatise relating to the Worship of God* (1694)

Tenison, Thomas. *A Sermon concerning the Wandering of the Mind in God's Service. Preached before the Queen at Whitehall....* (1691)

Thomas, William. *A Preservative of Piety* (1662)

Thorndike, Herbert. *Just Weights and Measures* (1662)

Thorndike, Herbert. *An Epilogue to the Tragedy of the Church of England* (1659)

Thorndike, Herbert. *Of Religious Assemblies, and the Publick Service of God: a discourse according to Apostolicall Rule and Practice* (Cambridge, 1642)

Thurlin, Thomas. *The Necessity of Obedience to Spiritual Governours, Asserted in a Sermon at an Episcopal Visitation in Kings-Lyn, Norfolk, on the Tenth day of May, 1686* (Cambridge, 1686)

Tillotson, John. *Six Sermons* (1694)

Triall of the English Lyturgie (1643)

True and Briefe Narrative of all the Several parts of the Common Prayer book, cleered from aspersions which some men cast upon it (1660)

True Notion of the Worship of God, Or a Vindication of the Service of the Church of England (1673)

Tullie, George. *A Discourse of the Government of the Thoughts* 3rd ed. (1694)

Turner, Francis. *A Letter to the Clergy of the Diocese of Ely* (Cambridge, 1686)

U, O. *Parish-Churches No Conventicles, From the Minister's reading in the Desk when there is no Communion* (1683)

Use of Daily Publick Prayers (1641)

Verney, FP and Verney, MM *Memoirs of the Verney Family during the Seventeenth Century* Vol. I (London, Longmans, 1907)

W, I. *Certain Reasons why the Booke of Common-Prayer Being Corrected should continue* (1641)

Warren, Erasmus. *A Defence of Liturgies* (1687)

Watson, Richard. *The Right Reverend Doctor John Cosin, Late Lord Bishop of Durham, His Opinion ... What slender Authority, if any, the English Psalms, in Rhime and Metre, have ever had for the publick use they have obtained in our Churches: Freely rendered in two Letters, with Annotations....* (1684)

Wells, John, (Minister of St. Olave, Jewry) 'How may we make melody in our hearts with singing of Psalms? [A sermon on Ephes. v. 19.]' in ed. S Annesley *A supplement to the Morning-Exercise at Cripplegate* (1676) pp. 174-190

Wemys, Thomas *Beth-Hak-Kodesh or the Separation and Consecration of Places for God's publick Service and Worship and the Reverence due unto them vindicated* (1674)

West, Richard. *The Profitableness of Piety, open'd in an Assize Sermon Preached at Dorchester* (1671)

Westminster Assembly of Divines. *Two Letters of Great Concernment* (1645)

Wetenhall, Edward. *Enter into thy Closet* (1666)

Wetenhall, Edward. *Of Gifts and Offices in the Publick Worship of God* (Dublin, 1679)

Whitby, Daniel. *The Vindication of the Forme of Common Prayers Used in the Church of England....* (Oxford, 1644)

Whitehall, Robert. *A Sermon concerning Edification in Faith and Discipline, preached before the University of Oxford. Sept. 1. 1689* (Oxford, 1694)

Whole Booke of Psalmes collected into English Meeter by Thomas Sternhold, John Hopkins, and others: conferred with the Hebrew, with apt notes to sing them withall. Set forth and allowed to be sung in all Churches, of all the people together, before and after Morning and Evening Prayer; as also before & after Sermons: and moreover in private houses, for their godly solace and comfort, laying apart all ungodly songs and ballads, which tend only to the nourishing of vice, and corrupting of youth (1661)

Bibliography - Secondary Sources

Addison, JT. 'Early Anglican Thought 1559-1667' *Historical Magazine of the Protestant Episcopal Church* September 1953, Vol. 22, No. 3, pp. 248-369

Arber, E., ed. *A Transcript of the Register of the Company of Stationers 1554-1640* Vol. 4 (1877)

Argent, A. 'Aspects of the Ecclesiastical History of the Parishes of the City of London 1640-49 (with special reference to the Parish Clergy)' (London University Ph.D. thesis, 1983)

Arnott, FR. - 'Anglicanism in the Seventeenth Century' in ed. More, PE & Cross, FL *Anglicanism* (London, SPCK, 1935 pp.xli - lxxiii)

Avis, P. *Anglicanism and the Christian Church* (Edinburgh, T&T Clark, 1989)

Bailey, HI. *The Liturgy compared with the Bible* (London, SPCK, 1853)

Ball, FE. 'A Liturgical Colloquy: An examination of the records of the Savoy Conference, 1661' (Oxford University B.Litt. thesis, 1958)

Barratt, DM. 'The Condition of the Parish Clergy between the Reformation and 1660, with special reference to the Dioceses of Oxford, Worcester, and Gloucester' (Oxford University Ph.D. thesis, 1949)

Baum, PF. *The Other Harmony of Prose ... an essay in English prose rhythm* (North Carolina, Duke University Press, 1952)

Bennett, GV. 'Patristic Tradition in Anglican Thought, 1660-1900' *Oecumenica* 1972 pp.63-85

Biderman, S. *Scripture and Knowledge - An Essay on Religious Epistemology* (Leiden, Brill, 1995)

Bolton, FR. *The Caroline Tradition of the Church of Ireland* (London, SPCK, 1958)

Bosher, RS. *The Making of the Restoration Settlement* (Westminster, Dacre Press, 1957)

Boyarin, D. *Intertextuality and the Reading of Midrash* (Indianapolis, Indiana University Press, 1990)

Bozell, RB. 'English Preachers of the Seventeenth Century on the Art of Preaching' (Cornell University Ph.D. thesis 1938)

Bradshaw, PF. *Daily Prayer in the Early Church* (London, Alcuin/SPCK, 1981)

Brewer, J. and Styles, J. eds. *'An Ungovernable People': The English and their Law in the Seventeenth and Eighteenth Centuries* (London, Hutchinson, 1983)

Bridges, R. *Milton's Prosody* (Oxford, Henry Frowde, 1901)

Brink, AW. 'A Study of the Literature of Inward Experience, 1600-1700' (London University Ph.D. thesis, 1963)

Browning, A. *Thomas Osborne, Earl of Danby and Duke of Leeds 1632-1712* Vol. 1 (Glasgow, Jackson, 1951)

Browning, A., ed. *English Historical Documents 1660-1714* (London, Eyre & Spottiswoode 1953)

Buley, DM. 'Eloquence as the essence of common prayer: Cranmer's liturgical language' (Drew University Ph.D. thesis, 2004)

Burke, P. *Popular Culture in Early Modern Europe* (London, Temple Smith, 1978)

Bussby, F. 'A History and Source Book on Training for the Ministry in the Church of England 1511-1717' (Durham University M.Litt. thesis, 1952)

Butt, J. 'The Facilities for Antiquarian Study in the Seventeenth Century' *Essays and Studies by Members of the English Association* Vol. 24, 1939, pp.64-79

Christianson, P. 'Reformers and the Church of England under Elizabeth I and the Early Stuarts' *Journal of Ecclesiastical History* Vol. 31 (1980) pp.463-482

Clark, G. *The Later Stuarts 1660-1714* (Oxford, Clarendon Press, 1965)

Clay, WK., ed. *Liturgies and Occasional Forms of Prayer set forth in the Reign of Queen Elizabeth* (Cambridge, University Press, 1847)

Cliffe, JT. *The Puritan Gentry Besieged 1650-1700* (London, Routledge, 1993)

Coleby, AM. *Central Government and the Localities: Hampshire 1649-1689* (Cambridge, Cambridge University Press, 1987)

Cragg, GR. *The Church and the Age of Reason 1648-1789 - Pelican History of the Church Vol. IV* (London, Hodder & Stoughton, 1962)

Cressy, D. *Birth Marriage & Death - Ritual, Religion and the Life-Cycle in Tudor and Stuart England* (Oxford, Oxford University Press, 1997)

Cuming, GJ. *A History of Anglican Liturgy* (London, Macmillan, 1969)

Cuming, GJ. 'The Prayer Book in Convocation, November 1661' *Journal of Ecclesiastical History* Vol. 8 No.2 1957 pp.182-192

Darlow, TH and Moule, HF. *Historical Catalogue of the Printed Editions of Holy Scripture in the Library of the British and Foreign Bible Society* Vol. 1 (New York, Kraus Reprint Corp., 1963)

Davies, DH. *Worship and Theology in England 1690-1850* (Princeton, New Jersey, Princeton University Press, 1961)

Davies, DH. *Worship and Theology in England from Andrewes to Baxter and Fox, 1603-1690* (Princeton New Jersey, Princeton University Press, 1975)

Davies, E. 'The Enforcement of Religious Uniformity in England 1668-1700 with Special Reference to the Dioceses of Chichester and Worcester' (Oxford University Ph.D. thesis, 1982)

Davies, J. *The Caroline Captivity of the Church: Charles I and the Remoulding of Anglicanism 1625-1641* (Oxford, Clarendon Press, 1992)

Dillow, K. 'The Social and Ecclesiastical Significance of Church Seating Arrangements and Pew Disputes 1500-1740' (Oxford University Ph.D. thesis, 1990)

Duffy, E 'Primitive Christianity Revived; Religious Renewal in Augustan England' in Baker, D., ed. Renaissance and Renewal in Christian History (Studies in Church History 14, Ecclesiastical History Society, 1977, pp.287-300)

Duffy, E. 'The Godly and the Multitude in Stuart England' *Seventeenth Century* Vol. I, 1986, pp.31-55

Dugmore, CW. *Eucharistic Doctrine in England from Hooker to Waterland* (London, 1942)

C Durston 'By the book or with the spirit: the debate over liturgical prayer during the English Revolution' *Historical Research* Vol. 79, No 203 (February 2006) pp. 50-73

Durston, C. and Eales, J., eds. *The Culture of English Puritanism 1560-1700* (Basingstoke, Palgrave Macmillan, 1996)

Edwards, DL. *Christian England* Vol. 2 (Grand Rapids, Michigan, Eerdmans, 1983)

Elmen, P. 'Richard Allestree and the Whole Duty of Man' *The Library (Transactions of the Bibliographical Society)* 5th Series Vol. VI No. 1, 1951, p.19-27

Everitt, A. 'Nonconformity in Country Parishes' in Thirsk, J., ed. Land, Church, and People: Essays presented to Professor H.P.R. Finberg Supplement to The Agricultural History Review Vol. 18 (1970)

Fincham, K., ed. *The Early Stuart Church 1603-1642* (London, Macmillan, 1993)

Findon, J. 'The Non Jurors and the Church of England 1689-1716' (Oxford University Ph.D. thesis, 1978)

Finnegan, R. 'Literacy versus Non-Literacy: The Great Divide' in Horton, R. and Finnegan, R., eds. Modes of Thought (London, Faber & Faber, 1973)

Finnegan, R. *Oral Poetry: Its Nature, Significance and Social Context* (Bloomington, Indiana University Press, 1972)

Fischer, B. 'The Common Prayer of Congregation and Family in the Ancient Church' *Studia Liturgica* Vol. 10 No. 3/4 1974

Foster, J. *Alumni Oxoniensis: The Members of the University of Oxford 1500-1714* (Nendelm, Liechtenstein, Kraus Reprint, 1968)

Fox, A. *Oral and Literate Culture in England 1500-1700* (Oxford, Clarendon Press 2000)

Fox, AP. 'Aspects of Oral Culture and its Development in Early Modern England' (Cambridge University Ph.D. thesis, 1992)

Garrett, C. 'The Rhetoric of Supplication: Prayer Theory in Seventeenth Century England' *Renaissance Quarterly* Vol. 46 No. 2 1993, pp.328-357

Garside, C. 'The Origins of Calvin's Theology of Music : 1536-1543' *Transactions of the American Philosophical Society* Vol. 69 Part 4 1979

Green, I. *Print and Protestantism in Early Modern England* (Oxford, Oxford University Press, 2000)

Green, I. *The Christian's ABC: Catechisms and Catechizing in England c.1530-1740* (Oxford, Clarendon Press, 1996)

Green, IM. *The Re-Establishment of the Church of England 1660-1663* (Oxford, Oxford University Press, 1978)

Greenwood, DS. 'The Seventeenth-Century English Poetical Biblical Paraphrase' (Cambridge University Ph.D. thesis, 1985)

Grell, OP and Israel, JI and Tyacke, N., eds. *From Persecution to Toleration* (Oxford, Clarendon Press, 1991)

Griffiths, DN. *The Bibliography of the Book of Common Prayer 1549-1999* (London, British Library, 2002)

Grisbrooke, WJ. 'The 1662 Book of Common Prayer: its history and character' *Studia Liturgica* 1962 Vol. 1 No.3 pp.146-166

Hamlin, H. *Psalm Culture and Early Modern English Literature* (Cambridge, Cambridge University Press, 2004)

Haigh, C. 'Communion and Community: Exclusion from Communion in Post-Reformation England' *Journal of Ecclesiastical History* Vol. 51 No 4 October 2000, pp.721-740

Hardacre, PH. *The Royalists during the Puritan Revolution* (The Hague, Nijhoff, 1956)

Harding, DW. *Words into rhythm: English speech rhythm in verse and prose* (Cambridge, Cambridge University Press, 1976)

Harley, J. *Music in Purcell's London* (London, Dennis Dobson, 1968)

Healey, FG. *Rooted in Faith: Three Centuries of Nonconformity 1662-1962* (London, Independent Press, 1961)

Hibbitts, JB. 'Henry Hammond (1605-1660) and English New Testament
    Exposition' (Oxford University Ph.D. thesis, 1954)

Hoffman, A. *Bocking Deanery - The story of an Essex Peculiar* (London,
    Phillimore, 1976)

Holland, J. *The Psalmists of Britain: Records Biographical and Literary* Vol. 2
    (London, Groombridge, 1843)

Holley, ED. 'The English Bible and English Primary Education in the Tudor and
    Stuart Periods' (Florida State University Ph.D. thesis, 1998)

Holmes, G., ed. *Britain after the Glorious Revolution 1689-1714* (London,
    Macmillan 1969)

Houlbrooke, R. *Death, Religion, and the Family in England, 1480-1750* (Oxford,
    Clarendon Press, 1998)

Hunt, A. 'The Art of Hearing: English Preachers and their audiences 1590-1640'
    (Cambridge University Ph.D. thesis, 1998)

Hunt, A. 'The Lord's Supper in Early Modern England' *Past and Present* Issue 161
    1998 pp.39-83

Hutton, R. *The Restoration: A Political and Religious History of England and
    Wales 1658-1667* (Oxford, Clarendon Press, 1985)

Hutton, R. *The Restoration: A Political and Religious History of England and
    Wales 1658-1667* (Oxford, Clarendon Press, 1985)

Ignjatijevic, Gl. 'The Parish Clergy in the Diocese of Canterbury and Archdeaconry
    of Bedford in the Reign of Charles I and under the Commonwealth' (Sheffield
    University Ph.D. thesis, 1986)

Jacobson, W. ed. *Fragmentary Illustrations of the History of the Book of Common
    Prayer....* (London, John Murray, 1874)

Johns, A. *The Nature of the Book: Print and Knowledge in the Making* (London,
    University of Chicago Press, 1998)

Jones, JR. *Country and Court: England 1658-1714* (London, Edward Arnold, 1980)

Joyce, P. *Visions of the People - Industrial England and the Question of Class
    1848-1914* (Cambridge, Cambridge University Press, 1991)

Kelly, FL. *Prayer in Sixteenth Century England* (Gainesville, University of Florida
    Press, 1966 - University of Florida Monographs: Humanities 22)

Kermode, F. *Forms of Attention* (London, University of Chicago Press, 1985)

Knachel, PA. ed. *Eikon Basilike* (Ithaca, Cornell University Press, 1966)

Knox, RB. ed. *Reformation Conformity and Dissent* (London, Epworth Press, 1977)

Lacey, A. *The Cult of King Charles the Martyr* (Woodbridge, Boydell Press, 2003)

Lacqueur, T. 'The Cultural Origins of Popular Literacy in England 1500-1850'
    Oxford Review of Education Vol. 2 No 3, 1976, pp.255-275

Leaver, RA. *'Goostly psalmes and spirituall songes': English and Dutch Metrical
    Psalms ... 1535-1566* (Oxford, Clarendon Press, 1991)

Letsome, Sampson *The Preacher's Assistant, ... A Series of the Texts of all the
    Sermons and Discourses Preached upon, and published Since the Restoration,
    to the Present Time* (1753)

Lewis, CS. *English Literature in the Sixteenth Century* (Oxford, Clarendon Press,
    1954)

McFarland, RE. 'The Response to Grace: Seventeenth Century Sermons and the Idea
    of Thanksgiving' *Church History* Vol. 44, No. 2, pp. 199-203

McLeod, MSG and James, KI and Shaw, DJ. *The Cathedral Libraries Catalogue. Books printed before 1701 in the libraries of the Anglican cathedrals of England and Wales. Vol. 1 Books printed in the British Isles and British America and English books printed elsewhere* (London, British Library, 1984)

Martz, LL. *The Poetry of Meditation: A Study in English Religious Literature of the Seventeenth Century* (New Haven, Yale University Press, 1954)

Maltby, J. 'Approaches to the Study of Religious Conformity in late Elizabethan and early Stuart England: with special reference to Cheshire and the Diocese of Lincoln' (Cambridge University Ph.D. thesis, 1991)

Maxwell, WD. *John Knox's Genevan Service Book 1556* (London, Oliver & Boyd, 1931)

Moorman, JRH. *A History of the Church in England* (London, A&C Black, 1967)

Morrill, J. 'The attack on the Church of England in the Long Parliament, 1640-1642' in Beales, D. and Best, G., eds. *History, Society and the Churches* (Cambridge, University Press, 1985, pp.105-124)

Morrill, J., ed. *Reactions to the English Civil War 1642-1649* (London, Macmillan, 1982)

Old, HO. *The Patristic Roots of Reformed Worship* (Zurich, Theologischer Verlag Zurich, Zürcher Beitrage Zur Reformationgeschichte, Band 5, 1975)

Oxford English Dictionary 2nd ed. (Oxford, Clarendon Press, 1989)

Packer, JW. *The Transformation of Anglicanism 1643-1660, with special reference to Henry Hammond* (Manchester, University Press, 1969)

Pocock, JGA. *The Ancient Constitution and the Feudal Law: A study of English Historical Thought in the Seventeenth Century* (Portway, Bath, Chivers, 1974)

Pointer, M. *The Glory of Grantham* (Grantham, Bygone Grantham, 1978)

Porter, HC. *Reformation and Reaction in Tudor Cambridge* (Cambridge, University Press, 1958)

Potter, L. *Secret Rites and Secret Writing - Royalist Literature 1641-1660* (Cambridge, University Press, 1989)

Pruett, JH. *The Parish Clergy under the Later Stuarts: The Leicestershire Experience* (Urbana, University of Illinois Press, 1978)

Reay, B., ed. *Popular Culture in Seventeenth-Century England* (London, Croom, Helm, 1985)

Richards, GC. 'Coverdale and the Cursus' *Church Quarterly Review* Vol. 110, April 1930, pp.34-39

Rohr-Sauer, P. von. *English Metrical Psalms from 1600 to 1660* (Freiburg, 1938)

Roots, I., ed. *Into Another Mould: Aspects of the Interregnum* (Exeter Studies in History No. 3. Exeter, University of Exeter, 1981)

Sharpe, K. and Lake, P. eds. *Culture and Politics in Early Stuart England* (Basingstoke, Macmillan, 1994)

Shaw, W. *The Succession of Organists of the Chapel Royal and the Cathedrals of England and Wales from c.1538* (Oxford, Clarendon Press 1991)

Simon, WG. *The Restoration Episcopate* (New York, Bookman Associates, 1965)

Simpson, RL. *The Interpretation of Prayer in the Early Church* (Philadelphia, Westminster Press, 1965)

Skoglund, JE. 'Free Prayer' *Studia Liturgica* Vol. 10, 1974, No.3/4, pp.151-166

Smith, SR. 'Religion and the Conception of Youth in Seventeenth Century England' *History of Childhood Quarterly* Vol. 2, Part 4, 1974/75

Somerville, CJ. *Popular Religion in Restoration England* (Gainesville, Florida, University Presses of Florida, 1977)

Spaeth, DA. 'Parsons and Parishioners: Lay-Clerical Conflict and Popular Piety in Wiltshire Villages, 1660-1740' (Brown University Ph.D. thesis, 1985)

Spaeth, DA. 'Common Prayer? Popular Observance of the Anglican Liturgy in Restoration Wiltshire' in Wright, SJ., ed. *Parish, Church and People: Local Studies in Lay Religion 1350-1750* (London, Hutchinson, 1988)

Spinks, BD. *Sacraments, Ceremonies and the Stuart Divines: Sacramental theology and liturgy in England and Scotland 1603-1662* (Aldershot, Ashgate, 2002)

Spurr, J. 'Anglican Apologetic and the Restoration Church' (Oxford University Ph.D. thesis, 1985)

Spurr, J. *The Restoration Church of England, 1646-1689* (London, Yale University Press, 1991)

Stanwood, PG. *Jeremy Taylor: Holy Living and Holy Dying* Vol.1 (Oxford, Clarendon Press, 1989)

Stevenson, K. *Covenant of Grace Renewed: A Vision of the Eucharist in the Seventeenth Century* (London, Darton Longman Todd, 1994)

Stranks, CJ. *Anglican Devotion* (London, SCM Press, 1961)

Sutch, VD. *Gilbert Sheldon: Architect of Anglican Survival 1640-1675* (International Archives of the History of Ideas: Series Minor 12; The Hague, Martinus Nijoff, 1973)

Targoff, R. 'The Performance of Prayer: Sincerity and Theatricality in Early Modern England' *Representations* Issue 60, 1997 pp.49-69

Targoff, R. *Common Prayer: the Language of Public Devotion in Early Modern England* (London, University of Chicago Press, 2001)

Tatham, GB. *Puritans in Power* (Cambridge, University Press, 1913)

Temperley, N. 'John Playford and the Metrical Psalms' *Journal of the American Musicological Society* Vol. 25, 1972, pp.331-378

Temperley, N. *The Music of the English Parish Church* (Cambridge, Cambridge University Press, 1983)

Thomas, K. *The Perception of the Past in Early Modern England* (London, University of London, 1983)

Thornton, M. *English Spirituality* (London, SPCK, 1963)

Townsend, RD. 'The Caroline Divines' in Wakefield, GS., ed. *A Dictionary of Christian Spirituality* (London, SCM, 1983) pp.73-75

Tripp, DK. *Daily Prayer in the Reformed Tradition: An Initial Survey* (Alcuin 1996)

Trott, FJ. 'Prelude to Restoration: Laudians, Conformists and the struggle for 'Anglicanism' in the 1650's' (London University Ph.D. thesis, 1992)

Trotter, E. *Seventeenth Century Life in the Country Parish with special reference to Local Government* (London, Frank Cass, 1968)

Venn, J. and Venn, JA. *Alumni Cantabrigiensis: Part I, from the earliest times to 1751* (Cambridge, University Press, 1922)

Vogelzang, ME. and Vanstiphout, HLJ., eds. *Mesopotamian Epic Literature: Oral or Aural?* (Lampeter, Edwin Mellen, 1992)

Ward, AW & Waller, AR., eds. *The Cambridge History of English Literature* Vol.8 (Cambridge, University Press, 1912)

Watson, J. *The Literary Qualities of the Prayer Book* (Dublin, APCK, 1949)

Watts, MR. *The Dissenters: From the Reformation to the French Revolution* (Oxford, Clarendon Press, 1992)

Weston, CC. *English Constitutional Theory and the House of Lords, 1556-1832* (London, Routledge & Kegan Paul, 1965)

White, HC. *English Devotional Literature (Prose) 1600-1640* (Madison, Wisconsin, 1931 - University of Wisconsin Studies in Language & Literature No 29)

Whiteman, A., ed. *The Compton Census of 1676* (London, Oxford University Press, 1986 (Records of Social and Economic History New Series X))

Whiteman, EAO. 'The episcopate of Dr Seth Ward, Bishop of Exeter (1662 to 1667) and Salisbury (1667 to 1688/9) with special reference to the ecclesiastical problems of his time' (Oxford University Ph.D. thesis, 1951)

Whiting, CE. 'The Study of the Classics in England during the Restoration Period' *Durham University Journal* Vol. 26 1928-30 pp.255-269, 339-348

Williams, RW. 'The Puritan Concept and Practice of Prayer' (London University Ph.D. thesis, 1983)

Wing, D. *Short Title Catalogue ... 1641-1700* (New York, Modern Language Association of America, 1972, etc.)

Woolfenden, GW. *Daily Liturgical Prayer: Origins and Theology* (Aldershot, Ashgate, 2004)

Wordsworth, C. *Who Wrote Εικων Βασιλικη?* (1824)

York, LS. 'In Dens and Caves: The Survival of Anglicanism during the Rule of the Saints 1640-1660' (Auburn University, Alabama University Ph.D. thesis, 1999)

Young, T. *The Metrical Psalms and Paraphrases* (London, 1909)

Zim, R. *English Metrical Psalms - Poetry as Praise and Prayer 1535-1601* (Cambridge, Cambridge University Press, 1987)

Zwicker, SN. *Lines of Authority: Politics and English Literary Culture 1649-1689* (London, Cornell University Press, 1993)

INDEX

Parish Clerk 5, 75, 83-85, 107-109,
116, 118, 119, 125
Parish Church 6, 7, 18, 31, 46, 75,
80, 85, 97, 104, 113, 127, 141,
151, 166, 167
Patristic Studies 20, 25, 27, 52, 53,
55-60, 168
Plague (1665) 69, 70, 81
Polyphony 156, 157, 164, 171, 172
Prayer Book of 1604 43, 45, 47,
49, 75
Prayer, Definition of 154-157
Press Act 9, 55
Private Prayer 10, 137-146, 171
Psalter 79, 80, 101-103
Puritan practice of prayer 6

Restoration 18, 20, 25, 26, 40-50,
53, 67, 68
Revision of the Prayer Book 40-50,
86-87

Savoy Conference 42-47, 125
Savoy Liturgy 43, 45
Scottish Prayer Book (1637) 45
Sternhold & Hopkins 18, 92, 106-
125, 128-130

Toleration Act 9, 57, 87, 169, 172

Unanimity 27, 48, 64-66, 74, 113,
147, 157, 169, 170, 172
Uniformity of Publick Prayers 41,
45-47, 50, 55

Visitations 7, 62, 63, 75, 78, 84,
86, 89, 100, 110, 161

Westminster Assembly 13, 21, 30,
120, 122
William & Mary 71-73, 86, 169